Twentieth Century
Rumania

TWENTIETH CENTURY RUMANIA

Stephen Fischer-Galați

Columbia University Press

New York and London

1970

Stephen Fischer-Galați is Professor of History
at the University of Colorado

Copyright © 1970 Columbia University Press
SBN: 231-02848-2
Library of Congress Catalog Card Number:
77-108838
Printed in the United States of America

To My Mother

PREFACE

FOR TEN YEARS now the rulers of Communist Rumania have
sought identification with the country's historic past, have
claimed that the Rumanian Socialist Republic represents the culmination of the Rumanians' ultimate historic aspirations. This
book seeks to provide an answer to the essential questions of
whether indeed the Rumanian historic tradition is compatible
with the present communist order, whether the communists'
claims are justified in terms of Rumania's historic experience in
the twentieth century. The accent is on the twentieth century
for two reasons. First, the direct ancestor of Communist Rumania
is the greater Rumanian state established only at the end of World
War I, and the contemporary national problems are rooted in
those of Greater Rumania. Second, the Rumanian communist
movement is also a product of the twentieth century, and its
evolution and problems parallel those of the greater Rumanian
state.

Although addressing itself to historic "continuity and change,"
the study encompasses related aspects of Rumanian civilization
as relevant to evaluation of the validity of the contentions of the
present rulers of Rumania. Nevertheless, the book is essentially
a study in political history in its broadest sense.

Preface

The book represents the essence of many years of thought and research devoted to contemporary and historic problems of Rumania. Its preparation was stimulated by the evolution of the so-called Rumanian independent course in the sixties and, more immediately, by the interest expressed by Columbia University Press in the preparation of a book specifically devoted to the problems of the twentieth century. I am grateful to the Press for having sought me out for that task as early as 1964, when the events of the year of the Czechoslovak crisis and the corollary formulation of the menacing Brezhnev Doctrine could not have been anticipated.

I wish to express my special thanks to colleagues in Rumania and the United States who have provided advice, information, and encouragement during the preparation of this study, particularly to William Griffith and Robert Tilley. I am also indebted to Margaret Logun for readying the manuscript for publication after first having been exposed to often incomprehensible written and oral drafts.

Stephen Fischer-Galați

Boulder, Colorado
November 1969

CONTENTS

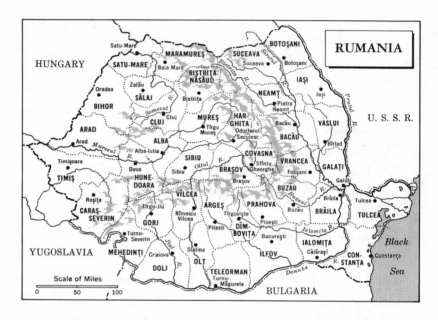

Twentieth Century Rumania

INTRODUCTION
The New and the Old

A s the visitor to Rumania crosses the border from Hungary at Episcopia Bihorului and proceeds through Transylvania on his way to the capital city of Bucharest, he is impressed by the strange mixture of the old and the new, the Rumanian and the foreign. Oradea, his first stopping place, retains the character of an old Hungarian town. The countryside around it, despite the numerous television antennas, has lost little of the rural comforts of early twentieth century Hungary. The atmosphere begins to change on the road to Cluj, Transylvania's principal cultural center. The inner city, with its monuments and cultural institutions, its pastry shops and restaurants, has a central European character. But the surroundings show the effects of Rumanization and industrialization, of the homogenization of Rumania's society that has taken place in the last quarter of a century. Hungarians and Rumanians live side by side, not only in villages but also in the modern apartment buildings constructed for the industrial workers and technocracy. They coexist harmoniously, at least by prewar standards. There is much intermarriage. Their children attend primarily Rumanian language schools although there are a few schools in which the language of instruction is predominantly Magyar. The university bears the name Babes-Bolyai.

1

The New and the Old

The leveling of national differences is less evident as the traveler reaches Sibiu, the Hermannstadt of old. The German minority is still relatively isolated from the Rumanian majority, probably because industrialization has made fewer inroads in this part of Transylvania than elsewhere. The atmosphere is serene and life leisurely. A few churches are still open but not well attended. Like Oradea, Sibiu is somewhat anomalous in terms of the dynamism of the next, nearby stopover, Brasov.

Indeed, as the traveler reaches the old imperial town of Kronstadt, in the foothills of the Carpathians, the old tends to fade away. It is not by accident that the Rumanian communists changed its name, temporarily, to the City of Stalin in the forties. In those years Brasov was destined to become a model industrial town, the city of steel and tractors. And that it became in a few short years with the concurrent disappearance of the nationality barriers separating, even physically, the Rumanian majority from the Hungarian and Szekler minorities. The historic sections of the town have been preserved as memorabilia. The Black Church, where the reformer Honterus preached in the sixteenth century, the old Town Hall, the gates—all are there for tourists to admire and for Rumanians to see as symbols of an historic past that has not lost its validity. Brasov is truly the historic melting pot of Rumania.

As one crosses the Carpathians into Wallachia en route to Bucharest, the momentum of change, because of industrialization, becomes even more evident. Sinaia, the former summer capital of the Hohenzollern dynasty and the wealthy Bucharest society, has become a resort town for industrial workers. A few factories have sprung up to use the water power of the region. More factories are under construction a few miles to the south on the way to Ploiesti, in the heart of the oil-producing region. Ploiesti dramatically illustrates the advances in technology. The refineries have been modernized and enlarged. The town itself has been

2

rebuilt to accommodate the army of workers and technicians employed by the petroleum industry. The horse and oxcart have disappeared as motor traffic toward Bucharest gains in intensity. At 40 miles from the capital city, Ploiesti is becoming an extension of industrial Bucharest. The main highway goes by renovated villages and building sites before entering the capital. It passes by the airport of Baneasa, still small by Western standards and filled with more propeller than jet aircraft. But traffic is heavy and international. Rumanian bureaucrats prefer to travel by train, at least within the country. Time has not yet become money, and it is not likely to do so despite the communists' clamor for greater efficiency. In fact, Bucharest is full of reminders of the need for and the reality of compromise between precommunist and communist aspirations.

The Rumanian capital has lost most of the characteristics of old. It is no longer the historic center of Wallachia, although relics of that distant past may still be seen here and there. The open-air central market, the dilapidated periphery, an old inn or two exist but do not reflect the *couleur locale*. The imposing residence of the Rumanian Orthodox patriarch on Metropolitan Hill, overlooking the city, is also there, but the symbolism is not. The former royal palace, the Atheneum, the parliament building, the imposing tribunal and university buildings—all of more recent vintage—are well maintained by their new communist occupants. The coffeehouses, restaurants, and movie houses of the twenties and thirties are all there, all full, all evidence of the continuity of a bourgeois tradition in proletarian garb. The customers are less well dressed than the once chic Bucharesters, the products eaten or screened less refined, but the essence of the past has been retained. The *Gemütlichkeit* is spoiled by poor service, noisy traffic, and high prices but no longer by the omnipresent secret police of the fifties.

But there is also much that is new in Bucharest. The suburbs

3

are new. Apartment buildings, shopping centers, and stadiums have replaced the picturesque shacks and single-family houses. Much of the population is new, relocated from the countryside, the provinces, and the periphery. The foreigners are different from what they were in the past. Organized tours of West Europeans, mostly Scandinavians and West Germans, are a novelty. But even more novel are African and Asian students, political and commercial officials—all unknown to Rumanians before the last quarter of a century. And yet Bucharest is not a cosmopolitan city in the modern sense; it is essentially Rumanian, more so than at any time in its recent history. It is also less significant than before in terms of the country's own requirements. Industrialization and modernization have resulted in decentralization. And this trend is most notable as one travels outside Bucharest on his way to eastern Wallachia, on his way to the Black Sea or to historic Moldavia.

Traveling eastward from Bucharest through the vast Wallachian granary, the Baragan, the uninitiated would hardly notice the impact of socialism and modernization on agriculture. The villages have changed little in appearance in the twentieth century. Collectivization applies to ownership and production but not to the configuration of rural society. Mechanization is more evident, but the number of tractors and other farm machinery is sufficiently small in comparison with animal-drawn equipment to dwarf the actual progress. On the surface everything seems peaceful and prosperous, and it may well be that way. Change becomes dramatic only as the road veers toward the Black Sea. The port of Constanta is active but not modern. The town itself has been modernized to accommodate tourists. It has also been transformed into an historic landmark. It is the seat of early Rumanian civilization based on the confluence of Roman and eastern civilizations. The historical museum and urban monuments all emphasize the Greek influence of antiquity and then the Roman,

as a reminder of the civilized origins and history of the Rumanians. The fact that parts of the historic province of the Dobrudja,
of which Constanta was the main center before World War II,
were involuntarily ceded to Bulgaria in 1940 is not obscured by
these reminders of the past. But competition with Bulgaria is
more evident in the development of the Black Sea coast for
tourism. Mamaia, Eforia, Mangalia, all resorts of the prewar elite,
have grown into replicas of the eastern Florida coast. They have
no specific Rumanian characteristics, any more than the neighboring Bulgarian coast has any Bulgarian ones. They provide the
hard currency required for industrial development and foreign
trade.

The validity of that financial purpose becomes evident as one
leaves the coast and drives northward toward Moldavia. In that
easternmost Rumanian province, neighboring the Soviet Union,
the impact of innovation has been most striking. The domain of
aristocratic comfort and of Jewish commercialism before World
War I, it retained most of the characteristics of the nineteenth
century even after 1918. Its enlargement through the annexation
of Rumania of the adjoining provinces of Bessarabia and Bukovina merely increased the number of Rumanian peasants and
Jewish merchants without transforming the static character of
provincial life. But after World War II Bessarabia and Northern
Bukovina were incorporated by Russia. Moldavia, without these
lands and minus most of the Jewish population, also lost during
those fateful years, was exposed to communist modernization.
New towns have appeared, industry has developed, agriculture
has been collectivized. In contemporary parlance, Moldavia is a
worksite of socialist construction. The areas close to the new
frontiers, however, have preserved their old Rumanian character.
The magnificent churches of Northern Moldavia have been re-
stored as monuments of Rumania's past. The city of Jassy (Iasi),
the center of the Rumanian cultural renaissance of the nineteenth

century, remains such a center within a few short miles of the new border with the USSR. Moldavia is symbolic of communist progress and identification with the historic past. It is the outpost of twentieth century Rumania facing the unfriendly giant to the east.

On leaving the Black Sea coast the traveler might choose an alternative route were he to exit through the west back into Hungary. If he were to seek that exit he could follow the course of the Danube, still peaceful and gray. Only as he approached the Yugoslav frontier would he notice change. At the famous Iron Gates, where the river narrows between Yugoslavia and Rumania, a giant hydroelectric power establishment is under construction. Driving again through peaceful rural areas on his way to the border, the traveler would reach first Timisoara and then Arad, both major industrial towns today. And as he crossed the border at Curtici, he would probably take stock of his impressions. His views would reflect the degree of modernization attained by his own country in the twentieth century. They would also be a function of his own awareness and prejudices. But no matter who he might be he would agree that at least in the second half of the twentieth century Rumania has become part of the modern world.

I

THE HISTORIC LEGACY
Greater Rumania

W<small>E ARE SUMMONED</small>, comrade deputies, to adopt the fundamental law of Socialist Rumania embodying the most
daring dreams of our people, the dreams for which our best sons
have fought, worked and died. Unlimited opportunities loom on
the horizon; no previous generation has been fortunate enough
to participate in such grandiose social changes, to be on the
threshold of national glory. What greater wish could anyone
have than to take part in the struggle and work for the attainment of the country's glorious future, for the progress and
prosperity of his Fatherland?

We are convinced that under the leadership of the Rumanian
Communist Party, the working people will spare no effort to
develop the socialist economy and culture, to pave the way for
the triumphant march toward the society in which all our people's activities will flourish and in which all who work will lead
a life of plenty and happiness—the communist society.[1]

With these words, strongly reminiscent of similar statements
by political folklorists of yore, Nicolae Ceausescu concluded his
address to the Constituent Assembly called in August 1965 to
immortalize the attainment of his Party's and the Rumanians'
penultimate goal—the national socialist society.

7

Greater Rumania

The establishment of a prosperous and a Greater Rumania has been, for over one hundred years, the historic dream of poets, patriots, and politicians. Balcescu and Bratianu, Alexandri and Antonescu, Eminescu and Ceausescu—each has spun his own version of the Rumanian epic, of which the latest version may be summarized as follows.

For centuries the Cinderellas of history, the Rumanian people, were prevented from attaining national liberation and political unification by the wicked stepmothers of Eastern European history, the Austrian Habsburgs and the Ottoman Turks. To their rescue came the Prince Charming of the nineteenth century, the Rumanian nationalists. These national heroes outwitted the wicked stepmothers and successfully fought all other dragons—Greeks, Hungarians, Russians, and Jews. But before 1944 they never uncovered the true villain, the Class Enemy. He was crushed by the true Prince Charming, the communists, who are still vigilantly protecting the beloved maiden against all potential enemies and seducers. Thus Cinderella and Prince Charming are engaged in the common struggle to attain their and their children's ultimate goal—eternal happiness in Communist Rumania.

To what extent is the communists' claim to the national historic legacy justified? How accurate is Ceausescu's version of the historic fairy tale?

Acceptance or rejection of the validity of Ceausescu's or all other nationalist versions of "manifest destiny" rests ultimately with the political philosophy of the historian of the Rumanians. The overwhelming majority of students of, or writers on, Rumanian affairs has tended to accept—occasionally *cum grano salis* —the theory that the moving force in Rumanian history has been the quest for national self-determination, the almost universal desire for national unification. No merit has been found in the possibility of coexistence with other nationalities in the multi-

8

national empires of the past; little if any attention has been paid to the significance of forces other than nationalism and opposition to foreign oppressors. Sophisticated analysts like Henry Roberts, Hugh Seton-Watson, C. C. Giurescu, and Lucretiu Patrascanu, whose appreciation of the role of socioeconomic forces in the process of historic evolution was far more acute than that of a James Upson Clark, R. W. Seton-Watson, D. Xenopol, or even Nicolae Iorga, concluded that the overriding motive force in the history of the Rumanians—even during periods of extreme hardship—was nationalism.[2] But to them that nationalism has a broader meaning than the creation and maintenance of a Greater Rumania; it is the sum total of the political, social, and economic aspirations of the Rumanians seeking to solve often insoluble and unsurmountable problems *en famille*, within the territorial and psychological framework provided by the nation-state. It is difficult to quarrel with that interpretation, but it is relatively easy to demonstrate that for historic reasons the national goal, no matter how defined, was not realized by 1944.

The history of the Rumanians has been turbulent. Formed as a national entity, under obscure circumstances, in the second and third centuries of our era through the union of the ancient Dacians and the Roman legions of Emperor Trajan and his successors, the Rumanians "disappeared" from recorded history for nearly one thousand years.[3] As the Daco-Roman territories (corresponding roughly to contemporary Rumania) were overrun by barbarians, the embryonic Daco-Roman state disintegrated, and many of its inhabitants migrated to neighboring regions less subject to devastation. The exact whereabouts of the Rumanian population during the period of "disappearance" are still unknown, but it is presumed that a substantial part took refuge in Transylvania and a smaller number in the Balkan Peninsula, south of the Danube. In any event, when the Rumanians' "reappearance" was confirmed and the first Rumanian states, Wallachia and Moldavia, were established around 1300, "national parcelation" became a *fait accompli*. Nearly half of the *Vlachs* (Rumanians) were subjects of the kings of Hungary or scattered throughout the Balkans outside the jurisdiction of the *voevods* (princes) of Wallachia and Moldavia.

The historians of that period would have us believe that the basic political goal of the rulers of the two provinces was the unification of all Rumanians, the liberation of their "brethren" from the onerous rule of the Hungarians.[4] The voevods' orientation was indeed anti-Hungarian as they themselves sought independence from their Magyar overlords. To characterize them as potential liberators and unifiers of the Rumanian nation is, however, unwarranted. Equally unfounded is the portrayal of these early rulers as defenders of the "nation" against all foreign foes. The depicting of men like Mircea the Old (prince of Wallachia between 1386 and 1418), Alexander the Good (prince of Moldavia between 1400 and 1432), and above all Stephen the Great (Moldavia's "Athlete of Christ," between 1457 and 1504) as Rumanian crusaders against the infidel Turk, treacherous Hungarian, and arrogant Pole overemphasizes the "heroic" and romantic aspects of these men's political motivations.[5]

By the fifteenth century, the voevods' *raison d'état* was self-preservation and maintenance of the existing sociopolitical order. It is true that the rulers of the Rumanian provinces, before the establishment of Turkish suzerainty in the fifteenth century, sought to organize states independent of external pressures and influences. The struggle for political emancipation from Hungarian and Polish vassalage by the voevods of Wallachia and Moldavia is a matter of historic record. So is the Rumanian "national heroes'" resistance to the numerically superior Turkish armies before acceptance of Ottoman suzerainty. But at no time did an Alexander, Mircea, or Stephen seek united political action by Rumanians outside Moldavia and Wallachia; at no time did they conceive of a Rumanian nation encompassing the historic frontiers of the destroyed Daco-Roman state. Nor did they regard their subjects as crusaders for the preservation of the "democratic nation." On the contrary, with rare exceptions, the heroes of historic folklore were perpetrators of the social inequities associated with the feudal states over which they ruled, instruments of the feudatories who elected them to office, tools of factions in the service of one or another would-be kingmaker, Hungarian, Pole, or even Turk.

The alleged "struggle for national preservation" (and later "national liberation") was clearly not carried on by the masses, whose primary concern was the safeguarding of their rapidly disappearing legal rights and earthly possessions. The peasants' support of military crusades against foreign enemies was rendered in the expectation of redress of grievances, as reward for military valor. But their regular "military" activities were the jaquerie. Whether, as maintained by "cosmopolitan" historians, the Rumanian peasants actually regretted the Turks' unwillingness in the fifteenth century to incorporate the Rumanian provinces into the Ottoman Empire and thus liberate them from their Rumanian masters, as was done in neighboring Bulgarian lands, or not, the very suggestion is indicative of the peasantry's dejection. And the situation went from bad to worse as the Rumanian provinces were caught in the giant struggle for hegemony in Eastern Europe involving first the Habsburg and Ottoman empires and later the Russians as well.[6]

First, the tribute exacted by the Porte from Wallachia and Moldavia, ultimately paid by the masses, led to the gradual pauperization and *de facto* enserfment of the Rumanian peasantry. Then, as the power of the Ottoman Turks began to wane and that of the Habsburgs to rise after a century of confrontation in East-Central Europe, the rulers of Wallachia, and to a lesser

11

extent those of Moldavia, engaged in political maneuvers adverse to the peasants' interests. The infidelity of the sultans' vassals, characterized by periodic shifts of allegiance from Turk to Austrian, provided grist for the mill of nationalist writers and politicians of later years who chose to interpret these actions as manifestations of Rumanian nationalism, as attempts to achieve the "national liberation" of all Rumanians from the Moslem yoke. To this day the great hero of the sixteenth century is Michael the Brave, the Wallachian voevod who temporarily "united" Wallachia, Moldavia, and Transylvania upon "liberating" these Rumanian territories from the infidel Turks and their accomplices, the princes of Transylvania.[7] Overlooked, however, is the fact that serfdom was legalized in Wallachia and reconfirmed in Moldavia during Michael's rule and that the corollary deterioration of the peasantry precipitated the ultimate dissolution of the "union" and the restoration of Turkish suzerainty over the "liberated" territories. In fact, the subsequent history of Wallachia and Moldavia in the seventeenth and early eighteenth centuries is also characterized by constant political maneuvering by voevods, feudal aristocracy, and churchmen with one or another enemy of the Ottoman Empire—Austrian, Pole, or Russian—and the constant deterioration of the social and economic status of the Rumanians.

Toward the middle of the seventeenth century, the unreliability of the rulers and the revenue from Moldavia and Wallachia prompted the Porte to start the policy of replacing native voevods by trustworthy Greeks from Constantinople; by the eighteenth century, because of growing Russian interference in the internal affairs of the Ottoman Empire, this practice became the rule. The takeover of Moldavia and Wallachia by the Constantinople Greeks—the so-called Phanariotes—resulted in the *de facto* displacement of the Rumanian aristocracy and upper clergy by Greeks, as well as in refinement of the methods of economic exploitation of the peasantry.[8] The Phanariote period, however, did provoke the first nationalist manifestations in Wallachia and Moldavia, political on the part of the Rumanian aristocracy, social on the part of the masses. The common goal, as the eighteenth century progressed, was the removal of Greek domination, albeit for different reasons: restoration of feudal privileges for the aristocracy, emancipation for the masses. This "nationalism" did not transcend the political and geographic confines of Moldavia and Wallachia. Indeed, it would be erroneous to assume that a common national motivation aiming at the unification of all Rumanians into a single Rumanian state existed in the eighteenth century. What did exist was a growing awareness of the common nationality of the "Ottoman" and the "Habsburg" Rumanians, and this awareness was particularly manifest in Transylvania.[9]

The unique position of the Rumanian inhabitants of Transylvania in the history of Rumania and of the formation of the national state of later years has been recognized by all but nationalist historians. The latter's suggestion that the historic experience of the Transylvanians was submerged in the supreme and constant desideratum of union with brethren in other Rumanian-inhabited lands and the creation of a United Greater Rumania is unworthy of serious consideration. Granted that the Rumanian inhabitants of that province were dissatisfied with their position of traditional subservience to the dominant "nations"—Hungarian, Saxon, and Szekler—and, in the case of the majority, also with their feudal servitude, it would be erroneous to assume that these grievances were to be remedied through common political action with the Wallachians and Moldavians.

The solutions propounded in the eighteenth century by the politically conscious Rumanians of Transylvania, the intellectuals and merchants, are characteristic of their own historic experience and of the history of Transylvania,[10] which had differed greatly from that of the Rumanian provinces under Turkish domination because of its intimate connection with Hungarian and Habsburg history and thus with events of Central and Western Europe. The Rumanians of Transylvania had been exposed to, and often were the victims of, the currents of historic change generated by the Reformation, Counter Reformation, commercial revolution, and struggle for political hegemony involving the Hungarians, Habsburgs, and the Western European state system. Many had been forcibly converted from their original Orthodox to the Uniate faith, the hybrid creed recognizing the basic elements of the Orthodox religion but accepting papal supremacy. Most were serfs on the lands of the Magyar feudal aristocracy. A few belonged to the privileged landlord class. More numerous than landowners were members of the merchant class. Although they were deprived of political rights and subject to discrimination by the privileged nations, the Rumanian merchants shared in the prosperity of the Habsburg Empire. A comparable position was enjoyed by the intellectuals, beneficiaries of the Habsburg educational system, offering opportunities for travel and cultural contacts with the West. Most of the Rumanians of Transylvania had been totally isolated from the historic experience of the Rumanians of Moldavia and Wallachia and were, as a rule, unconcerned with the problems of their geographically and historically remote brethren. This was true of the masses as well as of the bourgeoisie and intellectuals.

The first significant political demand voiced by the politically conscious was made in the name of and for the exclusive benefit of the Rumanian "nation" in Transylvania. The celebrated *Supplex Libellus Valachorum*, the petition submitted to Emperor Leopold in 1791 by the Rumanian intelligentsia and merchant class to secure political recognition for the Rumanian nation as the equal of the privileged nations, may indeed be regarded as the bible of Transylvanian Rumanian nationalism.[11] The essence of that nationalism was medieval and provincial. The key argument that the rights of the Rumanian nation were derived from the Latinity of its origin and consequent chronological primogeniture over the parvenu newcomers, the Hungarians, Saxons, and Szaklers, is far more representative of the then underdeveloped nature of the Rumanians' nationalism than the "modern" demands for representative government and humanitarian reform borrowed directly from the Enlightenment.

The historic separatism of the Rumanians of Transylvania from those of Moldavia and Wallachia continued in the nineteenth century, partly because of international factors beyond the Rumanians' control but also because of basic differences in nationalist doctrine and political aims. Whereas in Wallachia and Moldavia the dominant aristocracy sought emancipation from the Graeco-Turkish yoke for itself alone, in Transylvania elements of social reformism assumed increasingly greater doctrinal significance as the century progressed. In Moldavia and Wallachia the accent was on autonomy and independence from the Porte; in Transylvania it was on reform within the existing imperial framework.[12] These differing orientations clearly reflected the historic inheritances of the elite groups in the Rumanian-inhabited lands and played a far more significant part than consanguinity in determining the course of political action.

The intensification of contacts among the Rumanians on both sides of the Carpathian Mountains during the nineteenth century did not bring about reconciliation of political differences. Ideas from Transylvania were funneled into Wallachia and Moldavia by members of the intelligentsia. The Rumanians' Latinity, with the corollary emphasis on the continuity of a Latin oasis in a foreign sea—the doctrine so vociferously expounded by the Transylvanian "Latinist School"—was readily embraced by much of the Wallachian and Moldavian aristocracy as early as the eighteen twenties. The Transylvanians' views on social reform, focusing on the eventual emancipation of the peasantry, were accepted, however, only by a handful of "liberal" Moldavian and Wallachian landowners.[13] This limited acceptance of the reformist ideas of the Enlightenment and the French Revolution in Moldavia and Wallachia was precipitated by the abortive "social and national," anti-Greek revolt of 1821 headed by a member of the lesser Wallachian landowning class, Tudor Vladimirescu.[14] It is important, however, not to exaggerate the significance of the reformist elements in the political views of the Wallachians and Moldavians. With few exceptions, the aristocratic elite remained narrowly class-oriented, seeking oligarchic power for itself alone. The aristocracy, particularly the large latifundiaries (the boyars), collaborated as a rule with the conservative Russian tsarist regime, which, for political reasons of its own, encouraged emancipation from the Phanariotes and establishment of "boyar constitutionalism" in Wallachia and Moldavia. A pseudo-constitutional government was indeed set up in the Rumanian provinces in the early thirties by the Russian Governor-General Alexander Kisseleff, during one of several periods of Russian occupation of these provinces occurring in the first half of the nineteenth century.[15] The institutions established by the so-called Organic Statutes of 1832 perpetrated the continuation of the existing feudal order under Russian auspices, but with Rumanian rather than foreign rule. The Russians thus satisfied the class nationalist revendications of the conservative, anti-Greek, upper aristocracy and became the parents of conservative constitutional nationalism in Moldavia and Wallachia. Paradoxically, they became the stepparents of liberal constitutional nationalism as well.

The conditions for the ultimately successful attainment of a Rumanian national state were indeed created, ideologically and pragmatically, during the thirties under the Russian occupation regime. The beginnings of administrative reform, the establishment of a secular educational system, and, above all, the development of commercial and industrial establishments owned or manned by a rudimentary middle class all contributed to the development of a "bourgeois-nationalist" spirit and of bourgeois-nationalist aspirations compatible with those of the Transylvanians and, to a lesser degree, with western European liberalism.[16] The sons of the very latifundiaries who had been the greatest beneficiaries of Kisseleff's reforms joined forces in the thirties and early forties with the rising bourgeoisie against Russian conservatism and the ruling oligarchy. The young aristocrats who had left Wallachia and Moldavia for Paris, partly to further their education but mostly to escape the oppressive political atmosphere created by the Russians and their own fathers, adopted the ideas of socioeconomic and political reform expounded by the liberal thinkers of Louis Philippe's France. The political philosophy of the majority of those exposed to French thought was restricted to the attainment of "national liberation" from Russia and the Ottoman Empire and "constitutional democracy" for themselves and a few bourgeois friends. In a few instances, however, men like Nicolae Balcescu, Ion Ionescu de la Brazi, and C. A. Rosetti went beyond the narrow class interests of a liberal aristocracy by expounding programs of social reform favoring the peasant masses. The political philosophy of these men, summarized as emancipation of the peasantry and establishment of a truly democratic national state through a "national and social" revolution by at least the Rumanians of Wallachia and Moldavia, could not be translated into reality in the eighteen forties. It was, however, included in the platform of the aristocratic and bourgeois revolutionaries who staged the unsuccessful uprisings in Wallachia and Moldavia in 1848.[17]

Perhaps more important than the inevitable failure—in the face of joint Russo-Turkish opposition—of the amateurish revolts was the substitution of unenlightened nationalism for socioeconomic reform by the revolutionaries themselves both during and after the "debacle of 1848." Reneging on the promised emancipation, the "fighters for the democratic Rumanian state" lost the support of the peasants, whose interest in the unification of Wallachia and Moldavia was evidently secondary to their desire for land and freedom. Undaunted by their setback, the militant "generation of 1848" returned to France, where it devoted its political energies to securing French support for the establishment of a united Rumanian state for the Francophile "enlightened" aristocracy and to a lesser extent for the less Francophile and less enlightened bourgeoisie. For a few, such a Rumanian state was to include also Transylvania, the Banat, Maramures, and, in extreme cases, all territories inhabited by Rumanians no matter what their location.

The adoption of so narrow a political program presupposing no basic changes in the social order met with relatively little resistance from the aristocratic oligarchy. Any existing disagreement involved the choice of external supporters for the attainment of the nationalist goal. The "sons," opposed to reactionary Russia, preferred France; the "fathers" favored the Tsar over Napoleon III but took enough comfort in the Emperor's conservatism and readiness to assist his "Latin brethren" to dismiss most of their reservations. The submerging of the gradually narrowing differences separating two generations of landowners in the common goal of the aristocratic nation-state did not correspond, however, to the interests of the Moldavian and Wallachian peasantry or, for that matter, to those of the politically conscious Rumanians of the Habsburg Empire.

The masses' indifference toward the political plans of their masters may be ascribed to ignorance and lack of concern with problems transcending their immediate socioeconomic goal—emancipation. The indifference of the Transylvanians, or the inhabitants of the Banat, Crisana, or Maramures, to the national cause of the Wallachians and Moldavians was, however, due to

18

satisfaction of their immediate desideratum—improvement of their socioeconomic and even political status in the Habsburg Empire—following their own revolution of 1848. The Habsburgs' attempt, albeit temporary, to bring about the reconciliation of the conflicting interests of the various protagonists in the revolutionary upheavals that shook the monarchy to its very foundations aided the Rumanians. The attainment of equality with the previously privileged nations satisfied the politicians. The promised emancipation of the peasantry, although not immediately realized, placated the restless masses. The increased economic opportunities in trade and finance pleased the bourgeoisie. In short, the Habsburg policy of appeasement deepened the Rumanians' traditional *Kaisertreue* (loyalty to the emperor) and undermined the wild plan proposed by "extremist" intellectuals at the height of the revolutionary crisis—common political action with the Moldavian and Wallachian brethren.[18]

The divergent roads toward the most effective attainment of the interests of the nation propounded, on the one hand, by the Rumanians in the Habsburg Empire and, on the other, by those of Moldavia and Wallachia began to merge only in the sixties, when the Moldo-Wallachian formula appeared to hold greater promise of success than the Transylvanian. The history of the Rumanians took a decisive turn in 1866–1867, when, almost simultaneously, Carol of Hohenzollern became the ruler of the United Principalities of Moldavia and Wallachia while the aspirations for political equality of the Rumanians of the Habsburg Empire were frustrated by the Austro-Hungarian *Ausgleich*. The struggle for autonomy and union of Moldavia and Wallachia was crowned with success by 1859, when the United Principalities of Rumania were *de facto* recognized by the European powers. The union, promoted by France and Russia for independent political reasons, represented the triumph of the "forty-eighters'" cause. It did not entail immediate emancipation of the peasantry or other social reform because of opposition by the conservative aristocracy and acquiescence by the Francophile leaders of the unification movement. Nor did the union bring about the termination of Turkish suzerainty or of Russian influence as was desired by the unifiers. Social reform was the work of a minority that included the first prince of Rumania, Alexandru Ion Cuza.

The supreme achievement of the union, the emancipation of 1864, resulted in the ousting of Cuza and his "accomplices" by the outraged aristocracy, "liberal" and conservative. The official justification for the rebellion—the need to accelerate the attainment of total independence from the Porte through installation of a foreign ruler on the Rumanian throne—was a rudimentary alibi for the true reason, opposition to social change. Rumania belonged to the aristocrats; it was theirs to enjoy, not to share with the masses. It was theirs to expand, not to reform. A foreign ruler was useful for the achievement of their aims: he was outside the mainstream of Rumanian life and, if properly selected, could bring both prestige and foreign capital into Rumania, which in turn would facilitate the enrichment of the power elite and its bourgeois friends and the attainment of the ultimate goal of an independent Greater Rumania owned and ruled by them. Thus the enlargement of the national patrimony, narrowly identified with the interests of the landowners and "par la grâce du seigneur" the bourgeoisie, was the political *raison d'être* of the unifiers and soon also of their foreign prince, Carol of Hohenzollern.[19]

This unsavory formula for success, which because of its "nonbourgeois" and "nondemocratic" character would have been opposed in 1848 and for that matter until the mid-sixties by the *Romanii de dincolo* (the Rumanians of the Habsburg monarchy), became more and more acceptable to them as their own interests were sacrificed by the Habsburgs. The Rumanian leaders of

Greater Rumania

Transylvania and the other Habsburg lands had been only observers in the process of national unification on the other side of the Carpathians, regarding the union of Moldavia and Wallachia as a matter beyond their immediate concern. Their destiny was linked with that of the Habsburg monarchy, and by the early sixties they were optimistic about their future. Their economic and political power had increased after 1848, and the peasants' emancipation was a *fait accompli*. But the *Ausgleich*, which erased the Rumanians' political gains through the division of the empire between the Austrian and the Hungarian aristocracies, represented a major setback. In 1867, the Rumanians of the "Dual Monarchy" did not contemplate shifting their allegiance from the Habsburg emperor to the Prince of Rumania. Within a few years, however, the affairs of Carol's Rumania became of increasingly greater concern to Rumanians outside Moldavia and Wallachia. This was particularly true after the proclamation of Rumania's independence from the Porte in 1877 and the establishment of the "Old (Rumanian) Kingdom" in 1881.

The attainment of the original goal of the architects of the Rumanian national state, an independent Rumania, did not satisfy the ambitions of nationalist politicians unwilling to undertake the essential socioeconomic reforms that would have insured the viability of the national state. Convinced that the true emancipation of the peasantry and incorporation of the masses into the country's political life would spell economic and political ruination for the landlord class, the so-called Conservatives proposed programs of economic development within the framework of the agrarian-feudal order. The Conservatives, most influential with the monarchy, sought industrialization with foreign capital as compatible with their class interests. The so-called Liberals, comprising the last of the "forty-eighters," entertained similar views despite their demagogic advocacy of meaningful land reform and economic development by Rumanians rather than foreign capitalists. As the Liberals' primary goal was to dislodge the Conservatives and thus better enrich themselves in office, they cynically assumed the role of champions of Rumanianism and draped around themselves the mantle of xenophobic supranationalism. The Liberals conducted a virulent anti-Russian propaganda campaign after the loss to Russia of Southern Bessarabia in 1878, became the principal exponents of political anti-Semitism—accusing Carol and the conservatives of promoting the economic interests of Jewish tradesmen and industrialists—and took command of the movement for the establishment of the "true" Rumanian national state: the Greater Rumania of all Rumanians. The Conservatives, however, shared most of the Liberals' views, particularly those concerning Jews and peasants.[20]

At the beginning of the twentieth century the peasantry of Wallachia and Moldavia staged one of the bloodiest revolts in the history of Eastern Europe; it was put down in blood by the Conservatives then in power. The Liberals, whose agrarian policies in 1907 were undistinguishable from those of their political opponents, nevertheless exploited the events of that year of social revolution to promote the ultimate solution to Rumania's problems—territorial aggrandizement through the union of all Rumanians into a Greater Rumanian state. This magic formula propounded most vigorously by the Liberal Party's leader, Ion I. C. Bratianu, was eventually adopted by all politicians of the Old Kingdom as the possibilities for attainment of *Romania Mare* became evident during World War I. The total drive for a Greater Rumania was not accompanied by consolidation of the socioeconomic foundations required for supporting the enlarged national structure. The social, economic, and political blueprints drafted by Bratianu's Liberals and approved by nationalists in the Old Kingdom provided little room for new tenants and could not even pass the inspection of the international community of building inspectors and political architects. Rudimentarily conceived in terms of territorial aggrandizement at the expense of the vulnerable multinational Austro-Hungarian and Ottoman empires, it ignored the historic problems and desiderata of the future occupants of Greater Rumania.[21]

Disregarding the wishes of the masses was traditional with the politicians of the Old Kingdom. Even after the revolt of 1907 the Liberals concentrated on external political ventures such as the Second Balkan War, in which "Rumanian" territories were wrested from the Bulgarians in the Dobrudja. The corollary shift from the pro-German political orientation, to which the Old Kingdom had been committed since the 1880's, was also justified in terms of the greater national interest. The attainment of the supreme goal of total national unification presupposed the dismemberment of one of Rumania's allies in the Triple Alliance, which Rumania joined secretly shortly after its establishment— the Austro-Hungarian Empire. In fact, the principal arena for the fighters for a Greater Rumania had shifted from the Ottoman Empire to the Austro-Hungarian even before the Balkan Wars of 1912–1913. At least since the Bosnian Crisis of 1908, Rumanian propagandists sought with increasing intensity to draw the Rumanian inhabitants of Habsburg lands to the Greater Rumanian cause.

The courtship of the Rumanian population of Transylvania by nationalist politicians and intellectuals from the Old Kingdom was based on the assumption that their overtures would be irresistible after the rejection of the Transylvanians' Memorandum of 1891 by Francis Joseph. That celebrated political petition, aptly described as a nineteenth-century version of the *Supplex Libellus Valachorum*, demanded expansion of the Rumanians' political, social, and economic rights, so constantly circumscribed by the Magyar power elite. Although the imperial refusal to satisfy the Rumanians' grievances undoubtedly made future compromises more difficult and whetted the appetite of Transylva-

23

nian nationalists seeking union with the Old Kingdom, it did not per se destroy the Rumanians' *Kaisertreue* or affect the comparatively favorable socioeconomic status enjoyed by them. The majority of the Rumanian population continued to contemplate reform and change within the existing political framework rather than divorcement from the empire.

It is clear, however, that the unionist propaganda emanating from Bucharest gained momentum and converts after 1891. The Hungarians' intransigeance, most manifest after the turn of the century, helped the unionists' cause in the Rumanian areas of Transylvania, Crisana, and Maramures, but failed to drive any but the most extreme nationalists into the arms of Bucharest. The stumbling block to the Rumanians' unequivocal acceptance of the leadership of the Old Kingdom was the opposition to socioeconomic and political modernization displayed by the Bucharest politicians in 1907 and the years following. Indeed, only as the hopes for an Austro-Rumanian or Rumanian-Hungarian *Ausgleich* waned on the eve of World War I did the prospect of union with the Old Kingdom gain an increasingly larger number of adherents among the Rumanians *de dincolo*. As Bratianu's and his associates' gamble on the defeat of the Central Powers materialized and, correspondingly, the Habsburg Rumanians' alternatives other than political union with the Old Kingdom disappeared, union became inevitable in 1918. This is not to say, however, that the acquiescent leadership of the Transylvanians approved the plans for reorganization of the socioeconomic and political structure of a Greater Rumania propounded by Bratianu at the end of the war.[22]

Similar reservations were entertained also by nationalist leaders in the imperial Austrian outpost of Bukovina, wrested from Moldavia in 1775, and in Russian-controlled Bessarabia, despite their genuine proclivities for union with the Old Kingdom. In Bukovina and Bessarabia, Bucharest's nationalist propaganda with its strong anti-Semitic overtones had been well received at least since 1878. The actual or alleged economic exploitation of the Rumanian peasantry by the Jewish urban interests in Bukovina and Bessarabia aided the nationalists' cause as much as the intellectuals' traditional opposition to "foreign" domination. In the absence of moderating bourgeois influences, the intelligentsia persuaded the peasantry that union with the Old Kingdom would benefit the masses by providing them with a national home and corollary opportunities. Their failure to explain just what these opportunities would be did not dampen the interest of the peasants in unification as long as their property rights were guaranteed by the rulers of Greater Rumania. Verbal assurances were regarded as satisfactory, at least until the Bolshevik Revolution and Bucharest's reaction to it convinced the Rumanians of Bukovina and Bessarabia that formal assurances were necessary.

The impact of the Russian Revolution on the attainment of the nationalists' goal of a Greater Rumania has been generally recognized by students of Rumanian affairs. Fear of Bolshevism, it has been argued, pushed the Rumanians of Bessarabia and Bukovina into the arms of Bucharest. Valid as this explanation may be, it ignores the fact that fear of Bolshevism, particularly in Bessarabia, was far more pronounced among the nationalist intelligentsia and the Jewish commercial community than among the Rumanian peasantry. Whereas it is undeniable that the Rumanian peasant in Bessarabia had been dissatisfied with the Tsarist regime after the incorporation of the historically Rumanian land in the nineteenth century, it is far from certain that his lot was worse in the century of Russian domination than it had been under Rumanian rule or, for that matter, was less desirable than that of his brethren left behind in Moldavia. If anything, Russian agrarian policies benefited the Bessarabian peasant to a much greater extent than Rumanian agrarian policies did the Moldavian.

In the later nineteenth and early twentieth centuries, the Bessarabian peasant's hostility was directed against the Russianization of the province and the enlargement of the Bessarabian Jewish ghetto. His favorable response to Bucharest's unionist propaganda was thus largely determined by these noneconomic considerations. The relief held out by the Bolsheviks in October 1917, coupled with promises of land reform, however, upped the Bessarabians' and, for that matter, also the Bukovinians' price for union with the Old Kingdom. In fact, their demands for comparable guarantees from Bucharest and *de facto* flirtation with the Bolsheviks forced Bratianu and his colleagues to inject assurances of social reform into their shallow nationalist-unionist campaign.[23]

The political naïvete or cynicism of these politicians was evident from the very inception of hostilities in 1914. Reneging on the commitments to the Central Powers by persuading Carol I and, after his death in 1914, his successor Ferdinand to remain neutral, they engaged in not-too-covert negotiations with the Entente. The price for shifting alignments was fixed at recognition by the Triple Entente of Rumania's territorial claims. The negotiators for the Entente, more cynical than naïve, agreed on a Greater Rumania. In 1916, therefore, as the fortunes of war were smiling on the Entente, Bratianu persuaded Ferdinand to cast Rumania's lot with the French and Russians to attain the historic dream of Rumanian nationalism. Undeniably the commitment to the Allied cause had profound reverberations among all Rumanians within and without the Old Kingdom. Even if their initial enthusiasm was temporarily moderated by the defeat of the Rumanian armies and the subsequent occupation of the Old Kingdom by German forces, it reappeared as Germany's defeat by the Allies seemed imminent. Nevertheless, the Rumanians outside the Old Kingdom were not blind to the failure of the engineers of unification to make formal commitments to their interests and political representatives as the war came to a victorious end. It was for these reasons that "insurance clauses" were included in the celebrated Proclamation of Alba Iulia of December 1918, whereby the Transylvanians opted for union into a Greater Rumania. Their insistence on an unequivocal guarantee by Bucharest of their traditional rights and privileges and on an equal voice in the future of the new country reflected basic suspicion of Bratianu's sincerity. As a matter of fact, their demands were accepted by Bucharest in bad faith.[24]

The seemingly erratic behavior of Rumania's chief negotiator and Prime Minister, Ion I. C. Bratianu, at the Paris Peace Conference clearly reflected the Old Kingdom's unwillingness to share political power with anyone. The Alba Iulia stipulations were as incompatible with Bratianu's ambitions as the victorious Allies' demands that Greater Rumania inaugurate "a purely democratic regime in all branches of public life," benefiting all subjects regardless of religion, national origin, and social status. To avoid implementation of these stipulations so contrary to the historic tradition of the Old Kingdom, Bratianu assumed the mantle of anticommunist crusader and defender of the Allied interests in Eastern Europe. Arguing that a conservative Greater Rumania would be a bastion against Bolshevik Russia and Communist Hungary, he was able to secure the Allies' mandate to destroy Bela Kun's state in 1919. By the same reasoning, the Allies approved the incorporation of all Rumanian-inhabited areas claimed by Old Kingdom irredentists and paid only lip service to their initial demands for democratization and the participation by all inhabitants of Greater Rumania in the process of national construction.[25]

Thus by 1920, when the peace treaties had been signed, Greater Rumania had become a physical reality. The fundamental problems of national and international reconciliation, of economic development, of social integration—in short, of viability—were awaiting solutions that Bratianu and the Bucharest power elite were reluctant to provide. Indeed, these problems would have challenged even the most experienced and selfless of leaders and probably defied solution under all circumstances. There can be little doubt, however, that the solutions propounded by the victorious politicians of the Old Kingdom paved the road to disaster.

2

THE LEGACY TESTED
The "Democratic" Twenties

WHATEVER MODICUM OF political stability was enjoyed by Greater Rumania after its formal establishment was derived largely from a temporary and superficial reconciliation of the conflicting socioeconomic and political interests of the heterogeneous population and political organizations. In fact, it has been argued that it took the Rumanians all of three years to realize the calamitous nature of the compromises reached in 1919–1920 and the fundamental irreconcilability of conflicting interests before they were ready to express their displeasure and to seek remedies by political means.

Rumania's problems in the immediate postwar years may be ascribed ultimately to the unwillingness of the Bucharest politicians to provide adequate formulae for national and international reconciliation. The need for national unity based on a more realistic foundation than the euphoria of a Greater Rumania was evident to all initiated observers and politicians even before the formal establishment of the new state. After all, Greater Rumania was to be a multinational country with a socioeconomic structure far more complex than that of the Old Kingdom. The choice facing Bucharest was that of integration of the "foreigners" into the country's life, with resultant loss of

29

oligarchic political power, or of a *marriage de convenance, à la roumaine*, with the political leaders of Transylvania alone. The adoption of the latter alternative, regarded as the lesser of two evils, had far-reaching and disastrous repercussions.

Bucharest's disinclination to seek accommodation with the various national minorities, but primarily with the Hungarian and Jewish, was based on economic fears as much as on the need to perpetuate the nationalist-chauvinist and anti-Semitic traditions. The Magyars, Saxons, and Szeklers of Transylvania had, as businessmen, financiers, and industrial entrepreneurs, controlled the capital and dominated the professional and intellectual life of the province as well as of surrounding territories inhabited by Rumanians. They were the power elite—social, economic, and political—whose potential influence in the new state was incompatible with the aims of the politicians of the Old Kingdom. Whether these minority groups themselves would have welcomed an accommodation with Bucharest or whether they were fundamentally opposed to any compromise with the "despised Wallachians" is still a matter of dispute. The generally held view that the goal of the dominant Magyars was at all times reincorporation of Transylvania into Hungary (a goal allegedly shared by the Saxons and Szeklers) may be correct. Nevertheless, the basic question of what their reaction to Greater Rumania would have been had Bucharest evinced a genuine desire for national reconciliation after 1919 has never been satisfactorily answered.

In any event, the exacerbation of Rumanian-Magyar antagonism following the brutal suppression by Rumanian armed forces of the Bela Kun revolution and the subsequent plunder and devastation of Hungary by the Rumanians limited such possibilities of compromise as may have existed at the end of World War I. The corollary branding of the Magyars as historic enemies of the Rumanians by Bucharest, coupled with Budapest's ruthless denunciation of the Rumanian "criminal hordes," further poisoned the political atmosphere. The ensuing wholesale removal of Magyars from Rumanian governmental posts, the Rumanization of the bureaucracy and economic order, and, above all, the expropriation of rural property belonging to "foreign" landholders in Transylvania, Crisana, Maramures, and the Banat added fuel to the fires that the provisions of the Treaty of Trianon had fanned rather than extinguished.[1]

Bucharest's policies, however, transcended the avenging of historic national injustices. They were directed also against the traditional Rumanian leaders of the Transylvanian peasantry as Bucharest sought to demonstrate to the Rumanian masses both its power and its ability to implement its promises of agrarian reform. Indeed, Bratianu and his cohorts were staking their political future on Rumanianism and limited agrarian reform not only in Transylvania but also throughout Greater Rumania. The distribution of the lands of foreigners, absentee landlords, and large latifundiaries was designed to create a class of grateful if not satiated peasants, politically subservient to the "emancipators" and the king of all Rumanians, Ferdinand I. It is noteworthy that the most generous redistribution of land occurred in Transylvania, where peasant political consciousness was most highly developed. This relative largesse was credited to the Rumanian crown and the Liberals—to King Ferdinand and Ion Bratianu, rather than to Iuliu Maniu, Alexandru Vaida Voevod, and other leaders of the National Party of Transylvania. The effect of this double play was virtually erased as the cynicism of the politicians of the Old Kingdom became evident by 1922—but not entirely, since by that time the National Liberal Party had assumed control of the government of Greater Rumania as champion of social reform and executor and maintainer of the nationalist principles upon which Bratianu had built Greater Rumania.[2]

Similar tactics were pursued by the Liberals in the other provinces incorporated after the war, especially in areas where foreigners had held economic and political power. In Bessarabia, for instance, the affluent Jews were fleeced in the name of nationalism and economic justice, while the "benevolent" monarchy and Bucharest oligarchy reconfirmed and rounded out the redistribution of land begun during the Bolshevik Revolution.[3] These power plays, exercised throughout Greater Rumania—in violation of the spirit and often even the letter of the principles of national unification—were justified also in terms of resistance to the international forces of revisionism and communism. Hungarian revisionists and Jewish communists were singled out for special discrimination.

It is generally recognized today that neither Hungarian revisionism nor Russian communism posed a serious threat to the stability of the Rumanian state in the years of refinement of the doctrine of Rumania for the Bratianus. The possibility of the restitution of Transylvania to Budapest or of the re-establishment of the Austro-Hungarian empire was indeed remote in the early twenties. Moreover, the Magyar minority in Greater Rumania, although sympathetic toward the empty slogan of *nem, nem, sohot* ("no, no, never"), was nonmilitant and by and large predisposed to accepting a *modus vivendi* with Bucharest in the spirit of the "democratic" provisions of the peace settlement. The other "inimical" force, Communist Russia, would probably have pushed its claims to Bessarabia and used the Rumanian Communist Party as an instrument of general subversion of the ruling "bourgeois-landlord clique" had it had the power to do so. In fact, however, Moscow was unable to challenge the Rumanians and the Rumanian communists were impotent to undermine the political stability of Greater Rumania. As a rule, communist agitation for socioeconomic reform and "democracy" fell on deaf ears. Nevertheless, inasmuch as a substantial part of the membership of the communist movement was Jewish, the politicians of the Old Kingdom, true to their nationalist anti-Semitic tradition, readily associated the alleged threat from the East with the "Jewish peril."[4]

Since Jew, Hungarian, and communist were the enemies of the new order, their activities were to be restricted and the destiny of the state entrusted to elements untainted by association with the "enemy." Moreover, as these "hostile forces" also championed social reform for the benefit of the peasantry and working class or equality for all inhabitants of Rumania, their activities had to be rigorously circumscribed and the rights of the Rumanian peasantry and proletariat "carefully protected" by Bucharest. In fact, the "lower classes," suspected of left-wing tendencies or, in the case of the Hungarians, of political disloyalty, had also to be protected against exposure to "revolutionary" ideas expounded by "foreigners" or "foreign-influenced" organizations such as the various "peasant" and "workers'" parties that were generally formed immediately after the war or, occasionally, existed even before the union of all Rumanians. Thus political warfare rather than reconciliation, reaction rather than reform, were the rule in the formative years of Greater Rumania.

The vital political and socioeconomic problems facing Greater Rumania were not solved by the several governments that antedated the formal assumption of power by the National Liberal Party in January 1922.[5] And there were good reasons for their failure to find solutions. The crucial agrarian question was the most difficult to resolve since the nature of agrarian reform was to shape the country's political future. Had the wartime promises made to the peasantry of the Old Kingdom and the letter of the agreements of national unification been observed, and the agrarian reform assured therein been carried out in good faith, Rumania's destiny would in all probability have rested with the political representatives of the peasantry or with individuals sympathetic to the peasantry's aspirations rather than with Ion Bratianu and the National Liberal Party. But the Liberals, anxious to avoid political catastrophe, posed as champions of agrarian reform from as early as December 1918. The terms of their reform, affecting redistribution of land in the Old Kingdom alone, were spelled out in the decree law of December 15 of that year. Massive expropriation of lands belonging to the crown, foundations, foreigners, absentee landlords, and large latifundiaries whose domains exceeded 100 hectares was promised at the time. Generous as these provisions were on paper, they contained enough loopholes to prevent equitable distribution of the expropriated land. Legislation governing land reform in the incorporated provinces of Bessarabia, Bukovina, and Transylvania was not enacted concurrently because the differences between the generous provisions contained in the union contracts and the decree of December 15 would have exposed the Liberals' hypocrisy even to the illiterate peasantry of the Old Kingdom.

The reaffirmation of the principles of socioeconomic reform implicit in the agrarian measures of 1918 did, however, allow the Liberals to fend off the criticism and demands for a national election voiced by the political representatives of the masses until September 1919. At that time, a confident Bratianu resigned *pro forma* to demonstrate the Liberals' devotion to democratic practices and the principles of the agreements of incorporation. Of course, he acted on the assumption that his program of militant nationalism and social reform, together with the aid of tested techniques of electoral fraud, would insure his Party's continuation in power. The crushing defeat suffered at the polls by the Liberals belied Bratianu's assumptions and forced the Bucharest oligarchy to alter its tactics.

The temporary assumption of control over the government by a coalition of pro-peasant organizations—the National Party of Transylvania and the Peasant Party of Wallachia—provided the opportunity for Bratianu and all politicians of the Old Kingdom, other than the minority favoring majority rule and social reform, to unite against rule by "radicals" and "foreigners." The coalition headed by the Transylvanian Vaida Voevod and the leader of the Peasant Party, Ion Mihalache, was accused of committing two cardinal sins against the principles and practices of Old Kingdom politics. First, it advocated a comprehensive program of land expropriation and social reform in the village; second, it professed national reconciliation through observance of the incorporation agreements and of the provisions of the so-called Minorities Treaty—governing the treatment of minorities in Greater Rumania—which the allied powers imposed on Rumania in December 1919. These "treacherous" acts were branded as incompatible with the national interest by Bratianu and his entourage and, perhaps even more significantly, by the monarchy. Acting in consort with conservatives and nationalists, King Ferdinand dismissed the Vaida government in March 1920 at the moment when parliamentary approval of a play for agrarian reform that would have indeed satisfied the demands of the peasantry and consolidated the rule of pro-peasant or peasant parties in Rumania seemed assured.

The royal "coup d'état" of March 1920 was crucial in determining the course of Rumanian history in the interwar years. The entrusting of political power to General Alexandru Averescu, a popular military hero of conservative bent, *de facto* repudiated the promises and agreements made at the end of the war. The creation of an artificial political party, the People's Party, to serve as a vehicle for the advent to power of a man who stood for Wallachian supremacy, authoritarian government, rejection of social reform, anticommunism, anti-Semitism, and anti-Magyarism, together with the fabrication of an artificial electoral majority at "confirmatory" elections held in May 1920, dealt a fatal blow to the reformist and "democratic" forces of Greater Rumania. These irresponsible actions, culminating in the enactment of discriminatory legislation against the peasantry and advocators of social reform and the corollary strengthening of the political right, virtually precluded any possibilities for social and national reconciliation by the time Ion Bratianu succeeded Averescu in January 1922.[6]

Most students of Rumanian politics recognize that the agrarian legislation of 1921—the final legal version of Rumanian land reform—was far less liberal than had been expected by the peasantry. In fact, the restrictive provisions inserted into the law of 1921, favoring the conservative landowners and real estate interests, were designed to prevent the development of a meaningful political power base in the village. In 1921, Bucharest accepted land reform as a necessary evil, but not to the extent of its entailing the destruction of the political power of the expropriated. The former landowning class was provided with sinecures in the state bureaucracy and directorships in commercial and industrial concerns owned by Jews and foreigners. Together with the rapidly growing Rumanian commercial, financial, and industrial community, with the army, the King, and right-wing nationalist intelligentsia, they were to constitute the conservative bulwark against the "liberal" or "communist" intellectuals, minority groups, peasants, workers, and politicians. The consolidation of the political power of the conservatives at the expense of the peasantry and, even more so, of the disaffected industrial labor force led directly to the crystallization of the right and the left.

The left, consisting of socialists, communists, and politically unidentifiable workers and intellectuals, joined forces either in the Rumanian Communist Party (founded in 1921), in the Social Democratic Party, or in a variety of splinter groups of these major organizations, all at odds with one another but united in opposition to the "reactionary bourgeois-landlord" regime.[7] Averescu reacted by denouncing the "Jewish-dominated" left as alien and pro-Bolshevik, thus ushering in an era of persecution of all exponents of social and political reform and of implacable hostility toward their alleged protector and benefactor, Bolshevik Russia.

Concurrently, encouragement was given to the nationalist right, particularly in Moldavian and Wallachian universities—traditional hotbeds of anti-Semitic violence and ideological vituperation. It was hardly by accident that the first virulently anti-Semitic and anticommunist manifestations associated with the militant national Christian crusade of the infamous Iron Guard of later years occurred during Averescu's rule. Corneliu Zelea Codreanu, the *Führer* of Rumanian fascism in the thirties, received his political baptism in the Averescu period under the tutelage and protective umbrella provided by the Bucharest nationalists and Professor A. C. Cuza, the Moldavian ideologue of Rumanian anti-Semitism.[8] More significantly, perhaps, Averescu's policies alienated the peasantry and its political champions, driving them into a state of permanent opposition to the regime. Last but not least, the several national minorities, convinced that reconciliation was unlikely, fearful of nationalist reactions, and not infrequently encouraged by co-national political organizations outside Rumania, began to organize themselves into new, or to reactivate existing, political formations, along narrow national lines. National disunity had become an integral part of Rumanian political life by 1921.

Possibilities for international reconciliation were also substantially diminished through the pursuit of a chauvinistic foreign policy designed to nullify the provisions of the minority treaties granting economic compensation to expropriated Transylvanian landowners who opted for Hungarian citizenship at the end of the war and, in certain instances, even obligations formally incurred through the peace treaties themselves.[9] The conclusion of a complex "antirevisionist" system of alliances in 1921, supported by France and comprising the Little Entente of Yugoslavia, Czechoslovakia, and Rumania and the anti-Russian alignment with Poland, was allegedly based on the threat posed to Rumania's territorial integrity by bitter and hostile neighbors. In fact, these threats were minimal. But it was convenient for internal political purposes for Bucharest to brand the Hungarians potential aggressors and inveterate enemies of the Rumanian people in order to discredit the moderate Transylvanian political parties advocating adherence to the spirit and the letter of the treaties regulating Hungarian-Rumanian relations. It was also deemed desirable by Averescu to fan popular fears of Russia and to inflame Rumanian anti-Semitism and anticommunism by waving the red danger flag and dramatizing Russia's demands for reconsideration of the "illegal seizure" of Bessarabia. Whether any compromise would have been possible with the Bolsheviks in 1921—or in the following years for that matter—is uncertain, but it is noteworthy that the Russians voiced their claims in more dulcet terms than those of the Rumanians' riposte.

By the end of 1921 the Averescu regime had fulfilled its task of placing Rumania squarely in the camp of antirevisionism and conservative nationalism. To appease the clamor of the Transylvanian and other political parties opposing Bucharest's monopoly of power and seeking the establishment of a truly representative government, and also in effect to consolidate the policies of a Greater Rumania for the Old Kingdom, King Ferdinand dismissed Averescu and summoned Ion Bratianu to power. The old nationalist politician now assumed the mantle of the "great democratic" compromiser and leader of the only political party that could insure peace and prosperity in his Rumania.

Bratianu's formula for national consolidation and reconciliation was characteristic of the *raison d'état* and *politique* of the National Liberal Party.[10] It bore the veneer of liberalism but contained the essence of nationalism. The bitter pill that had to be swallowed by all but Bratianu's followers was sugar-coated by the supreme act of national reconciliation and unity, the Rumanian Constitution of 1923. The guarantees of democratic rights and equal opportunities for all inhabitants of Rumania, regardless of national, social, or religious background, failed to obscure, however, the political reality of National Liberal Rumanian supremacy. The citizens' rights and opportunities were to be ultimately determined and reviewed by legislative enactments and policies of the regime in power. In fact, national and socioeconomic discrimination continued unabated after 1923.

The fundamental political philosophy of the Bratianu regime was to let the sleeping peasant lie while the liberals governed the country for the benefit of the Rumanian bourgeoisie, upper bureaucracy, and professional politicians comprising the ruling party. The industrial worker, like the peasant, was to be *de facto* deprived of political rights; social and economic reform benefiting the labor force and peasantry was to be avoided. Suggestions for change were automatically branded as communist inspired. The outlawing of the Communist Party in 1924 because of its "revolutionary" activities and Russia's refusal to settle the Bessarabian dispute was symptomatic of this pernicious political climate. Falsification of electoral results, mass disenfranchisement, and adoption of the Italian fascists' electoral law guaranteeing an overwhelming majority in parliament to the party receiving as little as 40 per cent of the ballots cast in a national election assured the Liberals' continuity in office for six long years.

Nevertheless, the "Liberal period" was not barren of positive achievements. The years between 1923 and 1928, characterized by communist historians as ones of "relative stabilization of capitalism," were indeed marked by economic growth and relative prosperity. The communists' description of the period is accurate to the extent to which Rumanian economic progress was a function of the general development of Europe's economy before the Great Depression. However, it tends to disregard the efficacy of specific Liberal economic policies that provided the

The "Democratic" Twenties

Rumanian economy with stabilizers stronger than those on which the economies of most European countries rested in this period. These policies, based on high protectionist tariffs, limitations on the importation of foreign capital, and encouragement of industrialization through governmental subsidies and a favorable tax structure, did indeed insure a level of unprecedented prosperity. The regulated exploitation of Rumania's vast natural resources, primarily crude oil, by "Anglo-American and French imperialist interests" also helped the Rumanian economy by stimulating the growth of related and auxiliary joint foreign-Rumanian industrial and financial concerns and insuring a high level of industrial employment. The major and unsolved economic problems involved agriculture. The immediate and long-range difficulties arising from peasant economic self-sufficiency, agricultural overpopulation, and primitive techniques defied solution by a regime essentially opposed to the interests of the peasantry and by a peasantry essentially opposed to mechanization and modern agricultural techniques.

Nevertheless, the relative economic well-being of the population facilitated the creation of a "Liberal image" of national prosperity and progress that was difficult for the political opposition to demolish. That image was beatified by King Ferdinand's always standing beside Bratianu, especially since the monarch was revered by much of the peasantry as their "emancipator," friend, and symbol of political stability. Bratianu's posture of guardian of the principles of Rumanianism, defender of the national interest, and promoter of prosperity stood the Liberals in good stead until the King's and his own death in 1927. A new era in the history of Greater Rumania was to begin as the pillars of conservatism and Old Kingdom supremacy crumbled.

Political attacks on the Liberal regime, which had prompted King Ferdinand to adopt the tactical maneuver of replacing Bratianu with Averescu between March 1926 and June 1927, assumed conclusive proportions after Vintila Bratianu succeeded his brother Ion and the five-year-old Mihai his grandfather Ferdinand. Vintila Bratianu, although more liberal and sensitive to political pressure than his late brother, was unable to act decisively because of the shattering of the Bratianu-Ferdinand axis. Mihai, who succeeded Ferdinand only because Ion Bratianu in 1926 had forced the boy's less pliable father, Carol, to renounce his rights, was handicapped both by age and lack of a clear title to the throne. Carol contested the validity of the "forced renunciation," and this action was applauded by a substantial segment of the anti-Bratianu forces. The response to the exiled pretender's claims was particularly favorable among the leaders of the National Peasant Party, newly formed through fusion of the Transylvanian National Party and Mihalache's Peasant Party—by all counts the political organization most representative of the broad interests of Rumanian society. Moreover, the conservative regency, consisting of Carol's younger brother Prince Nicolae, the Rumanian Patriarch Miron Cristea, and the President of the Supreme Court, Gheorghe Buzdugan, was not totally unsympathetic to political reform and, more significantly, to the possibility of Carol's assuming the crown. Under the circumstances, Vintila Bratianu's regime, tainted by the prevalent image of a Bratianu oligarchy and Liberal corruption, was unable to resist the pressures for change as effectively as that of his predecessor. In November 1928 Bratianu resigned *à la roumaine*, over a trivial issue, on the assumption that the regency would ask him to form a new government. The regents, however, for reasons that remain obscure, entrusted the formation of a new cabinet to the National Peasant Party, and the this-time honest confirmatory elections held in December 1928 ratified the new order.

The crucial question in postwar Rumanian history, with profound reverberations to this day, is whether a democratic regime representative of the interests of all inhabitants of Rumania could ever have been established in that country. The test case occurred between November 1928 and October 1930 when the National Peasants were in power. The achievements of that government and its leader, Iuliu Maniu, have been appraised differently by various students of Rumanian affairs.[11] The general consensus is, however, that Maniu failed to realize the great expectations placed in his regime by the Rumanian people. His defenders argue that Maniu's failures were the result of unscrupulous maneuvers by opponents of reform and democracy. His detractors, on the other hand, attribute Maniu's undistinguished record to his inability to overcome the inherited political corruption and significantly to alter an historic legacy incompatible with democratic rule. Maniu's proverbial aloofness and sanctimoniousness are attributed by his critics to a basic unwillingness to carry out the drastic reforms so necessary for the political rejuvenation and democratization of Greater Rumania. According to these analysts, he deliberately evaded facing the realities of Rumanian life that were incompatible with his fundamentally conservative and nationalistic political outlook.

The record of the National Peasant Party during its term in office, as well as after its loss of power, tends to bear out the critics' contentions that even if the "democratic tendencies" of Maniu and other leaders were more pronounced than those of their rivals they were not sufficiently developed to bring about the long-overdue national reconstruction. It is likely that the National Peasant Party assumed power too late to be able to act as a truly effective democratic force. Not only had the die been cast but also the mold had hardened by 1928. The opportunities for meaningful domestic reform, short of radical measures that the National Peasants were unwilling to undertake, were limited by the conservative forces both within and without the party. Rumania's foreign policy, with its commitment to containing Hungarian irredentism and Russian communism, was irreversible

short of a "revolutionary" realignment that Maniu was also reluctant to attempt. Some of the difficulties were inherited from
the Liberals, some were a reflection of the political compromises
that permitted the very establishment of the National Peasant
Party in 1926, some again stemmed from factors over which
Maniu and his associates had no control—the rise of fascism,
consolidation of communism, and the Great Depression. The
National Peasants faced all these problems but resolved only a
few. How successful their rule would have been under the more
propitious circumstances prevalent at the end of World War I
is a matter of speculation. Probably they would have done better
than the political oligarchy of the Old Kingdom; they could
hardly have done worse. But by 1928, and certainly by 1930,
Maniu and his colleagues proved to be much less than men of
the hour.

The political immorality that had been the trademark of the
National Liberal Party was too deeply rooted in Rumanian political life to be altered by an ineffectual moralizer reluctant to
revamp the socioeconomic and political order. Maniu, as self-
styled guardian of national morality and protector of the national
interest, delegated the actual conduct of governmental affairs to
more imaginative but less principled subordinates. Most of these
men shared Maniu's suspicions of the "radicalism" of Mihalache's
wing of the party, whose reformist tendencies were regarded by
them as socialist and thus non-Rumanian. The internecine conflict between the politically conservative elements of the former
National Party of Transylvania and Mihalache's entourage on
matters of domestic and foreign policy resulted in doubtful compromises and unsatisfactory solutions to the country's outstanding problems. These problems ultimately centered, at home, on
the development of the economy and the corollary regulation of
the socioeconomic relations between the peasantry and working
class and the "bourgeois-landlord" oligarchy and, in foreign af-

fairs, on Rumania's relations with Communist Russia, Fascist Italy, and revisionist Hungary.

The solutions propounded for the development of Rumania's economy were formulated largely by the eminent economic theorist Virgil Madgearu. Madgearu's formulae, centering on rapid industrialization with foreign capital, ran counter to the *prin noi insine* (by ourselves) philosophy of the Liberals and also, more significantly, to the peasants' view on economic progress. Madgearu denied the need for further land reform, convinced as he was that the problems of agrarian overpopulation and inefficiency could be cured only through the creation of a modern, viable, industrial base. Whether his solutions would eventually have proved successful is difficult to ascertain. The fact is that the Great Depression prevented effective implementation of the National Peasants' economic plans and left the country with a still underdeveloped economy and disgruntled peasantry. The peasant, whose simplistic formulae for economic improvement were rejected by his own party, became disaffected with party politics and responded favorably to appeals for socioeconomic reforms on bases transcending those voiced by ordinary political formations. The monarchy, the fascists, and the proven friends and representatives of the peasantry—the nonbourgeois leaders of the National Peasant Party and other peasant organizations—soon vied for the allegiance of the masses. Disenchantment, though less significant politically, was also recorded among other followers of the National Peasant Party, the liberal intelligentsia and much of the working class. The hopes of the former for governmental reform, political decentralization, and, above all, national and international reconciliation were as frustrated as those of the latter for improved working conditions and living standards.

The foreign policy of the National Peasants was in fact similar to that of the Liberals.[12] No attempt was made to seek a rapprochement with the USSR through a compromise on the Bessarabian question. Mussolini's *Drang nach Osten*, pivoted on support of Bulgarian and Hungarian irredentism and undermining of French influence in Eastern Europe, was officially dismissed as benign on the assumption that France would honor her commitments to the Little Entente under all circumstances. An alternative formula for regional collective security propounded by several East European peasant parties and envisaging the establishment of a union of Europe's agrarian countries into a "Green International" was *de facto* rejected by Maniu. The Green International was too radical and internationalist for the taste of the conservative leaders of the National Peasant Party.

The irresolution and ineffectualness of National Peasant rule led to demands by the politically conscious and active for new solutions to Rumania's unsolved problems. As the Great Depression spread eastward, politicians with their eyes on their own future sought the restoration of the traditional alliance of a viable monarchy and conservative nationalist government to assure stability in times of crisis. Partly by conviction, partly by necessity, the National Peasant government agreed to the restoration of Carol's rights to the throne on the expectation that as king he would be guided by Maniu's advice and would rule as a responsible constitutional monarch. The recalling of the exiled prince in the summer of 1930 was designed to reinforce the faltering regime and to give the country a moral shot in the arm. But that action proved to be a simplistic solution to Rumania's problems.

3

THE LEGACY TESTED
Authoritarianism, Dictatorship, and War

T HE ROLE AND RULE of Carol II in Rumanian history remain subjects of continuing controversy. Condemned by most critics as a forerunner of fascism and a betrayer of the country's democratic potential if not tradition, Carol has also been characterized by defenders as the man of the hour who realistically faced if not solved the problems and challenges of the thirties.[1] It is unquestionable that Carol had little respect for, or confidence in, the democratic process. In this regard he differed only slightly from his father Ferdinand or, for that matter, from the entire crowned dynasty of the Hohenzollerns and the uncrowned succession of the Bratianus. His political philosophy, if he had one, was that of dynastic authoritarianism; the King was the ultimate source of political decision and initiator of meaningful political action. Whether these views were based on deep-rooted suspicions and contempt for Rumanian politicians, a desire to avenge the humiliations inflicted upon him by his political persecutors, the Bratianus, or an exaggerated confidence in his own abilities is a matter of conjecture. Probably a combination of all these factors was involved. In any case, his attitude toward Iuliu Maniu and the National Peasant leadership that recalled him from exile was not one of gratitude. It was not that he found any intrinsic incompatibility between Maniu's alleged democratic sentiments and policies and his own royal authoritarianism; rather he clashed with Maniu's authoritarianism and views on the role of the monarchy. Maniu favored controlled democracy in a constitutional monarchy; Carol clearly relegated the Prime Minister to the position of executor of the King's decisions.

The break in 1930 between Maniu and the monarch, regarded by most historians and politicians of Rumania as the end of the "democratic experiment" and a stepping stone to totalitarianism, was the consequence of the clash between parochial and "modern" authoritarianism rather than between democratic and antidemocratic forces. Maniu's resignation, technically over the issue of Carol's extramarital relationship with Magda Lupescu, could not obscure the true cause of the rupture—the King's unwillingness to take a back seat to the Prime Minister and follow the National Peasants' political course. It is nevertheless significant that morality should have become an issue in a country rank with immorality and that Madame Lupescu was of Jewish origin. Maniu knowingly touched on the Jewish issue in his search for support from all opposed to Carol's politics and his betrayal—to Maniu of the "democratic," but to many others of the "nationalist"—tradition. No matter how sincere his convictions, Maniu's denunciation of Lupescu, Carol, and royal authoritarianism facilitated, first, the consolidation of monarchic power and, later, the establishment of outright totalitarian fascism in Rumania.

The "directed democracy" à la Bratianu, reintroduced by the monarch in the fall of 1930 and practiced with varying degrees of success until 1938, provided no more satisfactory solutions to the country's outstanding socioeconomic and political problems than those attempted by Carol's political predecessors. But the failure of directed democracy and the subsequent establishment of a "monarcho-fascist" dictatorship in 1938 cannot be blamed

47

on Carol alone. The monarch's dictatorial instincts and his desire to manipulate the puppets acting on the Rumanian political stage certainly contributed to a growth in political instability and immorality. Even had a new political morality been introduced by the King, solutions to the crises generated by the Great Depression and fanned by the fascist powers were beyond the reach of Carol and his friends as well as of his enemies. Agricultural and industrial stagnation, with resultant discontent among the peasantry and working class, was beyond cure by standard Rumanian political methods.[2]

The governments that succeeded Maniu's did not distinguish themselves in office. The policies of Mironescu's and Iorga's cabinets, which followed each other in 1931 and 1932, were uninspired, maintaining, essentially, the status quo at the time of deepening economic crisis. Their *ad hoc* measures to fight the agricultural and industrial depression were palliatives rather than cures. The National Peasant regime, headed by Vaida Voevod during its term in office between June 1932 and September 1933, was also ineffectual in economic affairs. But the National Peasants' gravest error was the forcible suppression, in February 1933, of the railwaymen's strike (the so-called Grivita uprising) led by their nemesis of later years, Gheorghe Gheorghiu-Dej.[3] This political *faux pas* was first condoned and later, when a scapegoat was required to exonerate the King from the stigma of persecutor of Rumanian labor, used by Carol for ridding himself of Vaida. The replacement of a National Peasant by a National Liberal regime headed by the highly respected Ion Duca augured well for the restoration of a modicum of tranquility in the tense political situation and the improvement of the economic crisis. But the new premier, symbolic of honesty and conscientiousness, was promptly assassinated by a rapidly rising force in Rumanian politics, the fascist Iron Guard.[4]

It has been argued by students of Rumanian politics that Duca's murder and the subsequent acquittal of the murderers by a military tribunal virtually precluded the possibility of Carol's pursuing a moderate political course after 1933. According to this interpretation of Rumanian history, the internal pressures generated by fascism and the economic crisis, coupled with the external pressures exerted by Fascist Italy and Nazi Germany, inevitably led to Carol's assumption of dictatorial powers. Thus Carol's defenders emphasize the King's positive actions in the thirties and his prolonged adherence, under heavy pressure and against heavy odds, to the principles of directed democracy. It is true, for instance, that Carol supported the policies of the brilliant minister of foreign affairs, Nicolae Titulescu, seeking in vain the reconciliation of Rumania's differences with the Soviet Union over Bessarabia. It was also under Carol's guidance that reconciliation of the conflicting and divisive forms of Balkan nationalism and chauvinism was sought with a view to establishing a "zone of peace" in the Peninsula. Nor can it be denied that Carol resisted encroachment by Fascist Italy and Nazi Germany and steadfastly worked for the strengthening of the Little Entente and the League of Nations. However, there was also another side of the ledger.[5]

The King relied on a narrowly based and essentially corrupt political coterie for advice. His only prime minister between the time of Duca's assassination and the last free Rumanian election in 1937, Gheorghe Tatarescu, was a willing executor of Carol's wishes. Carol's coterie, headed by Ernest Urdareanu and Magda Lupescu, was definitely more influential than any minister of state. Carol appeased the right, when advantageous to his political interests, and persecuted the left in the same spirit. He supported the corporatist formulae for industrialization propounded by Mihail Manoilescu, which provided no solutions to the agricultural crisis and only negligible benefits for the economy in general.[6] Corporatism did lead, however, to the enrichment of the King, the royal camarilla, and the industrialists and politicians supporting it and clearly facilitated the establishment of the royal dictatorship in 1938.

Ultimately, however, the debate between Carol's defenders and detractors centers on the reasons for his abandonment of directed democracy in 1938. Was the assumption of dictatorial powers preventive—to avoid seizure of power by the Iron Guard—or was it a deliberate move reflecting the monarch's fundamental contempt for democratic processes? In all probability, the King's action was determined ultimately by his belief that the establishment of an outright fascist dictatorship by the Iron Guard—with external fascist support—was a distinct possibility after the last "free" parliamentary elections in December 1937 failed to provide the required plurality for the re-election of Gheorghe Tatarescu's National Liberals. The power of the nationalist rights and of the reformist ideas of the social-revolutionary, ultranationalist Iron Guard was certainly greater by the end of 1937 than had been suspected by the monarch and the vast majority of Rumanian politicians. It would not be inaccurate to assume that fascist solutions to Rumania's problems were contemplated by many at least since the exoneration of the Legion of Archangel Michael in Duca's murder. It would also be a fair assumption that the verdict reflected recognition of the fact that Rumanian fascism was not incompatible with the country's political tradition and mores. In fact, the Guardist movement was rooted in the history of Rumania and sought solutions for Rumanians.

Henry Roberts, the eminent student of interwar Rumanian politics, has distinguished four elements of international fascism that were in one form or another recognizable in the Rumanian movement.[7] In order of growing significance Rumanian fascism represented "the death rattle of capitalism," a national chauvinist manifestation, a form of dictatorship plus hooliganism, and an expression of anti-Semitism and racial glorification. Of these, the first element is the least significant. Capitalism, identified in Rumania with urban, Jewish-dominated ownership or control of the banking, commercial, and industrial network, was roundly attacked by the followers of Rumanian fascism. But historically the target of their attacks had been the Jewish *arendas*—the *locum tenens* of the absentee landlord of pre-World War I years. The forerunners of the anticapitalist fascists of the interwar era were the agrarian, anti-Semitic populists of the early nineteenth century, the followers of Constantin Stere. As glorifiers of the peasant and opponents of his exploitation by the then most powerful capitalist entity, the Jewish "corporation," the populists assumed the role of friends of the "masses" and defenders of their interests. But the masses were generally equated with the peasantry even after the "second emancipation" of 1917–1921 and the socioeconomic reorganization of the village after World War I. The industrial masses never enjoyed the same privileged position in fascist ideology as their rural counterparts. The distinction between agrarian and industrial capitalism remained valid throughout the interwar years: Guardists were friends of the peasant, and their anticapitalism bore that stamp. Industrial capitalists were tolerated, perhaps because they were the principal financiers of the fascist movement, whose doctrines had adverse effect on their industrial empires. Guardist anticapitalism therefore combined two strands, the populist and the anti-Semitic. The success of Rumanian fascism was as much a function of mass reaction to socioeconomic proposals by the Guardist leadership as to popular acceptance of anti-Semitic slogans and policies.

It is noteworthy that all Rumanian "fascists" at one time or another and in varying degrees advocated populist doctrines. Populism was vociferously expounded by the Iron Guardist movement led by Corneliu Zelea Codreanu. But even the exclusively anti-Semitic LANC (League of National Christian Defense), headed by Professor A. C. Cuza, initially sought the support of the peasant in its struggle against the League's constant whipping boy, the Jewish entrepreneur and merchant: "the exploiter of the Rumanian peasantry." In the twenties, as Cuza abandoned the peasant, whom he regarded as satisfied by the agrarian reform, and concentrated on the Jew, now the enemy of all Rumanians, Codreanu's Legion of the Archangel Michael and its activist political section, the Iron Guard, split with the Cuzists. Codreanu's group reiterated its commitment to the peasants' cause without renouncing Cuza's anti-Semitic vituperance. Thus, while the Cuzist movement spouted invectives against the Jew, Codreanu was developing a more complex socioeconomic and political philosophy that in the early thirties became the doctrine of "pure" Rumanian fascism.

In this doctrine anticapitalism remained a cornerstone. But as the peasants were unresponsive to Codreanu's appeals as long as the National Peasant Party was still regarded as the representative of their political interests, Codreanu's men concentrated temporarily on the Jew and his alleged friend and the peasants' enemy, the communist. It was during the early years of Carol's reign that the Guardist "anti-Judaeo-communist Christian crusade" assumed clear expression. To Codreanu and his associates the King stood for betrayal of true Rumanian values, as shown by his association with Magda Lupescu, appeasement of Jews in general, search for reconciliation with the Soviet Union, and basically unfriendly attitude toward Mussolini's fascism. Maniu's replacement by men of lesser nationalist orientation and particularly the appointment of the "pro-Jewish" Duca regime—which indeed eventually outlawed the Legion—provided a basis for testing the strength of nationalist anti-Semitic and anticommunist sentiments among the population at large. The assassination of the Prime Minister constituted that test, and the minimal consequences of that criminal action convinced Codreanu that national vindication was not a lost cause.

Authoritarianism, Dictatorship, War

It is indeed a misinterpretation of the events of the early thirties to attempt to equate the Legionaries' actual power with that recorded in the several popular elections held in that period. The official tallies reflected both falsification of actual results and the continuing allegiance of voters sympathetic to Codreanu's cause to more firmly established parties offering programs superficially similar to the Guard's. Any meaningful appraisal of the actual strength and following of the Legion of Archangel Michael became possible only after the establishment by Codreanu of a formal political party, *Totul Pentru Tara*, and publication of its program in 1934. The Guardists' power was by no means negligible.[8]

The development of that power after 1934 was intimately related to the broad dissatisfaction with existing economic conditions prevalent among the Rumanian peasantry and the unemployed or frustrated urban intelligentsia and bureaucracy. It would be erroneous, however, to assume that economic problems alone accounted for the success of Codreanu's Legionaries. Totul Pentru Tara promised palliatives and even solutions for the general malaise that engulfed Rumanian society in the mid-thirties. The traditional corruption, inaction, and ineffectualness of the political establishment, as well as the prevalent social injustice and immobility, seemed particularly oppressive and detestable at a time of growing economic insecurity. Codreanu held out national rejuvenation, moral rearmament, and, above all, a national Christian social and moral crusade against all betrayers of what the Legionaries believed to be the true national historic legacy. In specific terms the Legionaries identified that legacy with the supremacy of the Christian Rumanian peasant and his supporters and friends. The peasant, led by the Guard, would develop a Rumania for the Rumanians over the dead bodies of Judaeo-communists and all other exponents of non-Christian, non-Rumanian political and socioeconomic philosophies. Judaism was the plague of Rumanianism; it had to be eradicated. The Jew

53

was the mortal enemy of the Rumanian and of Rumania's progress; he had to be expropriated, destroyed economically as well
as physically. The Jew professed anti-Christian communism or
was in sympathy with it; that philosophy had to be extirpated
also. To cleanse Rumania and Christendom of the Jew and his
allies and to reorganize society according to the principles of
Christianity, as interpreted by Codreanu, was the "Captain's"
goal and his party's political program.[9]

In terms of Roberts' criteria and definitions, only anti-Semitism
could be identified as an integral component of Guardist fascism
in 1934. The Legionaries had no monopoly on chauvinism, hooliganism, and notions of dictatorship. Chauvinism was not an
indispensable part of their political philosophy; hooliganism was
held in abeyance; their ideas on dictatorship were still poorly
defined. In fact, an element of idealism and Christian mysticism
pervaded the movement. But this was to change under the impact
of domestic political reaction against the potentially explosive
doctrine of the Guardists and of the rapid progress recorded by
fascism in Germany, Italy, and Spain.

The transformation of the Guardist movement from an idealis-
tic, politically immature, Christian reformist crusade into a brutal,
hooliganistic, and fanatically anti-Semitic program occurred after
its expectations were frustrated by the political forces associated
with Carol II. Between 1934 and 1937 the Legionaries concentrated on preaching rural reform and anti-Semitic doctrine while
also condemning the mores of the political establishment. Their
moderation was due partly to the belief that accommodation with
Carol was possible, since he and some of his industrial friends lent
financial and occasionally ideological support to Codreanu's team,
but mostly to their expectation of the eventual conversion of the
masses to populist fascism. And they had good reason to believe
the latter, as the reception of Legionaries in the village was generally warm and frequently enthusiastic. The Guardists were also

welcomed by the clergy, anxious to participate in Christian reform, as well as by school teachers, students, and disgruntled
intellectuals and bureaucrats who for one reason or another believed in moral rejuvenation and, in any event, were anti-Semitic.

The extent of the penetration of the village and the effectiveness of the Guardist movement in the country at large were at
the time underestimated by all political parties except those concerned with the attitude of the peasantry. By 1937 the National
Peasant Party, the Plowmen's Front, and the latter's ideological
ally, the disorganized Communist Party, alone recognized the
depth of Guardist influence. Characteristically, their reactions
differed: the dominant conservative wing of the National Peasant
Party sought an *Ausgleich* with the Legion in the common political struggle against the National Liberals and their patron, the
King; the communists and leaders of the Plowmen's Front responded by intensifying their heretofore empty campaign against
fascism. It is fair to state that the responses of these political
groups, particularly the National Peasants, gave more direction
to the fascist movement in the crucial months immediately preceding and following the ill-fated election of December 1937 and
establishment of the "monarcho-fascist" dictatorship of Carol II
in February 1938 than Carol's own increasingly sharper reaction
to Guardist successes and the activities of the Legion's foreign
friends, Hitler, Franco, and Mussolini.[10]

Contacts, both ideological and financial, between the Rumanian fascists and their counterparts elsewhere were surprisingly
limited in the early thirties. Mussolini's flirtations and subsequent
engagement to Rumania's revisionist neighbors Bulgaria and Hungary did not entail the establishment of any meaningful relations
with Codreanu and his associates. If anything, the Legionaries
were as opposed as the monarchy to these Italian policies, regarding them as unjust and anti-Rumanian. The Legion also appears
to have been immune to the doctrine of Italian fascism. Similarly,

Authoritarianism, Dictatorship, War

Hitler's assumption of power in Germany and the initiation of his political and economic penetration into Rumania did not involve the Iron Guard. If anything, the Guardists were shunned by Berlin, which preferred orderly action through the King to working through illegal and untested ideological sympathizers. It is not improbable, however, that funds were made available to the Guardists for pursuit of anti-Semitic and pro-German propaganda, and the foreign activities of the Legionaries, chiefly as Rumanian volunteers in the Spanish Civil War, are known to have been largely financed by the Nazis. But the sums expended by the Germans on Rumanian fascists in Spain were apparently no larger, and probably smaller, than those spent by the Russians on the Rumanian communists who joined the antifascist forces in the same conflict.

Significantly, the Spanish Civil War provided the Iron Guard with both the political-military experience and the ideological exposure to militant fascism that was to place the Legionaries in direct and mortal combat with the national and international forces of "Judaeo-communism." The crusading spirit that developed during the war affected the entire movement, following the veterans of the confrontation between the totalitarian right and left. Similarly, the antifascist cause was fought with greater conviction and deliberation by the defeated communist returnees. It was not by accident that the first major clash between the fascist and the communist crusaders occurred in the regional elections of 1936 with both sides vying for the support of the masses for their respective reformist plans. The accompanying verbal and physical battles between the members of Totul Pentru Tara and those of the communist-dominated Popular Front were further proof of the growing threat of fascism in Rumania. The communists and their sympathizers alone preached against the dangers of organized and disorganized fascism in a futile attempt to discredit the Guardists with the peasantry and the working class.

Authoritarianism, Dictatorship, War

The struggle for the allegiance of the masses was, of course, unequal, as the left was overpowered and outnumbered by the right. But once the struggle was enjoined the right benefited from the assistance given it by all opposed to communism as well as by those opposed to monarchic rule. The inroads made by the Iron Guard in the village and among the population at large in 1936–1937, with the blessings of those seeking common action by all dedicated to "Rumanianism," were so extensive that, when translated into concrete terms in the national election of December 1937, they spelled the difference between victory and defeat for directed democracy.

The official results of this last so-called free Rumanian election recorded the defeat of the National Liberal government, which was unable to muster even the minimum 40 per cent of the vote required to insure its continuance in power. The defeat was ascribed to the unexpected size of the Guardist vote, reported as 16 per cent of the ballots cast. It is now conceded by contemporary political observers that the actual fascist vote was well above that percentage. In fact, the King's decision not to proclaim the National Liberals the winners but instead to hand over the government to the right-wing coalition of Octavian Goga and A. C. Cuza was a clear reflection of his realization that the country was leaning toward the extreme right. The appointment of the Goga-Cuza cabinet was a stopgap measure anticipatory of the establishment of an outright royal dictatorship. The King's maneuver of December 1937 revealed not only his great political acumen but also his shock over the extent of the Guardist penetration into the society at large.

It would be erroneous to assume, as some analysts of the Rumanian fascist movement have done, that the size of the Guardist vote merely reflected the anti-Semitic sentiment of the Rumanian population. That this was not the case was amply proven by the failure of the Goga-Cuza electoral coalition, whose platform was specifically anti-Semitic, to obtain more than 9 per cent of the total popular vote or to stay in power for more than a few weeks on the basis of a purely nationalistic, anti-Semitic program. The success of the Guard, as Carol realized, was based on the broad support it received from the village and urban bureaucracy and intelligentsia and on the electoral alliance that it had concluded with the National Peasant Party earlier in 1937. Even if the majority of the peasantry did not vote Guardist, enough did to insure the defeat of the National Liberals.

It has been suggested, with much validity, that the National Peasant leadership knew that it could not muster a majority on its own strength and therefore decided to collaborate with the Iron Guard on the assumption that the combined vote would force the King to accept the popular mandate and summon a National Peasant coalition, if not an actual National Peasant government, to power. This thesis is apparently correct. Also correct appears to be the corollary interpretation that the virulence of the opposition, the Guard's in particular, increased when Carol upset their plans, first by appointing the unrepresentative Goga-Cuza regime and then by assuming dictatorial powers himself. The monarch's decision to substitute monarcho-fascism for legionary fascism of the populist-Guardist variety forced an immediate and far-reaching modification of tactics, policies, and alignments by the "betrayed" Guard and its political supporters. After February 1938 a life and death struggle began between the King and the Iron Guard.[11]

The threat posed by the Iron Guard to the continuation of "directed democracy" was real, but it was not this threat that caused Carol II to resort to personal dictatorship. It must be assumed that the monarch's decision was based foremost on the knowledge that any free election held after that of December 1937 would bring to power a government committed, if not to his physical abdication, at least to the curtailment of his actual power. Whether the National Peasants, headed by Maniu, or a coalition government of National Peasants and Iron Guardists, or perhaps even an outright Guardist regime would have emerged victorious, "directed democracy" would have come to an inglorious end. Carol, however, provided another political rationalization by elevating "directed democracy" to "collective democracy." According to him, the threats posed to the democratic order by fascism, internal and external, were beyond that order's ability to resist. To cope with the essential problem of national unification and welding together of the forces of resistance to fascism it was essential for the representative of the entire nation, the monarch, to bring about a true "national rebirth." The corporate state established in the spring of 1938 was indeed that of the *Frontul Renasterii Nationale* (Front of National Rebirth), headed by the national saviour himself, Carol II.[12]

The internal threat posed by the Iron Guard in early 1938 was grave. The external threat to Rumania's independence, or at least territorial integrity, had also increased after the *Anschluss*. But it is doubtful that either threat, in the months antedating Munich, was serious enough to justify the assumption of dictatorial powers by the King. It is particularly noteworthy that the Germans preferred collaboration with the monarchy to subversion of royal authority through the Iron Guard and that Berlin contained the forces of territorial revisionism in irredentist Hungary. Similarly the Italians, whose influence in revisionist Bulgaria was on the rise in the late thirties, did little to foment Bulgaria's territorial ambitions vis-à-vis the Dobrudja. It is possible, however, to agree with the contention of his defenders that Carol's dictatorship was both preventive and farsighted and that by its very nature it sought and partly achieved the unification and strengthening of the nation.

The royal dictatorship—"monarcho-fascist," as it has been characterized by its detractors—had but few of the characteristics ascribed by Roberts to fascist movements. It was not anticapitalistic, it was only moderately anti-Semitic and chauvinistic, and it contained no elements of racial glorification or hooliganism. It was, however, a dictatorship that "borrowed" two essential tenets of Guardist philosophy: nationalist social-reformism and national renaissance. The abolition of political parties and the establishment of "collective democracy" under the leadership of the King were designed to steal the thunder from the Iron Guard and its supporters, who had advocated successfully both national rebirth and social reform.

Carol's policies proved to be a poor substitute, however, for the militant idealism and reformism of Codreanu and his associates. It is not that the King was unable to gain the support of politicians who had flirted or even collaborated with the Iron Guard. Nor was the monarch devoid of success in seeking to retain or regain the allegiance of the dissatisfied peasantry through advocacy and occasional execution of pro-peasant policies. Carol's tragedy was his inability to destroy the Guard as a political force in Rumania. His foolhardy decision to execute Corneliu Zelea Codreanu and the Captain's closest associates in November 1938, "while trying to escape," and his subsequent attempt to carry out a policy of mass extermination of Legionaries strengthened rather than weakened the determination of the Rumanian right to rid itself of Carol at all cost. And, for the first time, the fascists secured the support of a Nazi Germany dissatisfied with the monarch's wavering foreign policy for the pursuit of their destructive program and tactics. Forced underground, the survivors of the Guardist purge assumed the role of martyrs and avengers of the dead. Between 1938 and 1940 they became the executioners of Carol's "accomplices," hooligans and assassins dedicated to the physical annihilation of their mortal enemies—Jews, communists, and royalists.

The struggle for power between Carol and the Guard was

only deceptively uneven before 1940. If Carol had the upper hand in 1938, it was only because the Germans were not ready, before Munich, to impose their dictates on Rumania. Superficially and temporarily their interests were sufficiently safeguarded by the Carolist dictatorship and the efficiency of the King's major-domo, Prime Minister Armand Calinescu. Nevertheless, the Germans and their sympathizers in Rumania were not out of touch with the remnants of the Legion, which to them represented a lever and an alternative to the "monarcho-fascists." Certainly after Munich the balance of power began to shift in the direction of the Guard. Carol's dictatorship was suspect because of his refusal to side overtly with Germany. The King's succumbing to German economic pressures in March 1939, as recorded in the onerous Nazi-Rumanian economic agreement of that month, did not satisfy the aggressive and suspicious German leadership any more than it did the "rejuvenated" Guard.

The royal dictatorship became increasingly more threatened during the second half of 1939, particularly after the Ribbentrop-Molotov agreement ushered in World War II. Carol, still anxious to maintain Rumania's neutrality, became increasingly more expendable for the Germans and certainly *de trop* for the Legionaries. In September 1939, as Poland's defeat was recorded, the Guard assassinated Calinescu in cold blood. Its challenge to the royal dictatorship was unmistakable, and the public execution of the assassins did not deter the Legionaries from pursuing their antiroyalist campaign as martyrs and saviours of the Rumanians from Carol. Defections from the King's to the Guard's cause were slow, at least on the surface, until the "Judaeo-communist conspiracy" was finally and fully "exposed" in June 1940. The seizure of Bessarabia and Northern Bukovina by the Soviet Union during that month vindicated the Guardist cause. And as France also lay prostrate before the superior German armies, the Legionaries appeared as the champions of true militant Rumanianism, defenders of the interests of Rumania against Bolshevism and Judaism, avengers of treacherous royalism, rectifiers of all ills afflicting Rumanian society and politics.

In fact, however, reform was no longer an essential part of their program; revenge, power, extermination of the Jew, destruction of the Bolsheviks and all other opponents of their plans for unlimited control of the country had become their main credo. In September 1940, as the Germans had cynically given Northern Transylvania to Hungary and the Bulgarians had secured Southern Dobrudja with Germany's support, "monarcho-fascism" came to an inglorious end. Carol barely escaped alive, most of his followers joined the Guardists, and his son, now King Michael, entrusted power to the Iron Guard and the pro-Guardist military leaders headed by General Ion Antonescu. A new crusade, anticommunist, anti-Semitic, and anti-all opponents of the Guard, was initiated under the "new" Iron Guard led by power-hungry men like Horia Sima and other "betrayers" of original Legionary goals.[13]

The triumph of Legionary fascism was, however, short lived. The Guardists, coming to power late, at a time of major international crisis on the eve of the entry of the German forces of occupation into Rumania, had little time to carry out their program. In the race against time they so disrupted the country's economy and engaged in such acts of hooliganism and crime against their enemies that they were forcibly removed from power in a bloody revolution of their own doing in January 1941. That revolution was an unprincipled blood bath for political survival, totally devoid of the reformist idealism that had permeated the movement in the thirties. The hooligans were defeated by the forces of order headed by the Guard's ally, Marshal Ion Antonescu, and supported by the German High Command. But the decimation of the Guardists did not mark the end of fascism or of the Guardist movement.

Authoritarianism, Dictatorship, War

Antonescu ruled the National Legionary State, which he and the Guard had set up in September 1940, as a fascist military dictatorship.[14] His dictatorship, however, differed from that of his predecessors' and from contemporary European counterparts in significant respects. He adopted many of the corporatist features that had characterized Carol's regime. He sought the support of all traditional conservative political groups and of responsible Legionaries for the pursuit of an anticommunist, nationalist crusade of his own. It is noteworthy that Antonescu did not claim the racist and anti-Semitic Guardist legacy and that he rooted out all manifestations of hooliganism. His reformist tendencies were closer to Carol's than to Codreanu's, concentrating, albeit for military purposes, on the modernization of agriculture and industry. His crucial error, inherent in the *raison d'être* of his dictatorship, was focusing the national effort onto the pursuit of an anti-Russian, anticommunist military campaign. To stamp out communism and retrieve the territories lost to the USSR in 1940, he unflinchingly committed Rumania to the fatal war against the Soviet Union launched by Hitler in June 1941. This is not to say that his appreciation of the Rumanian mood was necessarily unrealistic. In fact, it may be argued that the Antonescu synthesis of the socioeconomic, cultural, and political currents at work in Rumania at the time of the German-Rumanian invasion of the USSR and at least during the first two years of the war was perhaps the most realistic of all syntheses attempted in the twentieth century.

The test of the effectiveness of Antonescu's dictatorship and of its significance in the history of twentieth century Rumania was the degree of support it received from the Rumanian population at large between 1941 and 1944. A meaningful and conclusive analysis of the factors and attitudes that contributed to the mass endorsement of Antonescu's aims and policies is difficult because of Rumania's defeat in World War II. In a desperate search for justification of political success or failure, for legitimizing their positions in victory or defeat, the communists and their opponents have distorted the true nature of the war years and of Antonescu's place in the Rumanian historical tradition.[15] A few facts are, however, incontestable. Antonescu enjoyed the overwhelming support of the Rumanian nation for his military activities against the Soviet Union. His domestic policies were consonant with the interests of the majority of the population. His personal integrity was unsurpassed in modern Rumanian history. He rallied the nation, provided it with a sense of purpose, and for a few short years established the bases for potential economic and social progress.

His critics, at all spectra of the political rainbow, have accused him of betraying the "democratic" principles with which they identified themselves and the history of the Rumanians. Antonescu's contempt for the democratic processes of government was undeniable, but few were the voices seeking the restoration of democratic practices in 1941 or even later years. Certainly such demands were not voiced by the Iron Guardists, who accepted Antonescu's leadership after January 1941. More significantly, the "traditional" parties, the National Liberal and the National Peasant, endorsed the Antonescu regime without seeking adulteration of its dictatorial nature. It has been argued by the defenders of collaboration between Bratianu and Maniu and the Antonescu regime that the venerable leaders of Rumanian democratic parties had little choice but to work with Antonescu. But such explanations are unsatisfactory and unrealistic. The fact is that the political leaders, like the vast majority of their one-time constituents, could and did subscribe to the essential aspects of Antonescu's policies.

There has been much debate in political and academic circles concerning the Rumanian attitude toward Nazi Germany during World War II. Whereas a substantial majority of the analysts of

Rumanian politics subscribe to the thesis that collaboration was forced upon the Rumanians by the defeat of France and a desire to save the nation from conquest by a determined Third Reich, the secondary thesis that collaboration was acceptable because of the common goal of defeating Soviet Russia cannot be taken lightly.[16] It is true that the traditional Francophilia of the Rumanian upper and middle classes and of "democratic" politicians precluded wholehearted support of France's conqueror. Nevertheless there was very little opposition to Antonescu's decision to join the Axis in war against Russia or resistance to the German forces stationed in Rumania. On the contrary, it is fair to say that the German forces in Rumania stood for law and order and commanded the respect if not the support of the Rumanian politicians and people. It is also true that the decision to commit Rumania to war against Russia was endorsed by the majority of the population.

This *de facto* betrayal of long-term sympathies for France is not surprising. The Rumanian peasantry and working class—the vast majority of the population—never had a sense of political or moral commitment to France in any way comparable to that of the intellectuals, aristocracy, and part of the bourgeoisie. Whatever sympathies the masses might have had at one time were gradually eroded through exposure to the views of the Rumanian right or left, neither of which had anything but contempt for the decadent French. The extent of the educated and propertied classes' commitment to France has also been exaggerated by historians and politicians alike. The intellectuals in particular, whose allegiance to the Franco-Latin cultural legacy had been heralded for decades, had by and large subordinated the French liberal inheritance to a right-wing Rumanian nationalism. The inroads made by the Guardists in the Rumanian intellectual community in the thirties were far deeper than were suspected by most observers on the eve of the war. The fall of France was taken in stride, with crocodile tears.[17] This is not to say that the Rumanian intellectuals were pro-German; they were Rumanian nationalist and largely anti-Semitic and anticommunist. And, as a rule, those who did not fit into this category were sympathetic to Russia and hence silent. The majority could support Antonescu, and most did.

Similar considerations apply also to the other politically conscious groups. The landowners of aristocratic origin, the clergy, the upper state and private bureaucracy, the industrialists, bankers, and directors of large commercial enterprises—unless Jewish—could subscribe to the conditions under which they had to operate under Antonescu and the German allies. If anything, their own power and fortunes reached unsurpassed heights in the early years of the war. True as it may be that this prosperity was entirely due to industrial development related to the war requirements, there was little evidence to show rejection of this effort by its beneficiaries.

Somewhat more disputable are the estimates of the attitudes of political leaders and of the masses themselves toward the Antonescu dictatorship.[18] Defenders of the "traditional parties" have staunchly maintained that the Liberals and National Peasants supported the war effort only to the extent to which it involved the recouping of Rumanian territories: Bessarabia and Northern Bukovina. Moreover, men like Iuliu Maniu and Dinu Bratianu have been represented as opposed to the dictatorial aspects of Antonescu's regime. The evidence, however, does not fully substantiate these contentions until such times as the drive to secure pure Soviet territories collapsed at Stalingrad. Opposition by the leadership of the former Social Democratic Party, which indeed refused to cooperate with Antonescu in any form, is, however, a matter of record. It may be argued that the cooperation of the Social Democrats was not sought by the dictatorship, whereas that of the National Liberals and National Peasants was. Still, in the late stages of the war the Social Democrats were regarded as uncompromised by the elements of the population seeking alternatives to fascism or communism, whereas the National Peasants and National Liberals generally attracted the support of those who had either agreed to collaborate with Antonescu or favored the right over the left. It is noteworthy that the preference for the Social Democratic leadership at the end of the war was expressed not only by much of the industrial working class but also by a substantial segment of the peasantry.[19]

The extent to which this political realignment reflected a mass response to Antonescu's policies is a matter of conjecture. In general it is believed that the peasantry accepted the regime without serious reservations in 1941 but grew increasingly more weary as the promised reforms fell short of their expectations. Antonescu had repeatedly expressed his love for the peasant, and this sentiment was apparently reciprocated by the masses at the start of his dictatorship. But the wartime measures adopted by the dictatorship did not satisfy the peasant, particularly the system of price controls and the requisitioning of draft animals. The peasant was aware, however, of the major efforts made by Antonescu to increase mechanization of agriculture, and it is probable that he saw better times ahead. In all likelihood the peasants' disenchantment with Antonescu was caused ultimately by the staggering losses of manpower on the Russian front rather than—as it has been alleged—by the belated realization that only the National Peasant leadership could satisfy their socioeconomic and political desiderata. The support given by the peasantry to the Social Democrats in the last stages of the war would substantiate this evaluation of mass attitudes. The Rumanian peasant's acceptance of leadership by the National Peasant in the twenties, by the Iron Guard in the early thirties, for a short time even by Carol in the later thirties, and finally by Antonescu was based ultimately on the expectation of socioeconomic reform. The failure of all those in whom the peasants had placed their tentative trust, or at least hopes, for change accounts for the partial shift toward the untested but presumably reliable Social Democrats. The significance of this deviation was not fully appreciated by Antonescu and the traditional parties in the closing stages of the war but was to play a crucial part in the revolutionary reorganization of the Rumanian socioeconomic and political order in the years to follow.

The attitude of the peasantry was remarkably similar to that of the industrial working class. Contrary to the claims of the communists that the workers rejected the Antonescu dictatorship even more violently than they had the "bourgeois-landlord cliques" of the interwar years, the industrial working class was one of the foremost beneficiaries of the war. The rapid expansion of industry and the related improvement in wages and technological progress provided a modicum of respectability for the working class. It is unclear whether the workers wholeheartedly supported the war effort against Russia. But any reservations they may have had were due to factors other than sympathy toward the Soviet Union and international communism. The disintegration of the Rumanian war effort made political realignments necessary; the workers opted overwhelmingly for the Social Democrats. This choice itself is significant because the Social Democratic Party stood for Rumanian solutions to Rumanian socioeconomic and political problems. In fact, the "national" character of the Social Democratic programs for socioeconomic change appealed to those seeking alternatives to traditional nationalist or outright internationalist, communist panaceas. But none of the alternatives that became available toward the end of the war repudiated Antonescu's synthesis altogether.

The war, in short, discredited Antonescu as a general and statesman but not as a patriot and nationalist. The unsuccessful war, however, rendered obsolete all traditional formulae for reconciliation of the socioeconomic and political forces in Rumanian society and hence also the supreme nationalists' goal of an unreformed Greater Rumania. A democratic formula for the construction of a modern, prosperous Greater Rumania may have been possible at the end of the war. It was probably desired by the majority of the population. Perhaps a nondemocratic, authoritarian but Rumanian solution would have been an acceptable alternative. But neither formula was feasible as Antonescu's regime was removed by a coup d'état and the Russian armies moved into Bucharest in August 1944.

4

THE LEGACY TRANSFORMED
Continuity, Change, and Legitimacy

A UGUST 23, 1944, is regarded as the day of enslavement by
opponents of communism and the day of liberation by the
communists and their supporters. To the anticommunists August
23 symbolizes the end of the old order, which, no matter how
imperfect, functioned according to Rumanian principles within
a national Rumanian framework. Indeed, in the summer of 1944
the *ancien régime* and its defenders were faced with two formidable inimical forces: Communist Russia and her agent in Rumania, the Rumanian Communist Party. The efforts of the politically conscious were directed at that time toward circumventing
the reality of August 1944, toward seeking formulae for compromise that would guarantee the continuation of the Rumanian
nation, Rumanian society, and Rumanian politicians within a
"democratic"—if necessary even socialist—but clearly independent Rumania. The coup d'état of August 23 was engineered by
the very forces that thought such a national solution to be feasible and attainable by the mere ousting of Antonescu and the
sudden and unilateral reversal of alliances. The efforts of the
communists, Russian and Rumanian, directly opposed to any
compromise other than one that would assure their eventual control of Rumania and the corollary transformation of the country's

socioeconomic and political order according to Soviet prototype, clashed directly with those seeking the reconstruction of the old order in a manner compatible with their interests. In the last analysis, the future significance of August 23 was to be determined by the relative accuracy of the traditional parties' and the communists' appraisals of the political realities of 1944.[1]

Of primary importance to the internal protagonists in the struggle for political power was the attitude toward Rumania of the United States and the Soviet Union. Of secondary importance was the attitude of the Rumanian population at large toward the Soviet Union and the Rumanian Communist Party. It is difficult to determine the grounds for confidence placed in the United States by General Constantin Sanatescu and his associates in the "democratic" regime established on August 23. Unofficial conferences conducted with representatives of the Western powers during the last months of the Antonescu regime should have been discouraging. The United States had few stakes in Rumania. Historically, relations between the two countries had been insignificant. Few Rumanians knew English, still fewer had visited the United States. Correspondingly, few Americans had been to Rumania before the war; in fact, not many were even aware of Rumania's geographic location. Rumanian emigration to the United States had petered out in the interwar years, and the second generation of Rumanian-Americans was small in size and generally apolitical. American economic interests were restricted to investments in oil companies, like Standard Oil, and in a few subsidiaries of lesser American corporations.

Nevertheless, the "traditional parties" regarded America as Rumania's saviour because of the collapse of France and their mistrust of England. And this illusion was shared by the population at large, for whom America represented utopia. It is possible that the Rumanian diplomats who had sought to persuade Antonescu to surrender to the Allies and who were discussing that possibility with United States and British representatives in Cairo in the early months of 1944 derived encouragement from American resistance to the British formula for dividing the Balkans into spheres of influence detrimental to Rumania. But it should have been evident to the Rumanians that the gradual weakening of American resistance to Churchill's proposed *quid pro quo* of Russian domination in Rumania for a British sphere of influence in Greece could have been fatal to their plans for an independent Rumania. It is known that the timing of the coup of August 23 was partly determined by the necessity to frustrate the implementation of the British and Russian plans for Rumania and to prevent their acceptance by the United States. But it is also known that the very doubts about America's readiness to oppose the establishment of a Soviet sphere of influence in Rumania caused King Michael and his closest political associates to allow the inclusion of a leading communist, Lucretiu Patrascanu, in the Sanatescu cabinet on August 23. The hope of American support entertained by the leaders of the traditional parties—the National Peasants' Maniu, the National Liberals' Bratianu, and the Social Democrats' Petrescu—and of their representatives in the Sanatescu regime was not shared by the communists, whose awareness of Russia's true intentions and Churchill's amenability to accepting solutions of Balkan problems favorable only to British interests determined their course of action. The communists' goal was the subversion of the Sanatescu regime and of American influence in Rumania.[2]

The main unanswered question of August 1944 concerns the extent to which the Rumanian population at large was cognizant of the aims of the Russian communists and of the Soviet Union. Little is known about popular reaction to the Rumanian communists or the Soviet Union—certainly not enough to accept without reservation the view that in the summer of 1944 the Rumanians were hostile to both. Such hostility did indeed develop by 1945, but even at that recognizable date it is difficult to differentiate between the anticommunist and the anti-Russian sentiments of the population. This very problem of potential sympathy with the aims of the Rumanian communists despite outright rejection of Soviet imperialism is of cardinal importance in evaluating the significance of the communist movement and the role of the Rumanian communists in twentieth-century Rumania.

The history of the communist movement in Rumania before 1944 is obscure.[3] The Rumanian Communist Party itself was established in 1921 as a splinter group of the Social Democratic Party. It was then as ineffectual as the parent organization, which had played only an insignificant role in Rumanian politics since its own establishment in 1893. The Social Democratic Party had suffered from lack of a power base, resulting from the virtual absence of an industrial working class in pre-World War I Rumania and the predilection of Rumanian intellectuals for nationalist causes. As a result, the Social Democratic membership consisted of uneducated workers and non-Rumanian intellectuals, and the party was led by such foreigners as the Russian Jew Constantin Dobrogeanu-Gherea and the Bulgarian radical Christian Rakowski. It was thus vulnerable to attack on both social and national grounds. The problems of the social democratic movement were compounded during and after World War II by the swelling of its ranks with alien and often extremist elements belonging to the social democratic and other workers' organizations from the newly incorporated provinces of Greater Rumania, chiefly Transylvania and Bessarabia. A fierce internecine struggle for power between the pro-Bolshevik Bessarabian faction, favoring allegiance to Moscow, and the moderate Old Rumanian and Transylvanian leadership, seeking a national basis for the party's operation in Greater Rumania, tore the organization asunder in 1921.

In May of that year the pro-Bolshevik "maximalists" deserted the Social Democratic Party to form the Rumanian Communist Party. The immediate reason for the split was the moderates' refusal to approve affiliation with the Third International, which the maximalists desired. The maximalists' decision to subordinate their new party to the Communist International did not provide a basis for effective operation of the communist movement in Rumania. The internal difficulties that had troubled the Social Democratic Party were transferred to the communist organization, where they focused on the crucial issue of relations with Moscow. The Rumanian workers and intellectuals who joined the Communist Party sought control of the organization and the right to overt political action in Rumania, albeit under Moscow's guidance. The Bessarabians and a few Rumanian radicals fought for the execution of Moscow's plans for the Rumanian movement: underground activities and unequivocal subordination to the Kremlin. In practice the struggle was resolved in Moscow's favor. The Communist Party, outlawed by the National Liberal government in power in 1924, was never able to maintain a position of even relative autonomy from Moscow through the twenty years of ensuing "illegality."

It remains a matter of conjecture whether the Rumanian Communist Party could ever have established itself as a viable organization had it not been driven underground in 1924. The prevailing view is that it could not because its tenets were unacceptable to the proletariat and the satiated peasantry of post-World War I Rumania. It has been pointed out that the membership of the organization was always very small and that the proletarian contingent was in the hands of individuals unrepresentative of the industrial working class. Men like Alexandru Constantinescu and Gheorghe Cristescu, the leaders of the "workers' wing," have been regarded as ineffectual demogogues speaking for themselves rather than their class. The intellectuals have also been branded as ineffectual because of their commonly Jewish or foreign backgrounds and consequent divorcement from the realities of Rumanian life. In the opinion of skeptics, Ana Pauker, Marcel Pauker, Bela Brainer, and other leaders of the Communist Party could never have secured the confidence of the Rumanian masses.

The validity of these views is generally confirmed by the events of the period antedating the party's Fifth Congress (1932), during which four inconsequential congresses were held at the behest of Moscow. The repeated purges in the organization's Central Committee on such charges as right- or left-wing radicalism reflected internal factionalism and Moscow's desire to assert its total control over the Rumanian communist movement. In practice, neither the ethnic nor the social composition of the Central Committee or of the party as such underwent meaningful changes in these years.

It is almost impossible to ascertain the exact conformation of the Rumanian Communist Party's central organs in this period. Educated guesses attest to the predominance of intellectuals over workers and the almost total absence of peasants. It is also believed that non-Rumanians constituted a majority in the Politburo and the Central Committee. Equally vague are data on the social and ethnic composition of the membership at large and on the actual size of the organization. It is likely that at no time during the interwar years did the membership exceed a few thousand. The communists' following was, however, more substantial. Despite the traditional falsification of electoral results, the political front of the illegal Communist Party, the Workers' and Peasants' Bloc, obtained close to 75,000 votes (or 2 per cent of the total ballots cast) in all parliamentary elections antedating the party's Fifth Congress of 1932. Most of the ballots were apparently cast by industrial workers and intellectuals; the peasantry is believed to have lent only nominal support to the communists in the years antedating the Great Depression.

Continuity, Change, Legitimacy

The Kremlin's estimate of the impact of the depression on international politics, rather than the relative lack of success of the Rumanian communists in Rumania, caused the reorganization of the Rumanian Communist Party and the adoption of a more militant course of political action at the congress of 1932. The party's upper echelons were packed with men and women, mostly non-Rumanians, committed to Stalin's precepts. "Foreigners" like Boris Stefanov, Stefan Foris, Remus Koffler, Vasile Luca, Iosif Chisinevski, Iosif Ranghet, Bela Brainer (and Ana Pauker in 1934) outnumbered and overpowered such Rumanian leaders as Lucretiu Patrascanu, Sorin Toma, and Constantin Parvulescu. On the other hand, a deliberate effort was made to enroll young members and to allow their representatives to assume positions of secondary leadership in the organization. It was in the early thirties that Nicolae Ceausescu, Miron Constantinescu, and Alexandru Barladeanu, for instance, assumed prominence in the Rumanian communist movement.

Stalin's goal, translated into the program of the Rumanian Communist Party, was first to exploit the socioeconomic dissatisfaction of the working classes and peasantry impoverished by the economic crisis and to appeal to the unemployed young and the disgruntled intelligentsia, and second, after 1933, to stir up the antifascist sentiments of all those opposed to Hitler's Germany and Codreanu's Rumanian Iron Guard. It remains a matter of dispute whether this Stalinist scheme was incompatible with the Rumanian political reality and consequently doomed to failure. The workers' dissatisfaction, which exploded as the railwaymen's rebellion of 1933 and propelled Gheorghe Gheorghiu-Dej to the forefront of the "fighting working class," lends at least partial support to the basic accuracy of the communist diagnosis.[4] The inroads made by young communists into the ranks of the unemployed youth and by such dissident peasant political formations as the Plowmen's Front into the village also tend to confirm the communists' awareness of Rumania's socioeconomic problems. But the communists' failure to establish an effective Popular Front against fascism reflects their basic political weakness. Branded as "foreign" instruments of an anti-Rumanian international conspiracy, they were unable to resist the formidable police pressures and corollary denunciation of their activities by nationalist and fascist politicians in the thirties. Ultimately, however, the communists' failure was ascribable to their blind identification with Stalinist dicta and policies. Their position became totally untenable in 1939, when the USSR seized the Rumanian territories of Bessarabia and Northern Bukovina subsequent to the Ribbentrop-Molotov pact. The destruction of the Rumanian Communist Party through the incarceration of the known activists and leaders who could not flee to the Soviet Union was officially justified on the grounds of national treason rather than of opposition to communist programs for socioeconomic reform, which often paralleled those of the Rumanian fascists in power in 1939 and the war years.[5]

The fate and fortunes of the Rumanian Communist Party were profoundly altered during World War II. Internally, the decimated party underwent a major reorganization. The Rumanian survivors of the fascist period, mostly secondary figures in the prewar communist movement, who were incarcerated at the beginning of the war emerged as the leaders of the organization by August 1944. The assumption of leadership occurred in 1944, when Gheorghe Gheorghiu-Dej and his closest associates ousted the then First Secretary of the party, Stefan Foris, and replaced him with Gheorghiu-Dej. The so-called Rumanian group of the Rumanian Communist Party, consisting of Gheorghiu-Dej, Chivu Stoica, Gheorghe Apostol, Nicolae Ceausescu, and a few others of the current leaders of Rumanian communism, was in control of the Rumanian communist movement, such as it was, at the time of the coup of August 23, 1944.

Continuity, Change, Legitimacy

It is true that their own power was insignificant at that time both because of the minuscule size of the Rumanian Communist Party (estimated at about 1,000 members) and because of the Russians' unwillingness to accept the Rumanian leadership as the actual leadership of communism in Rumania. This is not to say, however, that the Rumanian communists were hated by the population at large or that communism was discredited in Rumania. Antonescu's defeat appeared imminent early in 1944. A fairer statement would be that the Rumanian communists were unknown to the Rumanian people. Also unknown to the Rumanian people were the intentions of Russia. Many Rumanians were willing to hope that the Soviet Union, as an ally of the Western powers, would forgive and forget the nation's "involuntary" involvement in the war and would accept the olive branch extended by the King on August 23, when Rumania joined the side of the Allies against its former partner Nazi Germany. There were also many who believed that Rumania's socioeconomic problems could be solved by communist formulae. Few realized the basic incompatibility between political freedom and Russian communism, and even fewer were aware of Russia's true intentions toward Rumania.

Like the Rumanian communists, Communist Russia was an unknown quantity. The historic memory of the Rumanians was short and unclear. The educated had been for many years indoctrinated to beware of the dangers of Bolshevism and the Soviet Union. The Bolsheviks were reputed to be the historic enemy of the Rumanian people. According to propagandists and politicians, the Russians had tried, at least since the eighteenth century, to expand their sphere of influence into the Rumanian provinces and had often sought to and occasionally did incorporate Rumanian territories into a Greater Russia. The Russians were also depicted as brutish, unfriendly toward the Rumanian masses, and, since the Bolshevik Revolution, bent on erasing the gains attained by

78

the Rumanian people during and after World War I through the communizing of Greater Rumania. In short, Russia could not be trusted and Bolshevism had to be opposed at all costs.

The extent to which this propaganda affected these exposed to it directly or the Rumanian population in general, to whom it was carried by the educated, is difficult to ascertain. There were certainly many Rumanians in 1944 who believed that, had Titulescu and Litvinov survived politically longer than they did, a reconciliation between monarchist Rumania and Communist Russia might have been reached in the thirties. There were also many who held Antonescu and the Germans responsible for an unwarranted attack on the Soviet Union and who hoped that the spirit of Litvinov would reappear at the end of World War II. Was not the Soviet Union, as an ally of the democratic United States and Britain, also committed to the establishment of a new and better world? Although these views were held primarily by antifascist intellectuals and urban professional groups, it is probable that the Rumanian working class was open-minded about the inevitable Russian occupation of Rumania and that the majority of the peasant population was prepared to make its peace with the Russians in the early months of 1944. It is doubtful that the Rumanian population regarded the Russian armies as "liberators" and friends as they entered Rumanian territory in 1944, as has been claimed by communist propagandists, but it is equally doubtful that they regarded them as enemies bent on the destruction of Rumania and its people. Probably the hope for a *modus vivendi* between Rumanians and Russians was entertained by a majority of the Rumanian population.

Whatever optimistic expectations the Rumanians may have had in the summer of 1944, they were soon to be deceived. The crucial questions of why the Russians refused to accept a *modus vivendi* with the Rumanians, why they pressed for the unconditional surrender of the Rumanian people, political organizations, and even the Rumanian Communist Party, remain unanswered. A variety of explanations given for the Kremlin's attitudes and actions has ranged from premeditated intent for conquest and subjugation to a defensive reaction to anti-Russian plots engendered by fascist or profascist Rumanian leaders in the "pay of Anglo-American imperialists." The question of whether Russia was the aggressor in Rumania or whether the Russians merely responded to provocations by anticommunists defies a simple answer. Evidently, the Russians were determined to control Rumania or at least to establish an unequivocal sphere of influence there from the moment the victory over Nazi Germany was in sight. Since the fall of 1943, the Russians had sought Rumania's unconditional surrender in an effort to prevent the establishment of any meaningful "bourgeois" pro-Western regime. It would appear that the Russians were opposed, at least since crossing into Rumanian lands early in 1944, to the establishment of any government that could not be controlled by Moscow. Be this as it may, the regime summoned to power by King Michael on August 23 did not meet Russia's requirements and, receiving neither the undivided support of the Western powers or the backing of the Rumanian population at large, was doomed to failure. In fact, the Sanatescu government was unable to remain in office for more than three months.

By September 12, when the armistice convention between Rumania and the Allied powers (the United States, Great Britain, and the Soviet Union) was signed, the Western contingent had *de facto* accepted the irrevocable presence of the Soviet armies in Rumania and the assignment of Rumania to the Soviet sphere in Europe. It is true that the Americans regarded the presence of Russia as more temporary than did the British, but there is no reason to believe that the American government was at that time prepared to oppose Russia's policies and plans for Rumania. As for the British, they were fully prepared to commit Rumania to

Soviet domination in the fall of 1944. Churchill himself admitted to agreeing to a 90 per cent sphere of Russian influence in that country during talks held with Stalin in Moscow in October. Whether Churchill's generosity was motivated by recognition of Russia's determination to control Rumania at all costs or by the British desire to maintain its own sphere of interest in Greece at this same price is unclear. In all probability Churchill sought to obtain the greatest benefits for England in Greece on a correct reading of Russian intentions toward Rumania.

The corollary question of whether the United States and Britain would have been willing (and able) to support the Sanatescu regime and oppose the abuses of power perpetrated by the occupying Red Army in Rumania must be answered less equivocally. Neither ally was prepared to take a firm stand in support of Sanatescu at the risk of political confrontation with the USSR. The exigencies of the war in the West and in the Mediterranean area precluded positive action in Rumania in the fall of 1944. It is fair to say, however, that if Britain had in effect relegated Rumania to Russian domination and communism, the United States still believed, unrealistically, that these trends could be checked, if not reversed, at the end of the war. In any event, the policies of the United States and Britain confronted the Sanatescu regime and its supporters with alternatives that they were unprepared to accept.[6]

Sanatescu had few choices in August 1944 with the country at war and the Russian armies in Rumania. The obvious one was to collaborate with the Russians and the Rumanian Communist Party, at least until such times as the resolution of the country's political future could be made by the Allied powers. Sanatescu rejected that course of action as incompatible with Rumania's traditions and national interest. In his view and that of the leading Rumanian political organizations—the National Peasant Party, the National Liberal Party, and the Social Democratic Party—col-

81

laboration with Russia and the Rumanian communists could be considered only in the context of a coalition government dominated by the traditional parties. This position reflected a profound lack of insight into the realities of the national and international situation. It is uncertain whether enlargement of the communist membership in the Sanatescu cabinet and adoption of some of the political desiderata voiced by the Rumanian Communist Party would have affected the ultimate outcome of the political struggle between the traditional organizations and the communists. It is certain, however, that such actions would have altered the course of the dissolution of the old regime and that of Rumanian history as well.

The resistance to accepting the basic demands of the Rumanian communists—instigating agrarian reform, energetically pursuing war against Germany with a view to recouping Northern Transylvania, promoting workers' power in industry, purging war criminals and fascists, democratizing the army, etc.—was based on a multitude of reasons reflecting divisions in the coalition. The necessity to safeguard the political interests of conservatives, nationalists, propertied classes, workers, peasants, fascists, and all other components of the Rumanian socioeconomic and political spectrum allegedly represented by the Sanatescu regime precluded compromises with the communists. The communists' demands were shelved because they were deemed untimely during a period of continuing military action against Germany and because, in the view of the government, all major decisions had to await the end of the war. This holding operation was based on a series of unrealistic assumptions regarding the Rumanian communists, the Rumanian people, the Soviet Union, and the United States.

The Sanatescu government underrated the effectiveness of communist propaganda and activities and overrated the reliability of the groups that it thought to represent. It has been agreed by students of Rumanian politics that enormous inroads were made by the Rumanian Communist Party among the population in general in the weeks succeeding the events of August 23. Most writers have ascribed the enormous number of recruits to the organization (membership grew from an estimated 1,000 to a few hundred thousand in a few weeks) to opportunism and pressure. True as this diagnosis may be, the causes of the opportunism and the nature of the pressure have not been determined. Investigation does lead to slightly different answers from those previously supplied and to a somewhat different understanding of the country's and the communists' mood and intentions in the crucial summer and fall of 1944.[7]

It is too simplistic to assume that a substantial number of the upper echelons of the fascist elite, a substantial part of the intelligentsia, of the upper army cadres, and even of the business community, collaborated with the Rumanian communists and the Russians only because they wanted to save their own compromised positions. Evidently, there were many opportunists among the joiners, but also many sympathizers, or at least realists, who foresaw the inevitability of the establishment of a communist-dominated regime in Rumania. The industrial workers and peasants who joined the Communist Party or made their armistice with the Russians also sensed the reality of the situation or found the platform of the communists and their front organizations palatable if not altogether acceptable.

It is a matter of record, however, that Sanatescu and his supporters countered the inroads made by the communists by rallying the opposing elements in society, particularly those identified with Antonescu's regime. Thus, as the polarization of right and left became distinct in the fall of 1944, the "center" groups were forced to take sides at a time when they would have preferred not to. The Social Democrats were gradually leaning more and more to the left and the National Peasants and National Liberals to the right as the Sanatescu government, on the one hand, and the Rumanian Communist Party, on the other, became clearly identifiable as opposing forces. This is not to say that the population at large and the urban elite were procommunist or profascist; in fact, the vast majority appears to have been indifferent to the political wrangling involved or at least unwilling to choose sides. Whether the peasants would have supported the National Peasant Party and the workers the Social Democratic Party, had the polarization been avoided, is a matter of dispute. The fact is that they had no choice, given the intensification of communist and Russian pressures against the Sanatescu regime and Sanatescu's and his supporters' determination to resist those pressures at any cost. The conflict gained momentum during the winter, when the combatants formulated their respective positions in ideological terms: Sanatescu as the guardian of Rumania against communism; the Russians and the communists as the champions of a new "democratic" Rumania.

The ensuing struggle for power and for the control, if not the allegiance, of the masses assumed increasingly more dramatic proportions as the Sanatescu government was forced, under Russian pressure, to strengthen the communist contingent in the cabinet. Early in November, Gheorghiu-Dej assumed the position of Minister of Transportation, and Petru Groza, the head of the Plowmen's Front, of Vice-Premier. In turn, Sanatescu appointed N. Penescu, of the National Peasant Party, to the crucial post of Minister of Interior. The removal of Penescu, who controlled the police, gendarmeries, and local administrative officials, became the battle cry of the communists, while his maintenance in office was regarded as essential by Sanatescu and his political allies. The showdown came late in November, when Penescu forcibly put down a communist-organized demonstration seeking to oust him.

It would be difficult to argue, as has been done by several writers on Rumanian politics, that Penescu resorted to military action against the demonstrators in the interest of public order alone. The showdown between Penescu and the communists was symbolic of a life and death struggle between anticommunist Rumanians and the communists, Rumanian and Russian, which was in effect ultimately resolved in favor of the latter. The replacement of Sanatescu's cabinet by one led by General Nicolae Radescu on December 2 represented a major concession to the Russians and the communists.[8] Radescu's assumption of the post of Minister of Interior, while appointing Teohari Georgescu, a member of the Communist Party's Central Committee, as Under-Secretary in that ministry, emphasized the magnitude of the "traditionalists'" defeat. Nevertheless, Georgescu's appointment did not reflect any desire by Radescu and his supporters to come to final terms with the communists. If anything, the polarization of the conflicting political aims of the traditional parties and of the communists and their supporters in the country at large became more definite in the three months during which the Radescu regime was able to maintain itself in office.

In retrospect, Radescu's opposition to the establishment of a genuine coalition regime with the communists and his rejection of the communists' political platform may be attributed to his misreading the intentions of the United States toward Rumania. The Yalta Conference of February 1945 provided Radescu and his supporters with the hope that the Americans would not allow a Russian takeover in Rumania. Radescu's interpretation of Yalta was shared by the National Liberal leadership, as well as by the politically conscious or active anticommunists in the country at large. Unfortunately for them, the reading of American intentions was both incorrect and naïve; for them to assume that the United States would intervene in Rumanian internal affairs to support the Radescu regime or would oppose the Russians and Rumanian communists for their "misinterpretation" of the Yalta message was political self-deception.

Continuity, Change, Legitimacy

There can be little doubt that the Russians and the Rumanian communists sought to exploit the Yalta agreements to their advantage and to bring down the Radescu government as soon as possible. Evidently, the anti-Radescu demonstrations organized by the communists, which accused Radescu and the National Peasant and National Liberal parties of harboring fascists and promoting antidemocratic actions, were aimed at the establishment of a communist-dominated regime in Rumania. The nature of that regime and the timing of the replacement of Radescu's cabinet were profoundly affected, however, by Radescu's own actions. In February 1945, Radescu ordered a repetition, on a broader scale, of the actions that had caused Sanatescu's downfall a few weeks earlier. Troops loyal to his regime forcibly put down a communist-led demonstration in Bucharest on February 24, and he himself justified his action by denouncing the communist leaders Ana Pauker and Vasile Luca—Moscow's most trusted representatives in Rumania—as "foreign" agents of a "foreign power," the Soviet Union. This intemperate action, reflecting the attitude of a substantial segment of the leadership of the traditional parties, was exploited by Moscow to its immediate advantage. It provided the Kremlin with a rationale for demanding the capitulation of the "fascist" Radescu "clique" and the inauguration of a communist-dominated coalition government headed by Petru Groza on March 6, 1945.

It has been recognized by both communists and their opponents that the establishment of the Groza government marked the end of the *ancien régime*.[9] After March 1945, it has been claimed, the traditional parties could no longer hope to restore the political and socioeconomic patterns of the prewar period or to modify them according to a "bourgeois-capitalist" interpretation of the realities of post-"liberation" Rumania. Although there can be no quarrel with that interpretation, it is possible to challenge the corollary presumption of noncommunist writers that the traditional parties could have found viable solutions to Rumania's problems had the Soviet Union not imposed Groza's rule on Rumania, as well as of communist writers that the Groza regime was representative of the interests of the Rumanian people and enjoyed the confidence of the masses in March 1945.

Between August 1944 and February 1945 the traditional parties, through miscalculation and inaction, lost their opportunity to bring about the "democratization" of Rumania's political and socioeconomic order. Their unrealistic reliance on the United States and corollary failure either to promulgate a broad program of social reform independent of that of the communists, or to accept the necessity of meaningful collaboration with the communists—at the risk of losing their "traditional" political identity—played into Moscow's hands. By March 1945 the Russians and the Rumanian communists and their allies could claim that Radescu and the leaders of the National Peasant Party and the National Liberal Party associated with the "old regime" were bent on dividing the country, were committed to reactionary and regressive policies, were tolerant of fascism and inimical of communism—in short, were *de trop*. Exaggerated as the communists' condemnation may have been, it is evident that after Yalta and the polarization of pro- and anticommunist positions among the politically active and conscious Rumanians no possibility existed of Russian acceptance of a coalition government of the Sanatescu or Radescu variety.

On the other hand, the establishment of the Groza regime through Russian pressure did not necessarily preclude reconciliation of the "democratic" interests of the traditional parties with those of the "democratic forces" headed by Petru Groza in a new "people's democratic" synthesis. It is probable that the Russians would have preferred the establishment of an outright communist regime in March 1945. This thesis has been generally accepted by historians of the period who have argued that only fear of United States intervention and of an internal revolution in Rumania prevented the Kremlin's emissary, Andrei Vishinsky, from imposing on King Michael a government consisting almost entirely of communists. This explanation for Vishinsky's moderation is essentially correct and thus deserving of close analysis.[10]

The Russians were evidently unprepared to challenge the United States overtly in March 1945 by forcing a totally unrepresentative government upon Rumania. This disinclination was due, not to fear of American retaliation against a *fait accompli*, but to international political considerations transcending the Rumanian problem. More difficult to explain is the moderation displayed by Vishinsky in the selection of the membership of the Groza cabinet. Although the majority of the cabinet consisted of members of the Communist Party and the key ministries of the interior and of justice were controlled by such party stalwarts as Teohari Georgescu and Lucretiu Patrascanu, it is significant that the Russians insisted on a purely Rumanian regime and on the inclusion of four members of the traditional parties in the new government. The appointment of men like Gheorghe Tatarescu to the post of Vice-Premier and Minister of Foreign Affairs has been rightly regarded as window dressing for the Kremlin. But Moscow's insistence on a pure Rumanian regime reflected more subtle policies and concerns that would have far-reaching consequences.

It is improbable that the Russians' decision was based on a conscious policy of avoiding the appearance of interference in Rumania's internal affairs. The view that Russia desisted from including "foreigners" like Pauker and Luca in a Rumanian cabinet for that reason is refuted by the evidence. Nor is it possible to accept as an explanation the corollary theory that the Rumanian masses would have reacted violently to the inclusion of non-Rumanian communists in a Rumanian government in March

1945. The basic reasons for Russia's apparent moderation are related to the Kremlin's acceptance of the advice of the "moderates" in the Rumanian Communist Party, who urged the pursuit of policies of "persuasion" of Rumanians by Rumanians with a view to gaining the support of the masses for "progressive" ("democratic") reforms. It is now believed that the Rumanian communists who had been working among the industrial working class and the peasantry entertained the hope of neutralizing, if not converting, a substantial part of the Rumanian population. Through systematic propaganda and specific political action the workers and peasants were, in the communists' view, susceptible to alienation from the Social Democratic and National Peasant parties. Through class and personal identification with the desiderata of the have-nots in Rumanian society the communists hoped to get close to the masses, closer than the nonworker and nonpeasant leaders of the traditional parties. In the eyes of the moderates, the injecting of non-Rumanian and nonproletarian or peasant elements into the government would have weakened the chances for a nonviolent transition to "democracy." Violence, indeed, had to be avoided at any cost to prevent political embarrassment to the communists, Rumanian and Russian alike. This, it was argued, was all the more important because the "fascists" and their allies, the National Peasant leaders, headed by Maniu, would use nationalist and anticommunist propaganda to retain or regain the allegiance of the Rumanian people, presumably with a probability of success.

It is difficult to sustain or accept the thesis propounded by current Rumanian historians that the Rumanian communists and their allies were motivated primarily by the desire to create, by peaceful means, a political climate in Rumania that would assure their victory at the polls in free elections. Nor is it possible to accept the view that the communists' plan in February 1945 was to establish the bases for a "democratic" Rumania for Rumanians and by Rumanians through the adoption of "national-communist" policies.[11] The evidence allows only acceptance of the theory that certain Rumanian members of the Communist Party—men like Gheorghe Gheorghiu-Dej, Lucretiu Patrascanu, perhaps even Teohari Georgescu—sought to establish the bases for peaceful transition to a purely communist regime through "grass-roots" appeals and corresponding political actions albeit in accordance with the wishes of the Kremlin and under its direction. The evidence also attests to the fact that Moscow was agreeable to this formula and rejected the extremist solution advocated by non-Rumanian leaders, like Pauker and Luca, whereby Russia would have assumed total control over Rumanian affairs in March 1945 through the establishment of a hand-picked communist regime.

The Kremlin's decision, logical and necessary as it was under the "objective" national and international conditions prevalent in March 1945, allowed the Groza regime and the Rumanian Communist Party to assume the mantle of political legitimacy and of "democratic" continuators and executors of Rumania's "true" historic tradition. As Groza was sworn into office on March 6, 1945, it was evident to all that postwar Rumania was to be rebuilt on bases different from those of the past. But the foundations of the "new Rumania" would, apparently, be Rumanian.

5

THE LEGACY TRANSFORMED
The Loss of National Identity

IF AUGUST 23, 1944, recorded the presence of Russia as a decisive force in Rumanian affairs, March 6, 1945, recorded the presence of communism as an immovable force in postwar Rumania. The die had been cast in March 1945, but the mold of the "new Rumania" had not hardened. The recurring question of whether the new national synthesis of a "people's democracy"—which became a fact in 1947—would have been less violent had the anti-communists accepted the inevitable in March 1945, recognized the legitimacy of the Groza regime, and collaborated with the Russians and Rumanian communists, may be dismissed as academic. But the continuing strife between the right and the left, which could end only in the victory of the left, made the Rumanian "revolution" all the more rigid and violent. Also, these considerations are hardly academic because two separate revolutions were in fact occurring simultaneously between March 1945 and December 1947: the first directed at the destruction of the power base of the traditional political forces, and the second at gaining control of the Rumanian Communist Party. Neither of these struggles for power was ended by the time the old monarchic regime was proclaimed officially dead and the new "people's democratic" regime established in December 1947. And their continuation well into the fifties—with repercussions still felt in contemporary Rumanian political life—was rooted in the events of the crucial period from March 1945 to December 1947.

One fundamental advantage derived from the resistance in those years to the "socialist transformation" of the country was the maintenance of a Rumanian national identity. In the last analysis, the traditional political parties and their supporters opposed Groza, the communists, and their Russian patrons as enemies of the national political tradition, as antinationalist forces bent on destroying Rumania and Rumanianism. The Kremlin's and the Rumanian communists' reaction to this challenge affected more profoundly the course of Rumanian history and that of the Rumanian Communist Party than any other factor in the last twenty years, perhaps even in the twentieth century. The communists' identification with the Rumanian historical tradition was based on internal as well as foreign political considerations. To demonstrate to the Rumanian masses that the Groza regime was immediately concerned with the realization of their unfulfilled desideratum of 1918 and later years—socioeconomic reform in an independent Rumania—an ambitious program of land reform was promulgated on March 25. Groza, to win mass support for his government and for the Soviet Union (and thus counter the anti-Soviet and anticommunist campaign of the traditional parties), had announced only a few days earlier Stalin's decision to return Northern Transylvania to Rumania.[1]

The significance of these actions, characterized as crude and cynical manifestations of an alien regime, has been generally belittled by students of Rumanian affairs. Subsequent reappraisals of Groza's role in Rumanian politics in this period, however, tend to indicate that he and his closest communist associates may have been cynical but not necessarily alien. In fact, Groza, Gheorghiu-Dej, and Patrascanu, the principal members of the cabinet, were closer to the masses than had been assumed and did seek, in their own way, the reintegration of Rumania.[2] It may not be exaggerated to assert that these men were "communist patriots" to the extent permitted by the Soviet Union and by their own relations to the Kremlin and the rest of the Rumanian Communist Party hierarchy. It is also possible to ascertain, from this early date, a correlation between "state" action and "party" action, at least to the extent to which the Groza government represented the state. In the eyes of the traditional parties and, to a definite degree also the monarchy, the Groza regime was unrepresentative of the national interest and in fact constituted a state within a state. The Communist Party, in this view, was even less representative of Rumania and its interests than the Groza government; the party was merely branded as a tool of Soviet imperialism. The accuracy of these allegations and contentions, by historians and politicians alike, is questionable.

The return of Northern Transylvania to Rumania was clearly a Russian gesture of political support for Groza. It was designed to legitimize the national identity of Groza's regime rather than—as heretofore assumed—to place the Soviet Union on the side of the angels. Whether the restoration of the Hungarian frontier of prewar years attained the desired results is a matter of dispute. If indeed the Rumanian population at large was anticommunist and anti-Russian in March 1945, the return of Northern Transylvania per se could not have alleviated its suspicions. The cynicism of Russia's action should have been all the more evident in that the possible restitution of Bessarabia and Northern Bukovina remained unmentioned. This contradiction, stressed by the traditional parties, was evident to all concerned with territorial adjustments. It could be argued that the Armistice Convention of September 1944 had left the Transylvanian question in abeyance and that many a Rumanian nationalist feared the permanent loss of all or part of the territory ceded to Hungary by the Vienna Diktat. The United States and Britain, although believed sympathetic to the Rumanian claims, were noncommital, and Russia's unilateral commitment of March 1945 confronted the Allies with a *fait accompli* for which the Kremlin could take full credit. It would be unreasonable to assume that the Soviet Union committed itself to the restoration of Transylvania primarily to win over Rumanian nationalists to the communist cause, particularly as it considered the annexation of Bessarabia and Northern Bukovina as irrevocable. It should be assumed, therefore, that the Soviet action was intended to strengthen the power base of Groza's regime in Rumania in general, and in Transylvania in particular, and to allow the implementation of agrarian "socialist" programs with which Groza and his party, the Plowmen's Front, had been historically identified.

The selection of Groza as Premier had not been accidental. He and his party had enjoyed substantial support among the Transylvanian peasantry since the thirties. Groza had always advocated equitable redistribution of land and subsequent reconciliation of national antagonisms between Magyar and Rumanian peasants in Transylvania. His opposition to the Vienna Diktat and his militant antifascism were also known (and appreciated) in Transylvania. His identification with "democratic" causes rendered him suspect to the wealthier peasants, but he was not addressing himself to the privileged rural strata in March 1945. He thus had better qualifications to play the role of agrarian reformer and friend of the peasantry of all nationalities than any direct representative of the Rumanian Communist Party or, for that matter, any turncoat "nationalist" peasant leader may have had at that time.

This is not to say that the Rumanian peasantry was deluded by the nature of the Groza regime and its purposes. Undoubtedly the majority of the rural population would have preferred to entrust its problems to one or another of the traditional parties had such a choice been available in the spring of 1945. The essential question, however, is whether—given the political reality of that year—the peasantry's reaction to the agrarian reform and policies of the Groza regime was basically hostile.[3]

Statistical data alone cannot provide much insight into the peasants' views on the value of the agrarian reform of March 1945. The reform was politically rather than economically motivated, and its effectiveness should be appraised in terms of its intent. There are disagreements among students of agrarian economy on the economic value of the reform. But it is generally agreed that the redistribution of some 1,000,000 hectares of land among some 800,000 beneficiaries resulted in the parcelization of the distributed land into economically nonviable entities. Critics of the economic aspects of the reform have rightly pointed out that the reforms of 1919–1921 provided 1,000,000 peasants with slightly over 4,000,000 hectares and that even such relatively larger plots did not satiate the peasants' land hunger. Such comparisons, however, tend to minimize the significance of the "egalitarian" principle of the reform of 1945, according to which the size of privately owned property could not exceed 50 hectares. Granted that "egalitarianism" was political in inspiration and intent—as were, for that matter, the clauses directed against "collaborationists" with the Germans, war criminals, and absentee landlords—it is possible to assume that all these aspects of the reform made the inadequate economic features more palatable to the land-hungry village proletariat.[4]

It may be presumed that the "poor peasant," for whose benefit and political allegiance the reform was actually ordered, was satisfied by Groza's measures. Since the "middle peasant" was not affected either negatively or positively, it is difficult to assess his reaction although credence may be given to the prevailing view that his basic mistrust of communism was not alleviated by Groza's agrarian policies. It is clear that the "kulaks" were distinctly uneasy over the new reform and its long-range implications and hence gravitated more and more toward the opposition parties, most notably the National Peasant organization. However, inasmuch as the majority of the Rumanian peasantry was "poor" and not politically conscious, the results of the agrarian changes should be regarded as essentially favorable to the Groza regime. If Groza did not gain the allegiance of most peasants, at least he won their neutrality. The neutralization of the masses was pursued also in the industrial field, where Groza's closest associate, Gheorghe Gheorghiu-Dej, led a campaign entirely similar to Groza's in the village.

If in 1945 Groza was indispensable to the Rumanian Communist Party and Moscow, Gheorghiu-Dej made himself equally indispensable during the same year.[5] The two men had similar assets: they were both identified with the masses. Gheorghiu-Dej's position was, however, more vulnerable than the Premier's. Groza was strictly a cooperative front man, the undisputed head of a noncommunist political organization. Gheorghiu-Dej was the First Secretary of the Rumanian Communist Party, a position that he had appropriated without the explicit consent of the Kremlin, and held only the post of Minister of Communications in the Groza cabinet. His political strength and future rested on his maintaining the position of First Secretary against challengers closely identified with Moscow. His principal source of strength was his own identification with a Rumanian communist tradition. Gheorghiu-Dej was a "man of the people," a potential "hero" of the Rumanian working class movement because of his role in the uprising of 1933, his uncompromising attitude toward fascism, and his close contacts with the Rumanian railwaymen, who comprised the hard core of the Rumanian Communist Party.

None of his visible associates in the Groza cabinet shared his national stature. Patrascanu, the Minister of Justice and one-time First Secretary of the party, was an intellectual who did not enjoy Moscow's confidence. Teohari Georgescu, the Minister of the

Interior, was Gheorghiu's inferior in the Communist Party and lacked his political acumen. Gheorghiu-Dej's competitors for power in the party itself were either foreigners like Pauker and Luca or, if Rumanian, subordinate or inexperienced or young. Thus Gheorghiu-Dej had to capitalize on his Rumanian assets, which he did both at the government and the party level. He carried the communist message to the Rumanian workers, whose champion he was, to weaken the influence of the Social Democratic Party among the proletariat and, concurrently, imprinted a Rumanian character on the program of the Rumanian Communist Party that the Kremlin and its friends in the party could not repudiate.

Gheorghiu's successes are now recognized by all students of postwar Rumania. The importance and effectiveness of his activities at both the state and the party level in the crucial period 1945–1947 have generally not gained comparable recognition. It was in 1945, particularly, that Gheorghiu-Dej rendered major services to the Kremlin and the Rumanian Communist Party and consolidated his position in the party beyond the reach of all who sought at least his political demise.

Students of Rumanian affairs have, in our estimation, overemphasized the obvious political factors that permitted the repudiation of international agreements on Rumania by the Soviet Union and the corollary consolidation and expansion of the power of the puppet Groza regime. Thus authors like Ghita Ionescu, the eminent analyst of Rumanian problems, tend to regard the expansion of Soviet power in Rumania as the sole reason for the country's inability to assert its independence and to secure American support for the attainment of that goal in 1945 and 1946.[6] There can be little quarrel with that view. But the concurrent consolidation of the power of the Rumanian Communist Party and the shaping of its program and internal structure in a manner that could not be wholly controlled by the Kremlin were at least as important as the visible national phenomena recorded in those fateful years.

The Soviet Union established the bases for exclusive economic exploitation of Rumania in May 1945. The creation of a series of joint Soviet-Rumanian companies—the so-called *Sovroms*—for the "exploitation and development of Rumania's natural resources and industries" was tantamount to Russian control of the Rumanian economy.[7] Such joint stock companies as *Sovrompetrol* (for the exploitation of crude oil and petroleum products), *Sovromtransport* (in the transportation field) and *Sovrom-Lemn* (timber) precluded the free and independent utilization of Rumanian resources and the corollary development of the Rumanian economy. Their management was Russian, and their capital derived from invalidation of the rights and *de facto* confiscation of the capital of Rumanian and foreign investors. The significance of the *Sovroms* was clearly appreciated by the politically conscious Rumanians and, for that matter, even by the more naïve Western powers. The import of the limitations on political action and expression imposed on the traditional parties by the Groza government was similarly obvious.

The reaction of the West, however, was at best ineffectual. It is true that at the Potsdam Conference of July–August 1945 the American delegation reaffirmed the validity of the Yalta agreement regarding the creation of a democratic and representative government in Rumania and questioned Groza's fulfillment of these requirements. It is also true that the Americans were particularly adamant to the Soviet demand that the Allies recognize the Groza regime as properly constituted in terms of the principles enunciated at Yalta. However, the Western nations ultimately agreed to *de facto* recognition of the Rumanian political order and Russia's "special rights" (i.e., sphere of influence) in Rumania. The Western demands for "democratization" of the government through the inclusion of representatives of the opposition parties and the guaranteeing of free elections and of democratic processes were neither persuasive nor enforceable.

As Ionescu so clearly indicates, the Groza regime and its Russian backers chose to ignore the Western demands and interpretation of the Potsdam Declaration, whereby a representative and democratic regime alone would be acceptable, and defied the demands of King Michael, the recognized ruler of Rumania, that the provisions of Potsdam be enforced. Certainly the strongly worded but politically ineffectual American statement issued as late as October 1945 at the London Conference, designed to implement the Potsdam decisions regarding "democratic and representative government" in Rumania, had no visible effect on Groza or Stalin. Only the inconvenience created by the West's refusal to recognize the Groza regime eventually persuaded Moscow to agree in the so-called Moscow Agreement of December 1945 to the broadening of the "democratic basis" of the Groza government through the inclusion of one representative each from the National Liberal Party and the National Peasant Party. Ionescu rightly points out that the Moscow Agreement, which was followed by Western recognition of the Groza regime, marked the formal surrender by the West to Russia's demands and the legitimizing of communist rule and Russian domination over Rumania.[8] Under the circumstances, the actions and plans of the Russian Communist Party, as related to governmental policy and the party itself, assume paramount significance.

It is almost impossible to ascertain the extent to which the policies of the Groza government were initiated by the cabinet or by representatives of the Soviet Union. Nor is it possible to determine which communist members of the government were more influential in initiating or executing policies. In general it is assumed that all matters related to foreign affairs were predetermined in Moscow and that even in domestic affairs Rumanian initiative was circumscribed by Russian directives. Be this as it may, the Groza regime continued to identify itself wth Rumanian causes throughout 1945 and, for that matter, until the legitimizing of its power through the national elections of November 1946. But independently of such governmental actions as the 1945 trial and condemnation of Marshal Ion Antonescu and certain of his close wartime associates as "enemies of the Rumanian people," and the constant attacks against the traditional National Peasant and National Liberal parties for complicity with fascists and for other anti-Rumanian activities, the principal spokesman for the preservation and furtherance of the true Rumanian traditions was the First Secretary of the Rumanian Communist Party, Gheorghe Gheorghiu-Dej. It was Gheorghiu-Dej who most eloquently expounded the theory of the Rumanian party's leadership in the "armed uprising of August 1944" that liberated Rumania and the Rumanians from fascism. It was Gheorghiu-Dej who recalled the heroic struggles of the Rumanians against domestic and foreign oppressors. It was Gheorghiu-Dej, then, who draped the mantle of "socialist nationalism" around his and his party's shoulders and sought to identify the Rumanian progressive historic tradition with the plans and actions of the Rumanian Communist Party and, by identification and extension, of the Groza regime.

The basic reasons for the identification of the Rumanian Communist Party with the national historic tradition have been explained earlier. But the specific reiteration of the formulae devised before March 1945 in legitimate governmental context had far-reaching implications. Groza was clearly not a participant in the uprising of August 1944. Nor were other members of the cabinet. The "Rumanian legitimacy" of the *de facto* communist regime could be derived only through the crucial revolutionary action of communist Rumanians, that is, the revolutionary activists of August 1944. Groza's protectors and sponsors, the Russians, in their own effort to legitimize their position in Rumania, still deemed it necessary in 1945 to act as Rumania's friends and partners, as "coliberators" and "cobelligerents." Thus identification with the claimants of the Rumanian progressive tradition and engineers of the uprising that in effect allowed the "liberation" of Rumania by the Russian armies was sought and obtained.[9]

The unanswered question concerns the price that the Rumanian leaders of the uprising exacted for their collaboration with the Russians in 1945. The consensus among students of Rumanian politics is that the Russians had to make no concessions of any sort to the Rumanian communists, that in fact Gheorghiu-Dej and his closest associates owed their political lives to Moscow and could exert no pressures whatever on the Kremlin—in other words, that Gheorghiu-Dej, like Groza, was a pliant and subservient puppet. Although certain reservations may be voiced against this argument, it is evident that even if Gheorghiu-Dej and his closest associates willingly collaborated with Moscow they reaped substantial gains from their prostitution. By virtue of the monopolistic claims that they levied on their own behalf regarding the revolutionary nature of the armed uprising of August 1944, whereby non-Rumanian and even Rumanian communists absent from Bucharest at the time of the "liberation" were excluded, Gheorghiu-Dej's "team" was able to provide a Rumanian communist veneer to the program adopted at the memorable conference of the Rumanian Communist Party of October 1945 and to renew Gheorghiu's own tenure as the Rumanian First Secretary of the Rumanian Communist Party.[10]

The conference, whose importance became evident only in later years, laid down the fundamental principles for the socialist transformation of Rumania as envisaged by the Rumanian Communist Party. Inasmuch as the party was not formally in power and the principles enunciated in October 1945 were couched in platitudes, their potential significance was either ignored or minimized by contemporary political observers. The essential aspect of the party program, submitted by Gheorghiu-Dej himself in the First Secretary's report, was the construction of a Rumanian Communist state based as much on the traditions of the Rumanian communist movement and historic Rumanian conditions as on the generally valid principles of Marxism-Leninism. It is significant that agricultural collectivization and other specific and potentially onerous plans were not spelled out by Gheorghiu-Dej; however, no assurances were given that the Rumanian objective historical conditions excluded the necessity of such actions. In fact, Gheorghiu-Dej merely provided the assurance that may have been needed by an increasingly more apprehensive population: were the Communist Party to assume total power, it would carry out changes compatible with the Rumanians' historic interests as interpreted by Rumanian communists.[11]

Whether Gheorghiu-Dej's arguments and promises had any calming effect is still a matter of dispute. In all probability the majority of the Rumanian population, politically oriented or not, was becoming painfully aware by the fall of 1945 of the permanence of Russian and communist presence in Rumania. It may be argued that under the circumstances the relatively moderate statements of a Rumanian communist leader were more reassuring than those emanating from obviously alien agents of Russian communism, particularly the "Jewish" contingent headed by Ana Pauker. As a choice between two evils, Rumanians—even if communists—were preferable to Jews and Russians—particularly if communist.

Ultimately, however, the reasons for Gheorghiu-Dej's presentation of the Communist Party's program were transparent. The Russians were still anxious to maintain a Rumanian front for their operations and plans in Rumania, and Gheorghiu-Dej was a pliable tool. It was for this paramount Russian tactical purpose that Gheorghiu-Dej was re-elected as Secretary-General. His actual power in the party was clearly limited by his dependence on Moscow and by the inclusion in the Politburo of the Central Committee of such confirmed servants of the Kremlin as Ana Pauker and Vasile Luca. The reaffirmation of Moscow's "trust" in Gheorghiu-Dej by allowing the legitimizing of his position of Secretary-General through an open general conference of the Rumanian Communist Party was nevertheless an act of major political significance. Gheorghiu-Dej was clearly subservient to Moscow, as was Groza for that matter, but the state and the party were *pro forma* headed by Rumanians who could identify themselves with one or another segment of the Rumanian masses and be used to counter the attacks levied by nationalists and the criticism of Western powers that Rumania was becoming a province of Russia ruled by foreigners alien from and hostile to the Rumanian historical tradition, democratic aspirations, and national interest.

The lack of coincidence between the true traditions and national interests of the majority of the Rumanians and the communists' interpretations thereof was inescapable to almost all Rumanians after the Moscow conference and the party's conference. It was nevertheless essential to the Russians and the Rumanian communists to perpetrate their own interpretations until national elections prerequisite to a peace treaty between the victorious allies and Rumania, as well as the peace treaty itself, were concluded. Thus, throughout 1946, the Rumanian communists and Groza pursued their "nationalist" campaign while seeking to discredit the National Peasant and National Liberal parties as harborers of fascists, reactionaries, and betrayers of the Rumanian people's true interests. Concurrently, the communists consolidated their claims to the historic legacy of the workers' movement by splitting the Social Democratic Party into the proletarian and intellectual "left," which joined the Communist Party in May 1946, and the "reactionary right," which rejected the communists' claims altogether and sided with the National Peasant and

103

National Liberal opposition to the communist-led and Russian-sponsored National Democratic Front.

It has been generally assumed that the "free elections" of November 19, 1946, were anything but free and certainly fraudulent.[12] Contemporary observers and later students of the election have rejected the validity of the results, which gave the National Democratic Front 347 seats in the unicameral parliament and the National Peasants and National Liberals a mere 33 and 3 seats, respectively. The accusations levied against the Groza regime, which controlled the elections and counted the ballots, have ranged from arbitrary disenfranchisement of "fascists" and sudden enfranchisement of women, through police and armed pressure against the electorate, to actual reversal of the electoral count by crediting the 347 seats secured by the National Peasants to the National Democratic Front.

Although the results hardly mirrored the interests of the electorate and probably were falsified to a considerable degree, it is improbable that the National Peasant Party could have won the election in November 1946 under the "objective political conditions" of the time, even had foreign observers and neutral enforcers been able to insure a modicum of electoral regularity and to supervise the counting of the ballots. The fact is that by November 1946 the power base of the traditional parties had been largely eroded. The loss of support—at least of the type that could be translated into votes at a crucial moment—was only partly the result of the forcible prevention by the Groza regime of normal political activities of rival parties. The failure of the masses to support the National Peasant Party in November 1946 was a reflection of their general reconciliation to the political realities of 1946, of their realization that peace had to be made with the new order.

It is probably true that the peasantry, at least, took the communists' assurances of respect for private ownership of land at face value. Groza may not have been their idol, but his regime had not antagonized the village. Browbeating the rural electorate had been standard practice in prewar elections, and spectacular shifts in the voting pattern of the peasantry have been the rule rather than the exception in the electoral history of Rumania. This is not to say that, had the peasantry had an absolutely free choice in November 1946, and had the Russian army and the communists' village agitators been absent and the National Peasant elite and American and British observers present, the peasants would not have cast an overwhelming majority of their ballots for the National Peasant Party. In the absence of such conditions, however, the rural vote recorded by the National Democratic Front is probably closer to the actual count than has been generally conceded.

Certainly the vote of the working class was recorded quite accurately. The traditional leadership of the Social Democratic Party, headed by C. Titel Petrescu, was too closely identified with the conservative, nonproletarian wing of the organization. It was also impotent to meet the workers' desiderata in a manner competitive to that of the National Democratic Front. In fact, the only genuine supporters of the opposition parties were to be found among the politically conscious intellectuals, the middle-class and professional groups who had been unable or unwilling to come to terms with the communists. These politically sophisticated individuals were aware of the phony nationalism of the regime and of its long-range plans. Their only hope was American rejection of the validity of the electoral results and corollary refusal to sign a peace treaty with Rumania. But such hope was admittedly forlorn, as shown by the fact that many donned their walking shoes on November 19 to join, whenever possible, the clairvoyants who had sought asylum in the West even before the election.

Unfortunately for the historian, but understandably to the

politician, the electoral results, as published, did not provide any regional breakdown of ballots cast for the National Peasant Party and the National Liberal Party. It is probable, in terms of the subsequent actions of the "legitimate" Groza regime, that the majority of these votes were cast in Bucharest and in Transylvania and the Banat. In the latter provinces the Magyar population at least was aware of the defeat suffered by the communists in Hungary in a similar election, while the older Rumanian peasantry retained at least a sentimental attachment for Iuliu Maniu. In any event, the communists and their allies felt sufficiently confident after the ratification of the validity of the election by the West and the subsequent signing of the peace treaty with Rumania in February 1947 to gradually abandon the search for popular support by securing the allegiance of the masses for a Rumanian program. The denationalization of the Rumanian communist movement and of the Rumanian historic tradition started in February 1947 and apparently was completed in December of that year.[13]

The peace treaty itself denied the fulfillment of the "bourgeois" historic tradition and recorded a substantial diminution of Rumania's national sovereignity.[14] The "rape of Bessarabia and Northern Bukovina" by the Soviet Union was legitimized by Article 1. Rumania's position as a Soviet satellite was *de facto* legalized through the acceptance of the Russian formula that denied Rumania the role of "cobelligerent" in World War II and granted the dominant victorious power—the USSR—explicit rights of interference in Rumania's internal affairs. The Soviet armed forces alone were authorized to remain in Rumania as a *de facto* army of occupation. The excessive reparations, payable exclusively to the Soviet Union, for losses incurred by Russian military operations and for the maintenance of the army of occupation reduced Rumania to economic dependency on Russia. The enforcement of the provisions of the treaty was theoretically entrusted to the Groza regime; in reality the regime acted as the executor of the Kremlin's plans for the "socialist transformation of Rumania" into a Russian colony.

Russian policy in 1947 was directed toward the destruction of the "bourgeois-nationalist" legacy and of its chief exponent, the "bourgeois-landlord clique." The assault was political, aimed primarily at the traditional political parties identified with the historic past. The National Peasant and National Liberal organizations were dissolved in August 1947 after the mass liquidation or incarceration of past "activists." Late in October, Iuliu Maniu and seventeen leaders of the National Peasant Party were brought to trial and convicted for antistate activities. In November the last members of the traditional parties were removed from the Groza cabinet and replaced by non-Rumanian communists like Ana Pauker, Vasile Luca, and Emil Bodnaras. In December, King Michael himself was forced to abdicate and the Rumanian People's Republic was established.[15]

The condemnation, in 1947, of Rumania to the status of a colony of Communist Russia aroused the latent national sentiments of many who had been apolitical or unaware of the true intentions of the USSR. Whether this anti-Russian nationalism of the masses was rooted in the historic tradition or was motivated by more pragmatic considerations of the moment—primarily the actual or potential loss of property and liberty—is uncertain. But the total reaction was both anti-Russian and anticommunist, particularly after the ascendancy of well-known Russian agents to major governmental posts.

It would be erroneous to assume, however, that the opposition to Moscow or Ana Pauker or Vasile Luca was chiefly an expression of primitive nationalist anti-communist and anti-Semitic sentiments. Although these basic sentiments were aroused by the growing prominence of Russians and Jews in public life and the natural tendency to blame foreigners for unpopular actions, it would appear that the negativism of the Rumanian masses was caused by and was directed against the "social-revolutionary" measures associated with communist rule, be it Russian, Jewish, or Rumanian. These measures, in 1947, were restricted primarily to financial matters. The most drastic action—the currency reform of August 1947—was a destructive blow to the propertied classes and all bank depositors. The fact that workers and the majority of the peasantry were not penalized by the reform was hardly reassuring to these less privileged groups. Most Rumanians, regardless of social origin and economic status, blamed the Russians for the disastrous inflation that had preceded the reform and had rendered the majority of the population virtually destitute by the summer of 1947. Also, most Rumanians feared further and more sweeping attacks on personal liberty and property rights. The general apprehension translated itself into a nationalism of the scared, a nationalism directed against the foreign oppressor—Communist Russia and its agent, the Rumanian Communist Party.

Whether this nationalism was associated with the historic tradition to the extent to which that tradition guaranteed the socioeconomic interests of the society is difficult to ascertain. In all probability it was primarily a reflection of the anxieties of the moment. In any case, the communists' attack on "bourgeois nationalism" was an attack on "bourgeois" values and on the "bourgeois" aspirations of the Rumanian masses. "Proletarian internationalism" became the political slogan of all communists in power in Rumania, including such former spokesmen for Rumanian traditions as Gheorghiu-Dej himself. The establishment of the Rumanian People's Republic, symbolic of a new "people's democratic" order, represented the denationalizing of the Rumanian historical tradition at all levels.

6

THE NATIONAL LEGACY ABANDONED
Stalinism, Socialism, *Satellitenstaat*
(1948–1952)

THE PROCLAMATION of the "Rumanian Democratic Republic" on December 30, 1947, announced the "socialist transformation" of Rumania according to Soviet prototypes and directions. The Jacobin stage of the revolution was initiated in a most resolute and dramatic fashion seeking the destruction of the "bourgeois-nationalist" legacy at all levels of the social, economic, cultural, and, above all, political order. The eradication of the past, ordered by Stalin and executed by the Rumanian Communist Party, commenced early in 1948 and was *de facto* completed by 1952.

The violence and intensity of the socialist revolution in Rumania has perplexed most students of Rumanian affairs. The political history of Rumania has recorded less violence, at least by Southeast European standards, than that of Bulgaria or Yugoslavia, for instance. The relaxed nature of public life and the traditional venality of public officials alone should have insured a more "peaceful transition to socialism" than was possible in countries with higher standards of official morality. In fact it has been argued that the Rumanian revolution, even if directed by the Rumanian Communist Party, was not Rumanian in form, character, or execution. Were it not for such arguments and corollary explanations currently provided by the present leaders of Communist Rumania, which tend to emphasize the non-Rumanian influences and responsibilities for the "Stalinist abuses" committed in the revolutionary period, it would be necessary to conclude that in 1948 the communists, no matter what their nationality, dogmatic positions, and allegiances, were committed to the consolidation of their power and the destruction of all sources of actual and potential opposition.[1] Careful examination of contemporary explanations would not invalidate that conclusion since the evidence does not allow for differentiation between the actions and decisions of the Rumanian and the Moscovite contingents of the Communist Party's leadership and apparatus. No matter what their actual motivations may have been in 1948, Gheorghiu-Dej and his associates were as ruthless and radical as Ana Pauker and hers. If anything, Gheorghiu-Dej was probably more orthodox a Stalinist than Pauker if not than Stalin himself.

The Rumanian communist leadership performed the function of enforcing Moscow's blueprint for the transformation of Eastern Europe into a Stalinist empire and adapting that blueprint to a "specific objective" Rumanian conditions. And nobody was a better diagnostician of Rumanian conditions and a better executor of Stalin's orders than Gheorghiu-Dej. Nor was anyone more convinced of the necessity for radical action to attain communist goals.

The communist revolution in Rumania was directed first of all against the politically conscious and ideologically suspect. But it was also a social revolution whose aim was the leveling of all property-owning classes through the confiscation and socialization of their wealth.

The revolution was indeed non-Rumanian in that it followed Soviet prescriptions, but it did take into account the uniquely Rumanian threats to the establishment of the "people's democratic order"—"fascism" and "bourgeois values." The catch-all

110

Stalinism, Socialism, *Satellitenstaat*

"fascism," a standard cliché in communist political jargon, represented to the communists the sum total of actual or potential Rumanian opposition to communism. "Fascism" was the credo of all anticommunists other than Jews—the repository of nationalism, anti-Russianism, anti-Semitism, as well as of the socioeconomic aspirations of the peasantry. It was also the instrument for foreign subversion by "international" fascism and imperialism. Surely "fascism" in that context, and in 1948, had to be extirpated. The rooting out involved not only the mass imprisonment of intellectuals, professional groups, and members of the bourgeoisie who had been connected with the fascist movement in the past or was suspected of anticommunist attitudes in 1948, but also and more radically the destruction of the cultural and religious traditions and institutions identified with fascism.

Although this attack and subsequent alteration of traditional values and institutions was ultimately less significant than the socioeconomic transformation of Rumania, it nevertheless represented an unwanted modernization based on an alien ideology. Religion was deeply rooted in the history of the Rumanians.[2] Anticlericalism was an insignificant phenomenon. The subservience of the Orthodox hierarchy to the state had been traditional in Rumania, but all regimes antedating the communist one used Rumanian Orthodoxy as an instrument for securing the political allegiance of the population and identified themselves with the national Orthodox tradition. The church and the nation, the church and nationalism, were closely and inseparably interrelated. The adherence of a "progressive" segment of the Rumanian Orthodox hierarchy to the People's Democratic Republic was indeed secured by the communists in 1948, but that of the masses was not. The glorification of the revolution and the doctrinal reconciliation of Rumanian Orothodoxy with "Judaeocommunist" rule were politically necessary for the upper hierarchy of the church but not for the population at large or for the clerical rank and file. To defuse this politically explosive situation the communists purged the ideologically suspect clergy and discouraged, often by strong-arm methods, church attendance, thus reducing the organized Orthodox Church to a faithful servant of the "heathen" state.

The less centralized and less pliable religious organizations, identified with either a Catholic tradition or a non-Rumanian population, were *de facto* liquidated. The Greek Catholic (Uniate) church was a natural target inasmuch as its 1,500,000 members were Rumanian while its headquarters were in the multinational province of Transylvania. The possibility of union of the Greek Catholic and the Roman Catholic churches with resultant "papal interference in Rumanian affairs" precipitated the arbitrary and violent dissolution of the Uniate Church and its incorporation, in 1948, into the Rumanian Orthodox. The related Roman Catholic Church, with its 1,000,000 adherents of Hungarian, German, and occasionally even Rumanian nationality, was condemned as an instrument of "foreign imperialism" after the Vatican and its representatives in Rumania rejected the communists' attempts to regulate the affairs of the church. Catholicism was, in effect, banned in 1948. Other religious denominations, Lutheran, Calvinist, and minor Protestant organizations, as well as the Mosaic, which were prepared to adhere to the essential communist requirement for survival: subservience to the state and renunciation of all political activities, fared as well as the Orthodox Church. They continued to function as ritualistic organizations expounding doctrines of allegiance to communism to frightened and politically inactive members of rapidly waning congregations.

The forcible eradication of religious influences and values was accompanied by a massive attack on other alien, "fascist" cultural values and institutions. The primary targets were the national culture and the educational establishment. Writers and historians were the principal victims of the cultural purge inasmuch as they had been traditionally the principal exponents of "bourgeois nationalism." Artists and teachers survived the holocaust in better shape.

The attack against the national culture and its creators or exponents was politically justifiable.[3] The Rumanian writers of the interwar years and, for that matter, their predecessors of the nineteenth century had two major defects from the communists' standpoint: they were as a rule rabid nationalists, and their cultural inspiration was Western. Authors of the classics of the nineteenth century, men like Eminescu, Alexandri, even Cosbuc, had glorified the Latinity of the Rumanian people and expressed strong anti-Russian sentiments. In fact, the fascists had claimed Eminescu as one of their spiritual fathers. Alexandri's celebrated eulogy to Latinity, "Latina Ginta," was a household poem. The patriotic verses of the nineteenth century were the required attributes of a grade school education. The writers of the twentieth century were less distinguished but no less nationalistic and certainly more wedded to the West. Many had also been actively identified with the fascist movement. Few had devoted their works to meaningful social themes. Their writings were known only to the cultural elite except when, for political reasons, their lesser contributions were included in school textbooks. This is not to say that men like Victor Eftimiu, Mihai Sadoveanu, and Cezar Petrescu were less talented than Alexandri or Cosbuc; but they were men of the twentieth century, of the age of confrontation of communism and fascism.

The communists' solution to the problems of national literature was simple and radical. They banned all works of a "fascist" character and the literary activity of all writers who either were closely identified with the Iron Guard and Antonescu or refused to retool themselves into exponents of "socialist realism." This constituted a majority of the better known literateurs and poets.

After 1948 only classic social satirists like Ion Luca Caragiale, socialist realists like Ion Creanga or contemporary equivalents or converts like Mihai Sadoveanu, genuinely militant communists like Zaharia Stancu, or apolitical poets like Grigore Alexandrescu and Tudor Arghezi were acceptable to the communist regime. Most of the literary production was the output of incompetent, often illiterate party stalwarts, rendering second-rate Russian literature into Rumanian equivalents or emulating the sterility of Soviet literary *apparatchiks*.

The same fate was reserved for the historians, the traditional exponents of Rumanian nationalism and of the official political line. The history of Rumania, as depicted by such men as Dimitrie Xenopol, Nicolae Iorga, and Constantin C. Giurescu, was unacceptable in the age of communist conformity and permanent loss of Rumanian territories to the USSR. All references to nationalism and to the heroic figures of the Rumanian past were suppressed; all the facts relevant to Russo-Rumanian relations were eliminated. The history of Rumania and of the Rumanians was rewritten in accordance with Soviet precepts, with subsequent annulling of the national historical identity and "bourgeois-nationalist" historical legacy. By 1948 the denigration of the past and the glorification of the Soviet Union and its example had become the *raison d'être* of historical writing.

The eradication of the past and, whenever possible, that of the intellectuals connected with it—or at least aware of its actual and potential significance—was also attained through opening the doors of the previously restricted educational facilities to the masses.[4] Education for socialism, which involved *inter alia* a spirited campaign for the elimination of illiteracy, expansion of the network of primary and secondary schools and of institutions of higher learning, adoption of Soviet techniques and philosophy of education, elimination of "bourgeois-nationalist" teachers and students, and general "democratization" of education through

114

indiscriminate admission of workers, peasants, and their children to educational institutions, was initially designed to train propagandists and to indoctrinate all those subjected to the new education in the values and purposes of communism.[5] The educational "reforms" of 1948, which opened the traditional schools to the masses and created new vocational training centers, were aimed, however, not only at the "democratization" of the system but also, and perhaps primarily, at establishing the bases for the "socialist transformation of Rumania," for the "modernization" of the country.

It has been argued by sympathetic observers of Rumanian affairs that the denationalization of the historic tradition in 1948 was part of a communist tactic of *reculer pour mieux sauter*. The establishment of a viable and respectable Rumania was, in this view, not possible without the "modernization" of the historic legacy through the secularization and industrialization of the country. Opponents of this interpretation, according to which the communists would qualify as revolutionary modernizers of an irrevocably retrograde society and power elite, have in turn argued that the modernization of Rumania's society would have occurred under all circumstances after World War II and that the industrialization of Rumania, albeit with private capital, had gained sufficient momentum in the late thirties to be resumed as soon as propitious conditions for industrial growth reappeared. The supporters of the theory of inevitability of further industrialization after World War II have based their case on comparable developments in Greece, Turkey, and Western Europe, on a variety of statistical data, and on optimistic statements by Rumanian industrial magnates and political leaders in exile. Although prognostications are of doubtful value, the inevitability of progress in modernization by any Rumanian regime that might have emerged after World War II is now recognized even by communist leaders. The communists, however, claim that modernization would have been much slower and less thorough under a "bourgeois-democratic" regime, had such been established after the war, than under communist auspices and certainly quite inadequate without a radical transformation of the socioeconomic and cultural bases of society. The destruction of false "bourgeois-nationalist" values, the eradication of illiteracy, and the equitable redistribution of capital were the minimum requirements for modernization, communist style.[6]

Regardless of the relative, theoretical merits of the controversy the fact remains that the communists were in power in 1948 and carried out the modernization of Rumania according to Stalinist principles and Rumanian conditions. The validity of their socioeconomic measures and plans may be questioned on both economic and political grounds, but their program should ultimately be appraised in terms of its immediate and long-term effectiveness and repercussions. The socioeconomic and political aspects of the socialist transformation of Rumania are inexorably related. The socioeconomic changes, which started with the nationalization of private property, industry, trade, and banking institutions, gained momentum with the beginning of state planning in July 1948 and of agricultural collectivization in March 1949. Were these measures economically justified or politically determined?

The statistical data and analytical appraisals provided by leading students of the Rumanian economy tend to prove that the economic measures adopted in 1948 were essential for the reconstruction of the economy and for its future development. Although questions have arisen regarding the effectiveness of the economic program in Rumania, it is generally agreed that despite major mistakes in planning, grave shortcomings in the organization of the production process, low productivity of labor, and irrational utilization of manpower and resources, Rumanian industrial progress was impressive even in the early years of the planned economy.[7] If the standard of living of the population in

Wood Church in Banat.

The Three Hierarchs' Church
(Seventeenth Century).

The Voronet Monastery, Moldavia
(Fifteenth and Sixteenth Centuries).

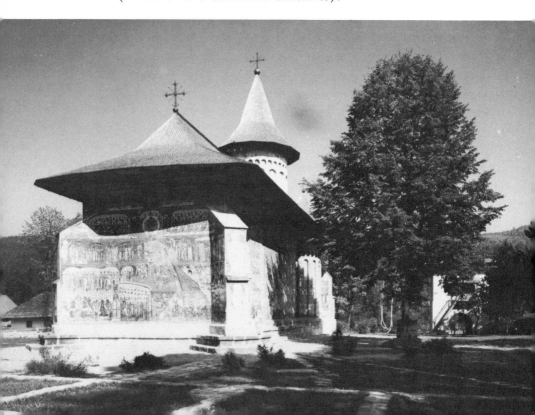

The North-South Highway, Bucharest.

Mangalia.

The Union Square, Iași.

The Caraiman Chalet in the Bucegi Mountains,
the Southern Carpathians.

New buildings in the Rumanian
seaside resort of Mangalia.

Center of the city of Bucharest.

The Church of the Cozia Monastery
(Sixteenth Century).

A few of the modern plants of the Brazi Combine near Ploiesti.

Apartment houses belonging to private owners
in the new quarters of the town of Bucharest.

Outer buildings of the wine-making center in
Panciu, lying in the middle
of the famous vineyards bearing the same name.

A factory in Bicaz
manufacturing asbestos and cement.

The lake of the Bicaz hydropower plant,
surrounded by hills
and forest-clad mountains.

Building ensemble in the center of Bucharest.

The Church, Curtea de Argeș
(Sixteenth Century).

The Bucegi Mountains.

1950 was lower than before the war, this situation was due to the economic exploitation of the country by the USSR rather than to economic stagnation in Rumania proper.

Less favorable is the opinion of economists on the effectiveness of agricultural collectivization. They are critical of the economic rationale behind the establishment in 1949 of *artels* (agricultural production cooperatives) but tend to ascribe the shortcomings in cooperative agricultural production to such political factors as coercion and peasant resistance. Political analysts, however, have offered valid political reasons for the socialization both of industry and of agriculture. They contend that the economic policies of the Rumanian Communist Party were motivated solely by political reasons and that these reasons were as a rule irrelevant to Rumanian "objective" conditions.

Economic planning and agricultural collectivization are fundamental to Marxist-Leninist theory and Soviet practice. Whether the Soviet blueprint was adequate for Rumania was a mute question in 1948, when political and even personal survival was a function of conformity to Stalinist orthodoxy and Russian dictates. The merits of blind adaptation of Soviet patterns to Rumanian conditions had been questioned and opposed by not only the Rumanian population in general but also the Rumanian Communist Party itself.[8] As early as 1946, when the legitimate parties were in vain expressing their fears and suspicions of the communists, Rumanian and Russian, a small but principled portion of the party's membership expressed similar fears of the Kremlin. The principal exponent of anti-Russian doctrine and practice and of a platform for the socialist transformation of Rumania in terms of Rumanian realities was Lucretiu Patrascanu, then Minister of Justice and for a long time one of the foremost members of the party. But Patrascanu's fears of and opposition to Stalinist imperialism were silenced by Gheorghiu-Dej and Moscow's trusted agents in the Rumanian party.

117

Stalinism, Socialism, *Satellitenstaat*

The decision to embrace Stalin's dictates for Rumania, to accept the loss of Rumania's national identity at the state and party levels, except as compatible with status as a *Satellitenstaat*, was made as much by Gheorghiu-Dej, the later champion of the principles advocated by Patrascanu, as by Pauker, Luca, and other non-Rumanian representatives of the Kremlin in the Rumanian party. The choice of the majority was realistic and, in the case of Gheorghiu-Dej, also rewarding. As the Soviet Union was determined to control Rumania and had the power to replace any suspect member of the Rumanian Communist Party and state machinery at will after the signing of the peace treaty in 1947, any anti-Soviet course would have certainly led to the demise of its advocates.

It is still a matter of dispute whether Gheorghiu-Dej and his close Rumanian associates believed that Stalin's variety of Marxism-Leninism in the socioeconomic sphere was compatible with Rumanian conditions. The evidence would support the view that Gheorghiu-Dej's blueprint for industrialization, presented as the program of the Rumanian Communist Party at the conference of 1945, accepted the validity of Soviet patterns in that sector of modernization. However, the evidence would deny acceptance by Gheorghiu-Dej and his associates of 1945 of the principle of economic exploitation by the USSR of the Rumanian national wealth in the name of reparations and economic partnership. Nor is it possible to find any evidence for acceptance of the principle of agricultural collectivization in Gheorghiu-Dej's pronunciamentos and programs in the period antedating the conclusion of the peace treaty of 1947. It may be possible that he had always favored collectivization, keeping his views secret for tactical political purposes. But it is also quite likely that such reservations as he might have entertained in 1948–1949 were subordinated to the attainment of his immediate goal: assumption of control of the Rumanian Communist Party as Stalin's most trusted agent. In

118

fact, the fundamental problem facing the Rumanian communists in 1948 was that of successful emulation of Stalin, of unflinching acceptance of Soviet dictates and on-time delivery of Soviet requisitions.

The balance sheet of the years 1948–1950—the crucial revolutionary years in Rumania—is by no means negative in this respect. The political power of the communists was total in 1950. The last of the traditional parties, the Social Democratic, had been absorbed into the Communist Party in February 1948. The change in appellation from Rumanian Communist Party to Rumanian Workers' Party (ostensibly to prove the fusion of the political representatives of the working class into a unitary organization) did not obscure the fact that power rested entirely with the communist contingent of the Workers' organization. In practical terms it legalized the one-party state and made the Rumanian Workers' Party the only arena for political struggle. And such struggles were by no means insignificant.[9]

Exaggerated emphasis has been placed by analysts of Rumanian problems in this period on the destruction of political traditions, internal and external. But the liquidation of political parties and the politically suspect, on the one hand, and the *de facto* breaking of relations with the West, on the other, were infinitely less significant phenomena than the Rumanian party's relations with members of the socialist camp and the relations within the party between the Rumanian and the Moscovite contingents. By 1950, Rumania was irrevocably a member of the communist camp and of the Soviet bloc. Also by that year, the Rumanian party's relations with the Kremlin were clearly, legally, and rigidly defined. The economic agreements of 1945, the Peace Treaty of 1947, and the Treaty of Friendship, Cooperation, and Mutual Assistance of 1948 formalized Rumania's dependence on Russia. The Rumanian Workers' Party seconded all international resolutions initiated by Moscow, including the violent condemnation of

Tito's heresy in 1948, and shelved all initiatives of its own unless such were required by the Kremlin. But the acceptance of the political reality of Soviet domination did not make internal political struggles within the party less fierce. In fact the bloodiest, most significant, and furthest-reaching phase in the "socialist transformation" of Rumania—that of gaining control of the Rumanian Workers' Party—was nearing completion by 1950.

The struggle for power for that end focused on the party's "national" composition, on whether the party would be dominated by Rumanian Stalinists, headed by Gheorghiu-Dej, or by Moscow Stalinists, headed by Ana Pauker, Vasile Luca, and erstwhile Rumanian allies. The nature of this internecine conflict has never been fully explained. Such simplistic views as Gheorghiu-Dej's personal lust for power, his reaction to popular discontent, the seeking of scapegoats for economic failures, which have been suggested by interpreters of Rumanian events, are clearly unsatisfactory. It is generally agreed that Gheorghiu-Dej, his associates, and supporters thought to rid themselves of control by Moscovites but not by Moscow. Whether their desire to downgrade and eventually remove Pauker and Luca was based on "nationalism" or on "opportunism" is difficult to ascertain. The evidence would favor the former motivation, but it would be erroneous to assume that their nationalism was in any way related to the "bourgeois nationalism" that the party as a whole was actively eradicating. Gheorghiu-Dej's nationalism was rooted in the belief that the Rumanian leaders were the legitimate heirs to the Rumanian revolutionary tradition and also the rightful executors of Stalin's orders in Rumania. As long as the compatibility, if not identity, of the Rumanian and Russian communist traditions and purposes was affirmed, Ana Pauker and Vasile Luca were *de trop*.[10]

Gheorghiu-Dej received support in his search for supremacy from the "xenophobic" contingent of the Rumanian party's mem-

bership. The extent and the nature of the opposition to the Moscovites have never been fully ascertained. It is believed that the
true proletarian elements were closely identified with Gheorghiu-
Dej and resentful of the revolutionary intelligentsia (which
Pauker had cultivated) and of such *apparatchiks* as Vasile Luca
and Iosif Chisinevski. It is probable that the resentment reflected
"nationalist" tendencies, at least to the extent to which Pauker,
Chisninevski, and other prominent members of the Moscovite
group were identified with Judaism. However, the opposition of
the proletarian rank and file was based on class rather than national diversity. In fact, at all times Gheorghiu-Dej's challenge to
the Moscovites emphasized their packing of the Rumanian party
with suspect "fascist" intellectual, nonproletarian, and noncommunist elements. Doctrinal purity and proper class structure were
claimed to be essential for the attainment of the goals imposed by
Stalin for the socialist transformation of Rumania.[11]

It is noteworthy that the Rumanians' first major challenge was
made in the spring of 1950 at a time when the basic measures for
that transformation had been successfully implemented. At that
time Gheorghiu-Dej used the report of the commission on "veri-
fication" of the membership of the party, appointed at the time
of the establishment of the Rumanian Workers' Party in 1948,
to denounce Pauker for having promoted the admission of alien
and hostile elements into the organization. The "purification" of
the membership through the strengthening of the proletarian contingent and the purging of nonproletarian elements from the
membership rolls was justified in terms of Stalinist precepts and
the socioeconomic requirements of Rumania. According to
Gheorghiu-Dej, the further development of the country's industry, the fulfillment of industrial and agricultural plans, the consolidation of the cultural revolution—all necessitated and made
possible the predominance of industrial workers and working
peasants in the party organization. The working masses—over-

whelmingly Rumanian—and their proletarian—and Rumanian—
leaders were thus entitled to rule the Rumanian People's Republic
and the Rumanian Workers' Party, albeit according to Stalinist
precepts and existing relations with the Kremlin.

Gheorghiu-Dej's case reflected his strength rather than his
weakness. The cultural revolution had been achieved.[12] The educational system was producing politically reliable and professionally semicompetent technicians and propagandists. Above all, the
economy was showing rapid progress.[13] The disaffection of the
population with the ruthlessness of the regime, with low wages
and lack of consumer goods, and with the total subordination of
Rumania to Soviet interests was repressible by a supremely effi-
cient police and the ever-present Soviet troops stationed in the
country. Indeed, Stalin could find no fault with Gheorghiu-Dej
as the first major test of the solidarity, stability, and cohesion of
the communist camp occurred in the Korean War in the summer
of 1950.

The Korean War elevated Stalin's requirements for subservience. But it also diverted the Kremlin's attention from the daily
conduct of Rumanian affairs, thus allowing greater latitude to its
underlings in determining Rumania's contribution to the common
war effort against the "American imperialists." Gheorghiu-Dej
evidently seized the opportunity for consolidation of his political
power provided by the war by maximizing the need for Stalinist
purity in times of crisis. The war itself was totally alien to the
country's historic tradition and to the population at large, acceptable only for defeatist purposes. The Rumanians, radically
opposed to Rumanian communism and Russian imperialism, entertained hopes that the defeat of the communist forces in the Far
East would lead to the "liberation" of Rumania from communist
rule. This unfounded optimism was mitigated, however, by the
reality of increased economic pressures for delivery of supplies
to the Soviet Union and North Koreans. The growing mass

opposition to the war and to Soviet exploitation was particularly manifest among the peasantry, who had resisted collectivization since its formulation in 1949 and regarded the acceleration of the drive for the socialization of agriculture, resultant from the unpopular war, as intolerable.[14] The industrial workers, mobilized for expediting the production of material and supplies, were also growing restless. These manifestations of unease were repressed with vigor by Gheorghiu-Dej, who, it is now believed, was also the principal architect of a general policy of intimidation and police terror against the population.

Gheorghiu-Dej concentrated his efforts, however, on the Stalinization of the Rumanian Workers' Party. The exact sequence of the events that began in June 1950 with the condemnation of the improper recruitment of party members by Ana Pauker and her chief lieutenant, Miron Constantinescu, in the immediate postwar period, and that ended with the purging of Ana Pauker, Vasile Luca, Teohari Georgescu, and other "Moscovites" two years later, is not entirely clear. But the result, the victory of the Rumanian Stalinists in June 1952, was carefully planned from the formal inception of the offensive in 1950.[15] The purging of 192,-000 members, announced on June 23, 1950, resulted in the strengthening of the Rumanian proletarian contingent, not through new recruitment but through removal of "foreigners" and "hostile" elements.

Significantly, the campaign of denigration of political opponents after that date was waged on a redefinition of the Rumanian national interest. That interest, still defined as the attainment of socialism for the sake of bringing about the ultimate victory of Russian-led communism, gradually reassumed a specific Rumanian character. The communist camp, according to Gheorghiu-Dej, consisted of a federation of Stalinist satellites, microcosms of Russia. As Stalin himself was assuming an increasingly more "national-communist" posture in the Soviet Union and was encouraging like manifestations of an anti-"cosmopolitan" and anti-Semitic character throughout his empire, Gheorghiu-Dej could safely emulate his master's dicta. The Moscovites were therefore condemned because of toleration of "fascism" and of "alien elements," presumably cosmopolitan and Jewish.

The corollary campaign for the "Rumanization" and "proletarianization" of the party and state apparatus, however, did not involve the restatement of the revolutionary legitimacy of the Rumanian leadership. No mention was made of rights derived by Gheorghiu-Dej and his associates from participation in the "armed uprising of August 1944," nor was the legitimacy of the Moscovites' position in the Rumanian party questioned because of their nonparticipation in that uprising. Rather the attack was directed against the Moscovites' incompetence resultant from their lack of acquaintance with Rumanian conditions. Nor did Gheorghiu-Dej try to hold his opponents responsible for the hardships imposed on the Rumanian people; on the contrary, he was quite prepared, because of political necessity and conviction, to assume full responsibility for the most onerous Stalinist features of communist rule. If anything, he was able to replace "conciliatory" elements in the party and state bureaucracy with hard-line Rumanian Stalinists, to impose standards of unprecedented rigidity for the training of party officials and propagandists, and to further the promulgation of Draconian labor and penal laws. He demanded total commitment to Stalinism, his and Moscow's.

It was thus in the name of Stalinist orthodoxy that Gheorghiu-Dej pursued the process of purification of the Rumanian Workers' Party and its front organizations, with resultant assumption of control by his supporters of the party and governmental apparatus by the summer of 1951. But it was in the name of Stalinist efficiency and the corollary attainment of the Stalinist prescriptions for the socialist transformation of Rumania that his team pushed through the radical currency reform of January 1952, which in effect destroyed the last vestiges of private capitalism among the kulaks and the peasantry in general and facilitated the socialization of agriculture.

Gheorghiu-Dej's actions apparently met with Stalin's approval. Whether Stalin actually approved or merely condoned the subsequent purging of the Moscovites in the Rumanian Party is not clear. The possibility of a negative reaction from the Kremlin was envisaged by Gheorghiu-Dej, as shown by repeated assurances of total loyalty to the Soviet leader both immediately before and after the removal of Pauker, Luca, and Georgescu from the top party echelons. But that possibility was minimized by the nature of the accusations levied against the Moscovites. The drastic action against them, completed in June 1952, was officially justified in terms of their having committed three major heresies: anti-Leninism, separating the party from the masses, and opposing Rumania's economic development. These were to be expurgated by Gheorghiu-Dej and his associates by firm adherence to the pure dogma, by strengthening the ties between the party and the masses, by increasing the party's vigilance against "communist deviationists" and "bourgeois nationalists," and by cementing Rumania's ties with the Soviet Union at both the party and the state level.[16]

Acceptable as these broad principles of reform and orthodoxy may have been to Stalin, it is far from certain that the explicit formulation of the communist goals of the revamped leadership was as palatable as has been assumed by students of Rumanian politics. In fact, there may be reason to believe that in time Stalin would have opposed Gheorghiu-Dej's "communist nationalism." The Korean War and the dictator's failing health and power, however, precluded any action unfavorable to the Rumanians' interests in the few months that elapsed between June 1952 and Stalin's death in March 1953.

The fact is that, even if Gheorghiu-Dej's triumph in June 1952 represented the total victory of Stalinism, it was also the triumph of a Rumanian Stalin. In his victory speech of June 3, 1962, as he assumed the dual role of head of the party and leader of the government, Gheorghiu-Dej enunciated two fundamental and far-reaching concepts of "communist nationalism."[17] The first was that the Rumanian Workers' Party was the democratic political organization of all Rumanians regardless of national origin; the second, that the democratic party was dedicated to the construction of socialism in the Rumanian People's Republic through industrialization of the country and the socialist transformation of agriculture. The blueprints for the attainment of these national communist goals were no longer exclusively drawn in the Soviet Union; rather, the new program was to be based on the principles for socialist construction formulated at the national conference of the Rumanian Communist Party in 1945. The realization of that program was to be the *raison d'être* of the new leadership and of all loyal members of the party. The attainment of socialism was to be the *national* goal of a party representing and acting for all inhabitants of Rumania.

The acceptance of this new formulation of the purposes of the regime, of the doctrine of "communist patriotism" as stated in 1952, was less than enthusiastic within both the party and state organizations and the country at large. The "Rumanization" of the all-important Politburo and Secretariat was incomplete in that men like Iosif Chisinevski and Miron Constantinescu, who were identified with the deposed triumvirate, retained their positions.[18] Moreover, there were "Moscovites" entrenched in the *Sovroms*, the state bureaucracy, and, occasionally, even in provincial party organizations. However, as long as Gheorghiu-Dej and his team pursued policies acceptable to Moscow, no possibility of reversal of his victory seemed possible.

It has been argued that, had it not been for the compromises which Gheorghiu-Dej had to make with Chisinevski, Constantinescu, and lesser Moscovites—reflecting his own insecurity vis-à-vis the Kremlin—he would have made certain "nationalist" concessions to the Rumanian masses in addition to the removal of the most objectionable foreign elements from power.[19] It has been suggested that the economic reforms, announced immediately after Stalin's death, were agreed upon as early as the summer of 1952. Such actions may have been comtemplated by certain members of Gheorghiu's teams, but apparently not by Gheorghiu-Dej himself. In the last analysis the Rumanization of the party was a narrow political action directed by Gheorghiu-Dej, unrelated to the economic or political interests of the Rumanian population. If anything, the unequivocal restatement of classic Stalinist positions in June 1952, particularly with respect to the eternal threat of "bourgeois nationalism" and the need for increased vigilance against all suspected of deviations from Gheorghiu-Dej's line and policies, would tend to invalidate any presumption of identification between "communist patriotism" and "bourgeois nationalism." The Rumanian population in general remained fundamentally opposed to the communist order. Whether Gheorghiu-Dej was more palatable than Ana Pauker because of his nationality is a matter of speculation. In all probability, the restatement of the national purpose in Rumanian communist terms was more acceptable than total subservience to the Kremlin. In any event, luck was on the side of Gheorghiu-Dej. Stalin's death facilitated the exploitation of his victory of 1952 in a manner advantageous to the furthering of his political cause, that of Rumanian communism and of Communist Rumania.

7

THE NATIONAL LEGACY RECLAIMED
Socialist Patriotism (1953–1960)

THE DEATH OF Stalin and the ensuing struggle for succession in the Soviet Union did not unleash the forces that were to lead to the reassertion of Rumania's sovereign rights in the socialist camp and the international community as a whole. In fact, Gheorghiu-Dej accepted the validity of Stalinist policies, foreign and domestic, and applied them rigorously in Rumania. He staked his future on the survival of Stalinism.

A variety of explanations has been provided for Gheorghiu-Dej's choice. The most persuasive, given by Nicolae Ceausescu himself, was political self-survival.[1] Gheorghiu-Dej was convinced in the spring of 1953 that the survival of the communist order, at home and abroad, depended on the continuation and consolidation of the practices devised by the late Soviet leader. Gheorghiu-Dej recognized two fundamental threats in Rumania: the "rising expectations" of the population, which he rightly equated with a mass desire for a change in the political order, and the possibility of the emergence of rivals within the Rumanian Workers' Party. It is not entirely clear whether he was aware of the intrinsicalities of the struggle for power in the Soviet hierarchy. But it is known that he was banking on the victory of what came to be known as the "anti-party group" of Molotov, Bulganin, and their lesser associates.[2]

Socialist Patriotism

The threat of counterrevolution by enemies of communism and the establishment of a noncommunist regime in Rumania in 1953 was nonexistent. The dissatisfaction of the masses, attributable primarily to poverty resultant from Soviet economic exploitation, was evident; but even more evident were the omnipresent forces of repression. Hence the threat to Gheorghiu-Dej's supremacy rested on a reformulation of Russian policies and possible exploitation of new trends by members of the Rumanian party less firmly identified with Stalin. To avoid any difficulties arising from that possibility, Gheorghiu-Dej was among the first of all East European leaders to adopt the "New Course" for economic development in August 1953.[3]

The economic significance of the New Course has been analyzed with admirable insight and clarity by Professor Montias.[4] According to Montias, the growth of exports required to maintain the level of planned economic development was rapidly becoming insufficient in terms of the regime's economic goals. Supplies of petroleum, timber, cement, and other primary materials were alarmingly scarce by the time of Stalin's death. The very basic needs of the expanding urban population could be met only with great difficulty because of the too-rapid expansion of heavy industry and the resistance by the village to the system of compulsory deliveries. Accurate as this diagnosis may be, it is still questionable that Gheorghiu-Dej was moved by economic reasons when the relaxation of the tremendous pressures exerted upon the population since 1948 was ordered in 1953.

More probably the decision to decelerate and adopt a less strenuous rate of economic expansion through the New Course was politically motivated. The decision of the party plenum of August 19–20, 1953, stressed the need for an improved standard of living for all people but particularly for those engaged in agricultural pursuits. The masses had little comprehension of such economic measures as reductions in the share of accumulation in the national income or investment outlays, but they did understand such positive measures as reductions in the quantities of agricultural products subject to compulsory delivery, cancellations of arrears in such deliveries, lowering of taxes, increments in monetary inducements for joining the socialist sector and for encouraging animal husbandry, and other steps designed to appease the peasant while strengthening the bases for further "socialist construction" in the village and the country at large. The masses also appreciated the significance of the corollary decision to raise the supplies of goods and the value of sales in the socialist retail market by 10 per cent in 1954 and by another 15 per cent in 1955. Whether they accepted as valid Gheorghiu-Dej's explanations for the adoption of the New Course—to the effect that the reforms were possible only because of the house cleaning carried out in 1952 and that they represented the first significant bonus paid by managers of Rumanian affairs truly concerned with the well-being and progress of Rumania and its people—remains a matter of dispute.

It has been argued that the decision of the plenum of August 1953 was the first clear formulation of the "national course" that distinguished Gheorghiu-Dej's subsequent career. His memorable speech on the occasion of the ninth anniversary of Rumania's "liberation" on August 23, in which he equated the party's, the people's, and the nation's historic goal with the socialist construction of a modern Rumanian state, and the related political and economic measures adopted at that time would tend to confirm the validity of that interpretation.[5] Moreover, a sense of change in the political orientation of the leadership, toward "domesticism," was perceived by the politically conscious elements in Rumania and apparently also in Moscow. The unresolved questions converge on the reasons that led Gheorghiu-Dej to drape around himself, in the summer of 1953, the mantle of nationalist reformer and of executor of the country's and party's historic legacy.

The prevailing hypothesis has been that the Rumanian New Course, like all those adopted in the Soviet bloc, was ordered by Stalin's successors in Moscow in their desire to reorganize the internal and external relations of the Kremlin, and that Gheorghiu-Dej was merely carrying out Russian orders. But this interpretation is based on the assumption that Malenkov, Khrushchev, and Bulganin were prepared to allow every member of the bloc the right to adopt reforms commensurate with each country's "objective conditions" as long as the essential degree of subservience to the USSR remained unimpaired. The evidence does not substantiate that view; on the contrary, it would appear that conflicting opinions regarding the character of the Rumanian leadership and the nature of the reforms necessary to improve the relations between ruler and ruled in Rumania were voiced at the plenum of August 1953.

Recent revelations of the events of the fifties provided by leading Rumanian officials have omitted mention of that specific meeting of the enlarged Central Committee. But it may be surmized from other evidence that Gheorghiu-Dej's Stalinism and unequivocal past identification with Stalin were then under attack.[6] In all probability the attack against Gheorghiu's errors in leadership was led by Miron Constantinescu and the intellectual wing of the organization identified with him. It was probably supported by Iosif Chisinevski, previously sympathetic toward the Pauker, Luca, and Georgescu group and reputedly the *porte parole* of the Kremlin. In any event, the "reformers" appear to have had enough support from a substantial segment of the members of the Central Committee to force Gheorghiu-Dej and his adherents to accept the principle of reform and "democratic centralism" in the party and to summon a congress of the Rumanian party in 1954. If it were possible to ascertain the extent to which Constantinescu and the "reformist elements" were encouraged, if not directly supported, by the Kremlin in their quest for emulation of Russian "anti-Stalinism," the missing parts of the puzzle of 1953 in Rumania would fall into their proper places. But such determination cannot be made with any accuracy. What appears certain is that the Rumanian opponents to Gheorghiu-Dej's *modus operandi* felt sufficiently secure to seek concessions from Gheorghiu and that Gheorghiu felt threatened but also powerful enough to mold these concessions into a compromise formula favorable to his long-range political survival.

It was easy for Gheorghiu-Dej to take credit for the New Course. More important to him was the necessity to defend his record on the basis of Stalinist theory and practice against the challenge of "reformists" and potential adherence to "revisionism" by the population at large. The "Decision on the Improvement of Party Work and Relations of the Party with the Masses," adopted concurrently with the economic reforms, was an unequivocal statement of Gheorghiu-Dej's determination to crush all actual and potential enemies and to maintain tight control over the party and the country. The "Decision" attributed to the discredited "anti-party" group of Pauker, Luca, and Georgescu all responsibility for the lack of rapport between the party and the masses, as well as for other "unhealthy" internal party practices. It also denounced the continuation of such improper practices by members recruited by the disgraced triumvirate and, by implication, Miron Constantinescu.

Far from promising democratization and less rigid relations with the people, however, Gheorghiu-Dej held out only the prospect of further purges in the party and of rigorous enforcement of the Stalinist principles identified with his rule. The call for eternal vigilance against the traditional enemies of the people—the foreign "imperialists" and their agents in Rumania, the "bourgeois-landlord clique," the "kulaks," and all those expecting a change in the political order resulting from Stalin's death—and the threat of dire punishment against all those who would succumb to the entreaties of the "class enemy" were far more strident than the call for greater identification with the people's interests and for emulation of Soviet reforms. The consolidation of the power of the police and the creation of an elite corps of some 100,000 loyal party vigilantes, ordered by Gheorghiu-Dej in August 1953, were most indicative of his apprehensions, strength, and ultimate reason for commitment to a nationalist-Stalinist course in Rumania: political self-preservation.[7]

It is now recognized that the crucial years in the history of Communist Rumania were the five that began with the plenum of August 1953 and ended with the plenum of November 1958. To the superficial observer of Rumanian affairs this period was characterized by continuing adherence by the Rumanian communist regime to the principles of Stalinism, indifferent economic progress, and rigid subservience to Moscow. But in fact, behind the facade of order, poverty, conformity, and repression, profound changes were taking place with respect to Rumania's emancipation from the Soviet Union and the "construction of socialism" *à la roumaine*.

The nature of the changing, all-encompassing Russo-Rumanian relations in these years was ultimately determined by the threat that Khrushchevism posed to Gheorghiu-Dej's Stalinism and to the political survival of Gheorghiu-Dej himself. The ascendancy of Krushchev in 1954 threatened the security of Gheorghiu-Dej in a variety of ways. The policy of peaceful coexistence with the West, particularly in the "spirit of Geneva," opened the possibility of a *détente* that could have been exploited by uncompromised members of the Rumanian party. Gheorghiu-Dej was identified, in 1954, with a policy of complete hostility toward the West and of ruthless persecution of Rumanians who had had even the most superficial ties with Western Europe and the United States. That policy was determined only in part by Moscow. The principal reason for its adoption and rigid enforcement

133

was Gheorghiu's persuasion that the pro-French and pro-Ameri-
can intellectuals and other "class enemies" of bourgeois and aristocratic origin were potentially subversive forces within the party
as well as outside. It is noteworthy that in 1954 Gheorghiu-Dej
and his proletarian associates were most reluctant to emulate
Khrushchev's policies toward the West and paid only lip service
to the principles of peaceful coexistence. In fact, the persecution
of individuals suspected of pro-Western sympathies continued
unabated for years to come; and, despite the objections of a
substantial number of intellectuals in the party, Gheorghiu-Dej
ordered the de-Latinization of the Rumanian alphabet in 1954 to
obscure the Western character of the Rumanian language. In the
last analysis, Gheorgiu's reluctance to alter the Stalinist policies
toward the West was determined by internal political considerations related directly to Russian interference in Rumania's internal affairs.

Although the evidence is still somewhat obscure, it is fair to
state that Krushchev was determined as early as the spring of
1954 to weaken the power base of Stalinists in the Soviet bloc
by encouraging "reforms" and "reorganizations" compatible with
his own plans for the Soviet empire. Whether these plans called
for Gheorghiu-Dej's "retooling" or for his outright removal from
power is uncertain. But it is clear that Krushchev was anxious to
limit Gheorghiu's powers through interference in the affairs of
Rumania at both the party and the state level and that certain
members of the Rumanian organization were prepared to encourage, or at least to support, such interference.

The intensity of Gheorghiu-Dej's struggle for survival before
the reconsolidation of his power at the Second Congress of the
Rumanian Workers' Party in December 1955 was revealed in
part by Nicolae Ceausescu in April 1968. Ceausescu confirmed
the validity of other evidence all focusing on the forging of a
"Rumanian road to socialism" and the casting of a "granite-like

foundation" for resistance to direct or indirect Soviet pressures against Gheorghiu-Dej's establishment. The formula for success was both simple and effective: at home, Gheorghiu-Dej resisted pressures for the calling of the party congress until such time as he felt confident that he could control it; abroad, he sided with the forces seeking to weaken Russia's hegemony in Eastern Europe and the communist world in general, while at all times professing loyalty to the Kremlin and the doctrines of Marxism-Leninism.[8]

The direct internal threat to his power and methods was met by purging all possible competitors. Gheorghiu-Dej had looked with alarm at the Khrushchev-inspired doctrine of "collective leadership." The separation of power between party and state was adopted in the Soviet Union early in 1954 and imposed on the satellites immediately thereafter. In Rumania, a plenum of the Central Committee decided in April 1954 to abolish the post of General-Secretary of the party and the unwieldy secretariat and substitute therefor a compact four-member secretariat headed by a First Secretary. That decision made Gheorghiu's control of the party and the state dependent on the reliability of the secretariat and on his own position of Prime Minister. The reasons for Gheorghiu's retaining the premiership rather than the post of First Secretary are by no means clear. It has been suggested that his resignation as Secretary-General was not entirely voluntary. This hypothesis may be at least partly correct, considering the turmoil in the party in 1954, but it is at least partly invalidated by the composition of the four-man secretariat. The new ruling body of the party was headed by Gheorghe Apostol, one of Gheorghiu-Dej's faithful collaborators, and included Nicolae Ceausescu, Mihai Dalea, and Ianos Fazekas. Dalea and Fazekas were politically insignificant, and Ceausescu's position is unknown. Even if the current revisions of previous interpretations of Ceausescu's relationship with Gheorghiu-Dej—all stressing basic incompatibilities rather than essential affinities—are correct, it must be assumed that Ceausescu was at least acceptable to Gheorghiu in 1954, even if not one of his men.

In addition to Gheorghiu-Dej, three others—Iosif Chisinevski, Miron Constantinescu, and Alexandru Moghioros—also left the old secretariat in April 1954, leaving Apostol as the only continuing member of the body. Moghioros' reassignment was seemingly unimportant, but Chisinevski's and Constantinescu's new posts were not. In all probability, a compromise was reached at the plenary meeting whereby the secretariat was reduced to the status of an administrative body; all meaningful political decisions were to be made elsewhere. The retention by all protagonists of their posts in the Council of Ministers did not per se make that body the principal organ of policy in Rumania, although it is certain that until Gheorghiu's reassumption of the position of First Secretary (*de facto* Secretary-General) in October 1955 the Council of Ministers was more prominent than the party.

The shifting of the locus of political activity from party to state, tactical as it was, represented more than the de-emphasizing of the party in times of internecine crisis in the organization. The existence of such a crisis is now well known, as are the reasons for it. Miron Constantinescu and his supporters, who challenged Gheorghiu's Stalinism and sought the adoption of a moderate "national" course, were making headway within the organization in 1954. The rehabilitation of East European communist leaders who had been destroyed by Stalinists began that year on Khrushchev's orders, and Gheorghiu-Dej feared the possible rehabilitation of Patrascanu and possibly also of Pauker, Luca, and Georgescu. Patrascanu in particular had been identified with "national communism," anti-Stalinism, and the intellectual wing of the Rumanian party. The possibility of his rehabilitation, or at least of encouragement by Khrushchev of individuals sympathetic to Patrascanu's views, prompted Gheorghiu-Dej to order the execution of his deposed rival only a few days before the opening of the plenum of April 1954. It also accounted for his packing the Council of Ministers with his own men until such time as he could reassert full control over the party itself. The constant purging of the party's rank and file and of its intermediate echelons assumed major proportions after April 1954. At the same time Gheorghiu's political rivals were isolated in an ever larger Council of Ministers, wherein they represented a diminishing minority.[9]

It is also likely that the new significance attached to the state was directly connected with Gheorghiu's determination to strengthen Rumania's national identity both at home and abroad. The year 1954 was one of major importance in the history of the communist movement, in international affairs in general, and in the evolution of Communist Rumania. Gheorghiu-Dej was a careful observer and exploiter of the opportunities available to him. Of these, the reconciliation of Moscow and Belgrade and the Chinese quest for equality with the Soviet Union in the socialist camp were the most beneficial in promoting his personal and, by extension, Rumania's national, interests. Moreover, the attainment of his primary goal, maintenance of power through identification of party and state by his and his close associates' contributions to Rumanian communism and Communist Rumania, could best be attained by stressing such identification.

It would probably be erroneous to assume that Gheorghiu-Dej was one of the moving forces toward polycentrism. That distinction must rest with Mao Tse-tung and Tito. However, the Rumanian communist leadership was quick to grasp the significance of the changing relations between Moscow, on the one hand, and Belgrade and Peking, on the other, and to promote the doctrine of "individual roads to socialism" in a specific Rumanian manner. Gheorghiu's principal contribution to polycentrism was his alignment with China and the adaptation of Chinese interpretations of Marxism-Leninism and international realities to the problems of East European party-states. It is indeed noteworthy that the Rumanians were the first of all satellite peoples to seek extension of the principles governing relations between Russia and China to the socialist camp as a whole. As early as February 1954, Gheorghiu-Dej stated that "complete equality of rights, mutual respect of national interests, a common desire for peace" should be the guiding political principles of all socialist nations.[10]

For a long time students of Rumanian and international communist affairs have interpreted that statement and similar ones emanating from Rumania in 1954 as expressions of Rumania's determination to oppose Western interference in the affairs of Eastern Europe, as, in fact, mere Rumanian parroting of Khrushchev. The evidence, however, has proved that interpretation to be in error. The Rumanian communist elite, whether pro-Gheorghiu-Dej or not, was united in furthering disengagement from Moscow and in asserting a national identity albeit within the limits set by the realities of the international situation. Thus, in March 1954, Miron Constantinescu himself took credit for negotiating the agreement with the USSR whereby the onerous *Sovroms* were to be liquidated.

It is noteworthy that these arrangements paralleled those leading to the dissolution of similar Sino-Soviet joint companies. Moreover, these negotiations occurred at a time of growing internecine conflict in the Rumanian party between Constantinescu and Gheorghiu-Dej. The latter's reliance on China for the furthering of his own cause was unequivocal by August 1954. On August 23, the tenth anniversary of Rumania's "liberation from fascism," Gheorghiu-Dej reclaimed for the Rumanian party the leading role in that liberation, and his claim was supported by the Chinese. Inasmuch as Gheorghiu was the leader of the "revolution" of August 1944, the legitimacy of his rule over Communist Rumania could not be denied by his opponents. Mao's endorsement of that position, at least to the extent to which Communist Rumania was created by the revolutionary efforts of its own leaders and therefore was entitled to its own national communist identity, strengthened Gheorghiu-Dej's position as the legitimate revolutionary leader of a national party-state.

Neither Gheorghiu's reiteration of long-silenced claims nor Mao's support could be ascribed to common opposition to the "Western imperialists"; both were, in fact, directed against Soviet hegemony in the socialist camp. The constant repetition of Chinese principles in Rumania and the extensive coverage given to the proceedings of the fifth anniversary of the establishment of the Chinese People's Republic in October 1954 led to the unequivocal formulation of Rumania's doctrine of "relations of the new type" among all nations—whether socialist or not—in November 1954. At that time it was formally stated that the Soviet formula for peaceful coexistence among countries with differing social and political systems—"respect for the principles of equality of rights and noninterference in the internal affairs of other countries"—should be extended to relationships among all nations, whether socialist or not. And, significantly, the Sino-Indian statement of June 1954 was invoked as the prototype of such broad relations of "the new type."

The affirmation of Rumania's sovereign rights, within the limits imposed by proximity to the Soviet Union and the realities of domestic opposition to Gheorghiu's regime, was intended ultimately to pave the way for the consolidation of Gheorghiu-Dej's position in international communist and Rumanian internal affairs. The conciliatory "spirit of Geneva," which affected both inter- and intracamp relations, provided the flexibility required for the attainment of these goals. By December 1955 Gheorghiu was successful on both counts.

Recent rehabilitations of party members convicted to long prison terms between the fall of 1954 and the summer of 1955 reveal the intensity of the house-cleaning process conducted by Gheorghiu-Dej in the crucial months antedating Khrushchev's visit to Rumania in August 1955 and the following Second Congress of the Rumanian Workers' Party of December 1955. The principal elements in that process were the destruction of Vasile Luca and his associates, condemned to life imprisonment in the fall of 1954, the downgrading of Constantinescu, the intensification of the purging of the party's rank and file, and the termination of collective leadership. The terrorizing of actual and potential opponents in the party was conducted by a special *aktiv* created by Gheorghiu-Dej for this very purpose; that of the population, by an ever more vigilant secret police. However, whereas no pity was shown for enemies in the party, a carrot and stick policy was pursued toward the population at large. The principal concessions were in the economic field, where rationing was abolished in December 1954. A major price reform followed. At the same time, intensification of the general economic development initiated by the New Course strengthened both the economy and Gheorghiu-Dej's rationale for seeking desatellization—the need for Rumanian solutions to Rumanian problems. It is indeed noteworthy that all actions beneficial to the Rumanian people were explained in terms of fulfillment of the national goal of socialist well-being and of the party's historic devotion to the realization of the people's aspirations. A mandate for a "Rumanian road to socialism," derived from the events of August 1944 and the directives of the conference of 1945, was assumed by Gheorghiu-Dej in his search for total power in Rumania.

The first formal confrontation between Gheorghiu-Dej and his opponents within the party and outside it occurred in August 1955 on the occasion of Khrushchev's visit to mark the eleventh anniversary of Rumania's liberation from fascism. Information on that visit and confrontation is obscure. Whether Khrushchev sought to encourage Constantinescu and other potential opponents to Gheorghiu's hegemony is uncertain. But it is known that Khrushchev insisted on the continuation of the division of functions between party and state, with a view to preventing too much concentration of power into the hands of Gheorghiu-Dej. Khrushchev apparently also objected to Gheorghiu's doctrine of legitimacy derived from Rumanian communist action in August 1944, preferring the traditional interpretation of Russia's having liberated Rumania, at best with the assistance of the Rumanians. In sum, desatellization and Rumanization, if not determined by the Kremlin, at least had to be closely coordinated with its interests. Khrushchev's speech on August 23 restated Moscow's positions on hierarchical subordination and ultimate power in the Soviet bloc. Gheorghiu's reply was surprisingly defiant. He reiterated the Chinese-supported views on the Rumanian party's role in the events of August 1944, on the nature of relations within the socialist camp, on individual roads to socialism, and, ultimately, on the inalienability of the sovereign rights of all nations regardless of their socioeconomic or political organization.[11]

Gheorghiu's courage may be accounted for by his awareness of Khrushchev's inability in the summer of 1955 to dislodge him from power. On the basis of that conviction he also reasserted his authority in Rumania in October 1955. At that time he reassumed the position of First Secretary of the party, removed Constantinescu as head of the State Planning Commission, and entrusted the premiership to his staunchest ally, the undistinguished and subservient Chivu Stoica. Thus strengthened, he enunciated the law of "socialist construction" *à la Gheorghiu-Dej* at the memorable Second Congress of the Rumanian Workers' Party.

That congress, which met in December 1955, represented a milestone in the history of Rumanian communism.[12] It marked the culmination of Gheorghiu-Dej's efforts to provide a Rumanian Stalinist imprint on the party's programs and on the development of the nation and to resist the re-establishment of "relations of the old type" with Moscow. In December 1955 Gheorghiu unequivocally asserted his determination to adapt Marxist-Leninist principles to the specific national interests and problems of Rumania. The socialist transformation of Rumania was to be based on the blueprints traced by the party in 1945. It would take into account the principles of interaction between socialist patriotism and proletarian internationalism on the basis of the correct intercamp and international relations of "respect of national sovereignty and equality of rights, nonaggression, and peaceful settlement of all problems, peaceful coexistence among countries with different social systems, and noninterference in internal affairs." It would be, not subordinated to, but rather harmoniously blended with, the interests of the socialist camp headed by the Soviet Union.

The formulation of these basic principles of Gheorghiu-Dejism was intended to secure a mandate from the Rumanian Workers' Party and, to a certain extent, from the Rumanian people, for pursuit of the country's socialist goals. Whether that mandate was directed primarily against Khrushchevism or against rivals in the party is not entirely clear; in all probability it was aimed at both. In practical terms it resulted in the simplification of the party's composition and in the packing of the upper and intermediate echelons with members devoted to Gheorghiu-Dej. The number of members and candidate-members reached the all-time-low of 595,000. Most of these persons were communists who had joined the party before 1946. The percentage of workers was still less than the majority, reaching only 43 per cent. However, the key positions in the organization were held by men of proletarian origin, and nowhere was this phenomenon more evident than in the uppermost echelons. The intellectuals were downgraded in December 1955, and the workers, both in industry and in agriculture, were heralded as the actual leaders of the massive process of socialist construction.

Socialist Patriotism

The anti-intellectualism manifested by Gheorghiu-Dej in 1955 was immediately related to his suspicions of Constantinescu and other members of the communist intelligentsia. The mandate of the party conference of 1945 was in theory given to the proletarian leadership, who best understood the needs and attitudes of the population at large. Identification between intellectuals and masses was unnatural in Gheorghiu's view, particularly as the intellectuals were in favor of a relaxation of tensions, reduction of the power of the police, and, in all probability, Khrushchevization. The existence of this state of affairs is confirmed by recent statements from Nicolae Ceausescu himself, indicating that Gheorghiu-Dej elevated Alexandru Draghici, then Minister of the Interior, to membership in the Politburo in December 1955 for the express purpose of resisting liberalization and pursuing the ruthless persecution of "honest" members of the party.[13]

Gheorghiu-Dej's hand in dealing with actual and potential rivals in the Rumanian party was strengthened by the record of achievement in economic affairs, which provided the necessary justification for the correctness of his rule. The balance sheet of economic progress was impressive. According to Gheorghiu-Dej, the First Five-Year Plan, which ended in 1955, brought the country's industrial development to a level nearly three times greater than that of 1938. The most dramatic increases in output were recorded in heavy industry, in electric power, crude oil, chemicals, and machine building. The number of factories had increased by over 100 since 1950, and that of industrial workers from 548,481 to 700,522.

Progress was less marked in agriculture. The production of cereals barely exceeded that of the prewar years (9,956,000 tons versus 8,016,000 tons), and the growth in productivity could be traced only to the period of the New Course. The concessions made to the peasantry after 1953 provided a modicum of incentive for agricultural production in that the collectivization drive was *de facto* arrested after Stalin's death. Collective farms accounted for only 5.5 per cent of the peasantry, and agricultural associations of the TOZ type only another 5.8 per cent. In terms of arable land, the whole socialist sector (state farms, state lands, collective farms, and agricultural associations) comprised only 26.5 per cent of the country's arable surface. However, the relative insignificance of the socialist sector in 1955 did not per se exclude the possibility of its enlargement. In fact, the uncertainty as to the future of individual landownership and farming made the peasantry suspicious of the regime and generally unwilling to commit either labor or capital to agricultural development. Whether it was the negativism of the peasantry or the dogmatism of the regime that accounted for the mutually suspicious relationship between the communists and the village is uncertain. Gheorghiu-Dej, however, promised the acceleration of socialization of agriculture during the Second Five-Year Plan (1956–1960) to the extent that by 1960 60–70 per cent of the agricultural output would be provided by the socialist sector. The assurances that the "socialization of agriculture" would be undertaken, not by forcible means, but on the basis of "strict adherence to the principle of free consent" were not reassuring. Nor was there any positive response from the peasantry to the rationale for socialization: "an objective necessityfor achieving higher socialist production in the national economy as a whole and for the harmonious development of agriculture."

The response of the industrial workers to the ambitious plans for development of Rumania's industry in the period of 1956–1960 was markedly more enthusiastic. It is fair to say that the workers, as well as the technocratic cadres, took pride in the growth of Rumania's industry. The planned increases in heavy industry, projected at 60–65 per cent over the production of 1955, and the corresponding growth of the national income could only augur well for their and their country's future. The lack of specific measures designed to insure a higher standard of living through increases in the production of consumer goods and wages must have dampened the enthusiasm of the proletariat, but not to the extent of contemplating changes in the political order. In all probability, the workers had confidence in Gheorghiu-Dej and his plans for the future. And this spirit of acceptance of the existing regime, which permeated the working class, assumed a broader national character as the echoes of Khrushchev's denunciation of Stalin at the Twentieth CPSU Congress reverberated in Rumania in the spring of 1956.[14]

Khrushchev's de-Stalinization speech confronted Gheorghiu-Dej with a major crisis. His own association with Stalin and Stalinism was irrefutable, and Gheorghiu-Dejism itself was a Rumanian variant of Stalinism. The precautionary measures adopted in 1955 rendered difficult the task of the anti-Stalinists at home and abroad who were seeking the removal from power of Gheorghiu-Dej's Stalinist team. Therefore Miron Constantinescu, Khrushchev himself, and the Kremlin's principal agent in Rumania, Iosif Chisinevski, had to work toward the erosion of Gheorghiu's strength in the party and the country instead of launching a decisive frontal attack on the Rumanian Stalinists.

Rather incredibly Gheorghiu-Dej, in his report on the proceedings of the Twentieth Congress presented in March 1956, sought total exoneration from any possible connection with Stalin and Stalinism.[15] The "cult of personality," according to Gheorghiu-Dej, was never practiced in Rumania except by the "anti-party group" purged in 1952. In fact, the purging of Pauker, Luca, and Georgescu was undertaken precisely because of their Stalinism and opposition to the democratic practices associated with Gheorghiu-Dej. Gheorghiu-Dej even went so far as to affirm the democratic nature of Gheorghiu-Dejism and its applicability to Rumanian conditions. The Rumanian party, according to his interpretation, would have applied at all times the proper forms of socialism, as determined by Rumania's objective conditions and the requirements of the socialist community in general, had it not been prevented in the execution of these principles by the deposed Stalinists. As all Rumanians realized, upon the removal of his enemies from power he, Gheorghiu-Dej, had worked faithfully toward the consolidation of democratic collective socialist rule in Rumania.

The absurdity of this interpretation of the lessons of the Twentieth Congress was self-evident. Nevertheless, the direct attack launched against Gheorghiu-Dej by Constantinescu and Chisinevski at the party meeting where he presented his interpretation of those lessons was unsuccessful in dislodging Gheorghiu. The Rumanian Stalinist team, entrenched in the party and fully in control of the forces of repression, agreed that the best defense was an energetic offense against "revisionists." And this course of action was pursued with relentless vigor and great skill.[16]

The principal victims of Gheorghiu's offensive were the intellectuals identified with liberalization. In May 1956 the Stalinists launched an all-out attack against the writers critical of Gheorghiu-Dejism and of Gheorghiu's interpretation of de-Stalinization. Gheorghiu-Dej himself ordered the purging of all revisionists and laid down the criteria valid for all intellectual activity. In simple terms, the function of intellectuals was to support Gheorghiu-Dej's road to socialism in Rumania. The attack on the writers was also directed against "cosmopolitan" elements, identified with the purged Pauker-Luca group. The principal victims, headed by Alexandru Jar, were Jews. By contrast, a corollary appeal was launched to all honest Rumanian intellectuals to support Gheorghiu-Dej's policies, with resulting rehabilitation of men and women previously barred from intellectual pursuits because of wrong social origin or, more frequently, "fascist" affiliations.

The effort to secure the support of true Rumanians for the

Rumanian road to socialism also entailed active propaganda among the population at large, with emphasis on the wisdom and positive results attained by the Gheorghiu team since 1952. At the same time, Gheorghiu-Dej sought Constantinescu's isolation from the student community and cleansed the Union of Working Youth of members who regarded his younger rival as a potential leader of the country's youth.

The precautionary internal measures were supplemented by closer relations with exponents of doctrines opposed to Khrushchev's. Gheorghiu-Dej rightly interpreted Khrushchev's message to the Twentieth Congress as an attack not only on Stalinists but also on those opposed to Soviet hegemony in the socialist camp. For Khrushchev was not inclined to alter the basic goals of Soviet foreign policy vis-à-vis the socialist community; he sought merely to re-establish Soviet domination in a manner more palatable to that community. As a would-be victim of any purge ordered by the Kremlin, Gheorghiu-Dej sought the support first of the Chinese and then of the Yugoslavs—the leading exponents of the doctrines of individual roads to socialism, equality of members of the camp, relations of the new type, and all other political aphorisms identified with independence from Soviet domination.

Relatively little is known about specific Sino-Rumanian relations in the period antedating the Hungarian revolution of October. However, in all exchanges of messages between Bucharest and Peking, the validity of the "relations of the new type" was stressed. Similarly, the marked improvement in Rumania's relations with Yugoslavia, following the reconciliation between Moscow and Belgrade, was motivated by Gheorghiu's desire to gain rights and immunities for himself comparable to those granted Tito by Moscow.

It is a matter of conjecture what Gheorghiu-Dej's political future—and for that matter Rumania's—would have been had the Hungarian revolution been either averted or successful. Under the revolutionary circumstances and conditions of October 1956 Gheorghiu's and Rumania's future were determined by the "correctness" of the Rumanian Stalinists' policies both before and during the revolutionary crisis and by Khrushchev's inability to seek Gheorghiu's removal from power in the wake of the Hungarian events. The reverberations of the Hungarian upheaval were minimal in Rumania.[17] Significantly, there were no anticommunist manifestations in the country. Isolated expressions of "bourgeois nationalism," inimical to the interests of the regime, were restricted primarily to high school and university students. The youth of Hungarian origin demanded greater cultural autonomy but not union with a free Hungary. Rumanian students in Bucharest and Iasi clamored for a greater measure of independence from the Soviet Union and for the abolition of Russian as a compulsory foreign language in academic curricula. Rumania's quiescence was reassuring to Gheorghiu-Dej; it vindicated his confidence in the efficiency and validity of Gheorghiu-Dejism.

The nature of the policies adopted by Gheorghiu-Dej in the wake of the Hungarian revolution has been generally misunderstood by students of Rumanian affairs. Gheorghiu-Dej did not support the Russian military intervention in Hungary unconditionally, nor did he necessarily approve of the rationale invoked by the Kremlin. In fact, the Rumanian leadership sought to capitalize on Khrushchev's embarrassment and promises made to the Hungarians in the days immediately preceding the crushing of the revolution. In December 1956, the Rumanians spelled out their demands to Moscow: recognition of the validity of their policies for a "Rumanian road to socialism," economic concessions commensurate for the attainment of the goals of Gheorghiu-Dejism, and legalization of the status of the Russian armed forces located on Rumanian territory. The all-encompassing request for Moscow's acceptance of Gheorghiu-Dejism was based on "The Declaration of the Principles of Development and Further

Strengthening of Friendship and Cooperation between the Soviet Union and other Socialist States" of October 1956, an albatross around Khrushchev's political neck.[18] The demands for a revision of the economic obligations incurred by Rumania were based on the same declaration and on the country's need for extended credits and raw materials for the attainment of its economic goals. The demand for legalizing the status of the Russian armed forces had no theoretical basis other than an evident desire to bring about the eventual removal of a long standing instrument of Soviet interference in Rumanian affairs. Evidently, Gheorghiu's demands were designed to lessen the degree of Rumanian dependence on the USSR and to allow for consolidation of Gheorghiu-Dejism and the Gheorghiu-Dej team in Rumania.

The concessions made by Moscow were less than expected by Bucharest, revealing Khrushchev's awareness of the Rumanians' motivations. The Russians refused to formally reiterate the validity of the "Declaration" but paid lip service to the right of each individual socialist nation to pursue its own road to socialism. In the economic field the Russians agreed to grant modest credits for the development of heavy industry and to postpone the repayment by Rumania of existing credits but would not cancel these obligations altogether. The agreement to limit the presence of Russian troops to a specified period of time, vaguely referred to as "temporary stationing," was of greater importance than generally recognized. The official rationale for the stationing of troops was the necessity for member nations of the Warsaw Pact to take military measures for the defense of the socialist community against the "revanchist forces" of West Germany, the American imperialists, and the threat of NATO. To this the Rumanians, as members of the Warsaw Pact, could hardly object. They were apparently able, however, to secure the provision that the stationing would be "temporary"—subject to the ability of the Rumanian armed forces themselves to secure Rumania's integrity against aggressive forces—because of support rendered to their demands by the Chinese representatives who attended the meeting of the Rumanian and Russian delegations.[19]

It is now believed that the Chinese were anxious in December 1956 to prevent the consolidation of Soviet power in the camp through military control of the member nations and therefore encouraged the demands for limitation of the power and number of Soviet forces stationed in Rumania. It is also believed that the Chinese supported the other demands of the Rumanians to the extent to which Rumanian interests coincided with theirs;—in this instance, in the right of individual members of the socialist camp to map their own roads to socialism.

As far as Gheorghiu-Dej was concerned, the concessions wrested from Moscow, minor as they were, provided him with the opportunity to pursue a program of socialist largesse toward the working class and the working peasantry with a view to consolidating their allegiance to Gheorghiu-Dejism. In practical terms, a series of economic measures intended to encourage the production of consumer goods, to provide incentives to workers through the payment of bonuses, and even to decentralize the industrial production process was adopted between December 1956 and the spring of the following year. These measures, coupled with an overall increase in wages of approximately 15 per cent, transcended appeasement of the working class. They were symptomatic of the embryonic development of autarchic economic policies designed to strengthen Gheorghiu-Dej's bargaining power with Moscow.

It has recently been revealed that as early as the spring of 1956 Gheorghiu-Dej feared the reactivation of the Council for Mutual Economic Assistance (COMECON)—the organ for the economic integration of the bloc founded by Stalin in 1949—in a manner disadvantageous to Rumania's interests.[20] Khrushchev's more subtle methods of imperialism, through economic rather than direct political domination of the "satellites," had resulted in the reviving of the dormant COMECON in 1955. By May 1956 the pattern for future development of the Council became clear. The economically developed members of the bloc, the USSR, Czechoslovakia, and East Germany, favored the relegation of the less developed nations, including Rumania, to the role either of suppliers of raw materials or, failing that, of secondary producers of specified industrial commodities.

The assignment of an inferior status to Rumania would have impaired the attainment of the goals for industrialization set by the party congress in 1955. Gheorghiu-Dej's opposition to the plan of the dominant nations in COMECON, however, was not rooted in economic considerations. Rather, Gheorghiu-Dej was persuaded that the controlling of Rumania's road to socialism through economic limitations was in effect an instrument of pressure by Moscow against his regime, a means for political interference in the affairs of Rumania by a power hostile to his own rule. Therefore, persuaded that Moscow's stinginess in the negotiations of December 1956 reflected a determination to press for its positions on economic integration and corollary controls, he decided to redraw Rumania's plans for economic development to render them independent of regulation by Moscow. The basic economic reforms in industry were therefore accompanied by similar reforms in agriculture and by cautious attempts at expanding Rumania's economic relations with countries outside the Soviet bloc.

In agriculture the appeasement of the peasantry was limited to the elimination of the system of compulsory deliveries of basic agricultural products on January 1, 1957. But the introduction of a series of financial and technological inducements to would-be members of collective farms was specifically designed to stimulate agricultural efficiency and the eventual completion of the socialization of agriculture.

In the area of foreign trade with noncommunist countries, progress was made toward lessening Rumania's dependence on the USSR and her partners in COMECON. As indicated by John Michael Montias in his masterful study of Rumania's economic development, the importation of machinery and equipment from "capitalist countries" more than doubled between 1956 and 1958 and comparable changes were recorded in the general acquisition of products developed by Western technology.[21] Montias rightly indicates that this westward movement was partly the result of a desire for emancipation from COMECON's clutches and partly an expression of Gheorghiu's conviction that Rumania's economic independence at least might best be secured through superior Western know-how.

If the rate of economic growth and emancipation from the USSR was relatively slow in 1957, this was due to Gheorghiu-Dej's concern for his political safety, which, in his view, was threatened by liberals and Khrushchevites headed by Miron Constantinescu. The major political crisis of the fifties was probably that of July 1957, when Constantinescu sought Gheorghiu-Dej's political demise.[22] The immediate antecedents and details of the confrontation between Rumanian Stalinists and Khruschevites, which ended in Constantinescu's defeat, remain obscure. It has been surmised that Constantinescu's challenge to Gheorghiu's authority and the legitimacy of Stalinist rule in Rumania was coordinated with Khrushchev's own challenge against the Stalinist "anti-party" group in Russia. It has also been suggested that Gheorghiu's group was acting in conjunction with Molotov's and Bulganin's forces in seeking the formal reassertion of Stalinism and the elimination of Khrushchevism. The only known facts are that relations between Gheorghiu and Constantinescu worsened after the Hungarian revolution and that the Rumanian Central Committee met in plenary session at exactly the same time as its Russian counterpart, late in June 1957.

Socialist Patriotism

Gheorghiu's fears of Constantinescu were based, as previously indicated, on the latter's standing with the intellectual community and university students. Since 1956 Gheorghiu had sought to win the support of the intellectuals for Gheorghiu-Dejism and to strengthen proletarian and peasant representation in the Union of Working Youth. However, during the Hungarian revolutionary crisis, Constantinescu was appointed Minister of Education, presumably as a conciliatory gesture to the students. Whether he used his influence with the youth and anti-Stalinist intellectuals to establish a power base for himself is unknown. In all probability he kept his ear to the ground for possible rumblings in Moscow in the aftermath of the Soviet intervention in Hungary. It is evident that Gheorghiu-Dej was also looking for signals from Moscow while keeping a close watch on Constantinescu. In any event, when the showdown occurred in both Moscow and Bucharest, Khrushchev's forces ousted Molotov's while Gheorghiu's defeated Constantinescu's.

In terms of subsequent internal actions it must be assumed that Gheorghiu-Dej was fearful of Khrushchev and of the possibility of subversion by the Soviet leader and Constantinescu's supporters in the Rumanian party. The most ruthless purging of all suspected of opposition to Gheorghiu-Dejism, within the party and without, began in July 1957 concurrently with the adoption of a national policy of building economic and political bridges with nations, within the socialist camp and without, that sought the lessening of Soviet power throughout the world.

The destruction of the party cadres suspected of affinity with Constantinescu and Khrushchevism was pursued relentlessly between the summer of 1957 and the fall of 1958. As usual the "cosmopolitan" intellectuals were the victims of the purge. Within the party "cosmopolitanism" was more and more identified with "non-Rumanians," primarily Jews. The reign of terror unleashed against all suspected of entertaining "bourgeois-nationalist" her-

153

esies was directed mainly against Jewish technocrats and "fascist" intellectuals. The corollary international actions focused on the consolidation of ties with Peking and the assumption of independent "political initiatives" by Bucharest.

The exploitation of the Sino-Soviet conflict for Rumanian purposes assumed major proportions in 1957, when the Rumanians realized the far-reaching advantages that might be derived from the disunity within the socialist camp. The Chinese exceptions to Russia's views on the nature of the camp and Moscow's role in the socialist world provided Gheorghiu-Dej with the political leverage required to secure one of his main objectives—the withdrawal of Soviet troops from Rumania. Recent studies of that momentous event, which occurred in June 1958, have revealed the coordination of Rumanian and Chinese actions toward the attainment of that paramount Rumanian goal.[23] Specifically, Peking sought the lessening of Soviet military domination over the socialist world through the sharing of nuclear power and reduction of the size of conventional military forces. The Chinese, like the Rumanians, were fearful of Russian nuclear blackmail and control over national armies. The Chinese fears were ultimately expressed in Peking's rejection of the views on the role of the Warsaw Pact forces in guaranteeing the security of the communist world expressed by the Kremlin at the Warsaw Pact meeting of May 1958. It is believed that the Rumanians sided with the Chinese at that meeting and that the Russians, seeking to reduce Peking's opposition, agreed to emulate China's own policies toward client states. Thus the oft-quoted Chinese view that the agreed-upon withdrawal of Chinese volunteers from Korea should be reciprocated by Moscow found application in Rumania. The Rumanians, who had stressed the correctness of Peking's views on several occasions since the Moscow Conference of 1957, bore witness to the accuracy of Peking's contentions and, with the aid of their Chinese comrades, secured first a promise of military withdrawal and later the actual withdrawal of the Red Army from Rumania. This major triumph facilitated the evolution of a national foreign policy by Rumania.

The "nationalizing" of Rumania's foreign policy began in the summer of 1957, when Ion Gheorghe Maurer, the present Prime Minister, became Minister of Foreign Affairs.[24] Maurer, if not the architect of Rumanian policy, was certainly intimately connected with the formulation of the Rumanian course in foreign affairs. An intellectual closely identified with the West and occasionally with Gheorghiu-Dej, Maurer executed the policy of assertion of national interests with great skill and remarkable finesse. The principal element of that policy was the reestablishment of links with Rumania's historic allies. Therefore in September 1957 the Rumanians, through the so-called Stoica Plan, re-enunciated the prewar policy of peace and prosperity in the Balkans through the formation of a Balkan federation. The historic past was also invoked in the quest for expansion of economic and cultural ties with Rumania's traditional friends in the West. By the fall of 1958 Gheorghiu-Dej assumed that the objective internal and external factors permitted a long-range commitment to the development of Rumania as a self-governing member of the socialist camp and as a distinct entity in the international community in general. The formal commitment of Rumania to the pursuit of national policies designed to insure the successful execution of Gheorghiu-Dej's blueprints for the Rumanian road to socialism, indeed the formal commitment to a policy of national communism, was made at the plenum of the Rumanian party's Central Committee in November 1958.

The principal decisions made at that time involved the country's economic development.[25] In the industrial field they promoted self-reliance and independence from external sources in the production of ferrous and nonferrous ores, steel, machine building products, and complex chemicals. The socialization of agriculture was to be accelerated. Within a year from the plenum, 72.2 per cent of the total arable area was indeed in the "socialist sector," and by the end of the following year the percentage reached 81.9. Most spectacular, however, was the development of foreign trade with Western Europe during the year following the decisions of the plenum to seek gradual economic independence from the Soviet bloc. Although the actual sums and volume of trade did not show spectacular gains in 1959, or for that matter even in 1960, the bases for eventual disengagement were indeed laid in 1959. In that year trade missions headed by senior communist officials explored possibilities of increased trade with France, Great Britain, Western Germany, Italy, Switzerland, Belgium, Holland, and even the United States and concluded agreements with several West European companies. The drive was continued in 1960 with increased energy and even greater success. By the end of that year, official statistics indicated a decrease in Rumania's trade with Russia from approximately 46 per cent in 1959 to 40 per cent in 1960; a corresponding increase in Rumania's trade with Western countries was recorded.

The plenum also decided to seek such national reconciliation as was necessary to withstand external reaction and insure the execution of the far-reaching economic policies. However, this reconciliation had to be strictly compatible with the party's interest and intolerant of any "bourgeois-nationalist" deviations. The basic element of the policy was the strengthening of socialist patriotism and the establishment of "granite-like" unity among all inhabitants of Rumania for the execution of Gheorghiu-Dej's plans for the "socialist fatherland." The movement that emerged clearly in 1959 was one of "socialist nationalism" with distinct chauvinistic characteristics. Intellectuals, primarily writers and historians, were directed to stress national themes, albeit socialist, and to minimize international socialist subjects. The reiteration of the soft-pedaled, if not altogether forgotten, doctrine of the patriotic achievements of the Rumanian communist leadership in August 1944 was indicative of the nationalist trend. The minimizing of the Russians' contribution to the country's historic development in 1944, and for that matter before and after that year, was implicit in the statements made on the occasion of the fifteenth anniversary of "Rumania's liberation" and explicit in Gheorghiu-Dej's own version of that event and of his subsequent role in Rumania.

The process of Rumanization of the history of Rumanian communism to the extent of seeking once again direct identification of Communist with historic Rumania assumed more negative forms, however, in the annulling of specific priviliges granted to national minorities after World War II. It is indeed noteworthy that in June 1959 the Rumanian regime ordered the merging of the Hungarian Bolyai University with the Rumanian Babes University into the unitary Babes-Bolyai University of Cluj on the grounds that all students and professors were constructors of socialism in Rumania. The dispersion of the Hungarian population from the "compact" Magyar Autonomous Region the following year was also justified in terms of national homogenization and common Rumanian socialist purpose. Similar measures affecting the German and Jewish populations were instituted on the same theoretical grounds.[26]

The actual motivation for the new minority policies was somewhat different. Granted that the regime sought a broad national commitment for the successful execution of its plans, it is also true that it feared the dissemination of "bourgeois-nationalist" propaganda among the national minority groups by the Soviet Union, Hungary, and the international forces of "Zionism" and "German revanchism" for the purpose of undermining Gheorghiu's policies. Paradoxically, although the emphasis in official propaganda was directed against the "nonsocialist" enemies of Rumania, the regime's main fears were caused by the activities of its socialist partners. As Gheorghiu-Dej knew, his autarchic policies, lack of docility in COMECON, flirtation with the West, and reassertion of the national communist and historic legacies were clearly offensive to the USSR. Moscow's displeasure became evident to Gheorghiu-Dej on the occasion of the Twenty-first Soviet Party Congress, held in January 1959. He feared the encouragement of Magyar nationalism by the Kremlin through Kadar's Hungary and the stifling of Rumania's own independent efforts in all other branches of political and economic activity. Consequently, the decisions adopted at the plenum of November 1958 had to be reinforced after that congress, as indeed they were in the spring of 1959. By 1960 the policies promulgated in 1958 were sufficiently developed and implemented to permit the calling of the Rumanian Workers' Party Third Congress, which spelled out the basic tenets of Rumanian national communism. The wheel of nationalism was rapidly closing the circle.

8

THE NATIONAL LEGACY RECLAIMED
National Communism (1960–1965)

THE DRAMATIC assertion of Rumania's independence from the Soviet Union contained in the now celebrated "Statement of the Rumanian Workers' Party of April 1964"[1] was the climax of a long process of disengagement from Soviet tutelage and exploitation. The roots of the doctrine of national communism spelled out in the "Statement," as has been shown, may be traced to the mid-fifties. But the springboard for the systematic development of plans for independence was the Third Congress of the Rumanian Workers' Party of 1960.[2]

The significance of that congress transcends the formulation of specific measures for the economic development of Rumania, incorporated in the Six-Year Plan, and the projected long-term fifteen-year program for economic growth. Actually, the economic plans were the blueprints for the modernization of Rumanian society in a manner compatible with the national historic tradition and the interests of the party. It is still a matter of dispute whether the formulation of a national communist program was motivated by Gheorghiu-Dej's and his associates' "socialist patriotism" or by the more primitive instinct of political self-preservation from the monolithically inclined Kremlin. There are arguments in favor of both hypotheses and perhaps for other ex-

159

planations of the clearly nationalist orientation confirmed by the Third Congress. In all probability, the party's leadership was encouraged by the gradual enlargement of the country's economic potential and the possibilities for further development through rational economic relations with the noncommunist world. In fact, students of the economic questions raised and solved at the congress have agreed that the Rumanian demands for industrial modernization under terms favorable to Rumania—specifically the establishment of a modern steel complex at Galati—constituted the test case of Russo-Rumanian relations in 1960. They have also indicated that the Russians' reluctance to agree to the Rumanians' terms prompted the search for alternatives in the West and marked the first formal manifestation of a rift between the two countries. What is not clear is whether the Galati steel mill was a political or an economic football, whether a satisfactory economic compromise could not have been reached had the political climate been more favorable in 1960.[3]

Inasmuch as economic issues in the communist world were by definition political in 1960, as they are now also, it is impossible to divorce the political from the economic. In his penetrating study of Rumania's economic development in that period, Professor Montias traces the economic as well as the political antecedents of the "Galati steel mill question."[4] There can be little argument with his basic contention that for the Rumanians that question was one of determination of the extent to which their economic development wast to be controlled by the Soviet Union and its supporters in COMECON and to which national decisions could be made by Bucharest. For Bucharest COMECON was an instrument of Soviet political imperialism, an economic subterfuge for maintaining and extending control over Rumania. Even if Gheorghiu-Dej's interpretation of Moscow's economic policies was incorrect, it is clear that he would not allow the substitution of multilateral economic pressure for direct military coercion only two years after the withdrawal of the Red Army from Rumania. The doctrine of "eternal vigilance" alluded to by Gheorghiu-Dej in his report to the Congress was applicable to Khrushchev, COMECON, the "Western imperialists," and the domestic "class enemy" indiscriminately.[5]

The Kremlin's reluctance to provide the Rumanians with the capital, equipment, and assurances for unhindered economic development confirmed Gheorghiu-Dej's suspicion of the Russians' imperialistic motives. To secure the attainment of his economic and political goals he resorted to a classic stratagem: exploitation of the "objective conditions" prevalent in the summer of 1960. The most favorable factor was the disunity of the socialist camp, which was dramatized by the open split between China and Russia at the Rumanian Party's Third Congress.[6] The Rumanians were aware of the growing friction between Moscow and Peking from at least the spring of 1959 and could not have ignored the anti-Russian tirade issued by Peking in February 1960 under the title "Long Live Leninism!" The Rumanians shared the Chinese views on the equality of members of the socialist camp and on rejection of Russia's unique position of leadership of that camp; in brief, like the Chinese, they thought to liberate themselves from Russian domination. The overt attack on Khrushchevism and Russian policies made by the Chinese in Bucharest in June 1960 persuaded Gheorghiu-Dej that Russia would have to make concessions to Peking and to the supporters of China's views on equality unless it chose to formally destroy the unity of the international communist movement. But Gheorghiu-Dej also understood that the Sino-Soviet conflict would accelerate the Russian trend toward "peaceful coexistence" with the West and thus provide opportunities for all adherents to that doctrine, Bucharest included. In 1960 Gheorghiu was interested only in economic opportunities, in securing the Western credits and equipment required to strengthen the economic foundation of communist

161

Rumania. Political leverage against Moscow was to be secured through Peking and the internal unity of the Rumanian party.

The stratagem reflected the party's continuing fear concerning the prevalence of "bourgeois nationalism" among the population at large and particularly among the technocrats and intellectuals whose contributions were needed for the implementation of the Rumanian road to socialism. The principal theme on matters other than economic development was the consolidation of the "granite-like" unity of the party organization. That unity was to be perfected through a constant increase in the size of the proletarian and peasant membership and through rigorous political indoctrination in Gheorghiu-Dejism. It is noteworthy that the political education branch of the party was drastically strengthened with the establishment of a core of some 800,000 agitators and propagandists under the direction of the leading propagandist Leonte Rautu. It is also noteworthy that the principal task of that team was the "mobilization of the masses for the implementation of the targets of the Six-Year Plan," although proper attention was to be paid to the "elimination of the influence of bourgeois education on the people's consciousness" and the fight against the revisionists' anti-Marxist outlook." The crusade against bourgeois values and ideology, however, was specifically entrusted to the Minister of the Interior, Alexandru Draghici, with a view to eradicating all such manifestations.[7]

Gheorghiu-Dej obviously realized the danger inherent in disengagement from the Soviet Union and the potential threat to his Stalinist rule from resumption of meaningful economic relations with the West and "coexistence" in spheres other than economic. The pro-Western professional cadres and intellectuals as well as the disgruntled masses were suspected of equating "coexistence" with the liberalization if not the outright termination of Gheorghiu-Dej's rule. Gheorghiu, therefore, denied the validity of such assumptions by declaring that "peaceful coexistence necessarily implied a battle between socialism and capitalism" and ordering Draghici to act according to these principles. Gheorghiu was also aware that numerous members of the party, even at the highest echelons, had views at variance with his and, in fact, favored democratization, at least within the party machinery. Such tendencies had to be contained and controlled by assigning priority to the attainment of goals acceptable to all segments of the Rumanian Workers' Party and the majority of the population. National self-assertion and economic growth were regarded as suitable for all Rumanians. In 1960 the accent was on economic growth; by 1961 it had shifted to national achievement.

The planned economic changes envisaged the rapid and consistent development of heavy industry, particularly the fuel, power, metallurgical, and chemical areas. Only a moderate increase was contemplated in the production of consumer goods, a deficiency that would be offset by heavy investment in the housing industry. The collectivization of agriculture was to be accelerated with total socialization envisaged within the span of the Six-Year Plan. The seemingly overambitious plan, which provided for more than doubling the production of such industries as electric power, chemical, rubber, paper, and cellulose, proved entirely feasible with resultant strengthening of Gheorghiu-Dej's position both within Rumania and in the international community. By the end of 1961 Rumania was showing the fastest rate of industrial growth in Eastern Europe, a development related in no small measure to the autarchic policies of the regime. These policies and particularly the rapidly expanding foreign trade with the capitalist and noncommitted world increased the political friction between Rumania and other members of COMECON and expedited the evolution of national communism under Gheorghiu-Dej's guidance.

Whether the Rumanians' reorientation to the West caused Russia to increase its pressure for conformity under COMECON or whether that pressure forced the Rumanians to turn westward is still a matter of dispute among students of Rumanian affairs. In any event, Rumanian trade with the West had assumed significant proportions by the end of 1961.[8] Imports from West Germany, France, and England, for instance, more than tripled between 1959 and 1961, and similar increases were recorded in exports to Italy, France, and Switzerland. Although Rumania's reliance on the Soviet bloc was still overwhelming at the end of 1961, the trend of disengagement was evident to other members of COMECON as well as to the politically conscious Rumanians. In fact, statements in support of Rumania's autarchic economic policies appeared in specialized publications in 1961 and were made publicly by the Chairman of the State Planning Committee, Gheorghe Gaston-Marin, at the meeting of the party's Central Committee in November-December of the same year. That meeting was characterized by the rejection of more than one Soviet position and the reaffirmation, in clear terms, of the validity of Gheorghiu-Dejism in the construction of socialism in Rumania.[9]

The Central Committee meeting marked the culmination of a process of gradual assertion of the correctness of the policies adopted in 1960 and search for national support for those policies. It has been suggested that the clarification in November-December 1961 of the decisions of 1960 was motivated by the implied threats to the Rumanian leadership contained in Khrushchev's celebrated report to the Soviet Party's Twenty-second Congress. The violent attack on Stalin's practices and the denunication of his crimes, as well as those of surviving Stalinists everywhere, could have been regarded as a direct warning to Gheorghiu-Dej his Stalinist team. The exponents of this interpretation have emphasized the specific denunciation of the "anti-party group," removed from power in July 1957, and of the Albanian and Chinese leaders of 1961, all of whom were identifiable with Gheorghiu-Dej and Gheorghiu-Dejism.[10]

National Communism

The accuracy of this interpretation of the significance of Khrushchev's statements for the Rumanian leadership cannot be denied. However, it is necessary to emphasize that Rumania's disengagement from Russia and the basic anti-Russian elements of Gheorghiu-Dejism were defined before the Twenty-second Congress. In fact, Gheorghiu-Dej sought a specific popular mandate for his Rumanian policies as early as February 1961 during the electoral campaign for the Grand National Assembly. The entire campaign stressed the role of the Rumanian party, headed by Rumanians, in the creation of the "objective conditions" for progress and prosperity in the "fatherland" and appealed to the peoples' love of country and patriotism as the essential prerequisite for the consolidation of actual achievements and the corollary development of a great socialist Rumania. The emphasis on the Rumanian character of the party's leadership and political traditions as opposed to the non-Rumanian, was striking and at no time was there any discussion of the fundamental ideological issues confronting the socialist camp—Stalinism, revisionism, dogmatism, liberalization, and the like. The national communist theme was also heralded during the crucial meeting of members of the Warsaw Pact and COMECON, held in Warsaw early in August, during which Khrushchev specified the formulae for closer integration of the military and economic activities of the member nations. The Rumanian delegation at that meeting refused to accept the Russian views of subordination of the national to the general interest, without, however, rejecting the desirability of bilateral understanding among equal, sovereign members of supranational organizations. The Rumanian doctrine of equality of members of the camp and clear identification of the national interests of parties and states was reiterated on the occasion of the anniversary of Rumania's liberation from fascism on August 23, this time in conjunction with the party's paramount role in the process of liberation and socialist construction since 1944.

National Communism

At the time of the Soviet Party's Twenty-second Congress relations between Russia and Rumania, as well as between Rumania and Russia's main supporters in COMECON, Czechoslovakia and East Germany, were definitely less than "cordial and fraternal." Khrushchev's attack on Stalin and Stalinism and his commitment to de-Stalinization and the consolidation of the camp, however, exacerbated the latent conflict between the Rumanian and Russian communist leaderships and between Rumania and the Soviet Union. It led, in Rumania's case, to an unequivocal restatement by Gheorghiu-Dej and his closest associates of the rectitude of the Rumanian leadership's policies and of the tenets of national communism.

Gheorghiu-Dej's thesis, enunciated at the meeting of the Central Committee of November–December 1961, was to accuse the "Moscovites"—Ana Pauker, Vasile Luca, Teohari Georgescu, and their accomplices, Miron Constantinescu and Iosif Chisinevski—of Stalinism and to identify Stalinism with an idealogy alien to the Rumanian communist. The Rumanian party, headed by Gheorghiu-Dej, alone stood for the Rumanian communist tradition and the Rumanians' interests, while the "Moscovites" stood for Moscow's. Only by carrying out the policies and plans of the Rumanian leadership, only by adhering to Gheorghiu-Dejism—the ultimate synthesis of Rumanian communist ideology and practice—could the glorious future of Communist Rumania be assured. Gheorghiu-Dej further identified Stalinism with Moscovite imperialism, with Soviet interference in the internal affairs of fellow-socialist countries, with Khrushchevism. Rumania and the Rumanian Workers' Party would not tolerate "Stalinism" in 1961 anymore than they did in 1952 or in 1957, when "de-Stalinization" was effectively carried out.[11]

The specific Rumanian definition of Stalinism—so at variance with the customary interpretation of dictatorial in juxtaposition to liberal communism—was in keeping with the dogmatism of

Gheorghiu-Dejism. In 1961, this philosophy was in effect Rumanian Stalinism, nationalist, authoritarian, and irrevocably opposed to both "bourgeois ideologies" and democratic centralism.

Gheorghiu-Dej's statements were apparently understood by Moscow, which intensified its pressures against Rumanian separatism in COMECON and Stalinism throughout the camp. It was also understood by the politically initiated in Rumania, who reiterated the validity of Gheorghiu's pronunciamentos and intensified the campaign for national self-determination and popular support for the pursuit of the Rumanian road to socialism. It is noteworthy, however, that the encouragement of the latent anti-Russian sentiments of the population, the inclusion of that essential historic ingredient of Rumanian nationalism into the national communist doctrine, was deferred until 1962. It was in that year alone that the reclaiming by Gheorghiu-Dej of the national historical tradition and the equating of that tradition with that of the Rumanian communist became a matter of fact.

The year 1962 was one of consolidation and completion of Rumanian programs. It was a test year for peasants, workers, and intellectuals. It was a test year for acceptance of the party's policies by the Rumanian people, the Soviet bloc, the socialist camp, and the international community at large. As a result of fortuitous international circumstances but also because of relaxation of tensions resultant from Rumania's own internal achievements, Gheorghiu-Dej became the respected leader of a sovereign national communist state.

It is difficult to determine whether the greater acceptance of Gheorghiu-Dejism by the Rumanian population was the consequence of concessions made by the communist leadership to that population, of realization of the value of the attainments of the regime, or identification with the nationalist tendencies and policies adopted by Gheorghiu-Dej and his lieutenants. In all probability the population as a whole realized that, no matter what the leadership's motivations, the policies were in the interest of the nation and a *modus vivendi* was possible with Gheorghiu-Dej.

The most significant phenomenon in the process of mutual reconciliation of party and people was the completion of agricultural collectivization in April 1962. The finalization of a measure theoretically so opposed to the aspirations of the Rumanian peasant did not elicit any negative response from the peasantry. Rather it was accepted as a tolerable solution to the agrarian problems of Rumania by the vast majority of the rural population. It has been suggested, and rightly so, that major concessions were made to the peasantry in the process of collectivization. Of particular importance was Gheorghiu-Dej's willingness to allow the retention by individual members of collective farms of private plots and farm animals for economic exploitation independent of collective responsibilities. Similarly, the providing of financial incentives for production over and above quotas subject to acquisition at regulated prices under state contracts was attractive to the rural population. The satisfaction of the peasants' concern with private ownership and monetary incentive, politically motivated as it was, anesthetized the masses and made them at least tolerant of communist treatment if not responsive to the patriotic messages emenating from Bucharest.[12] It is, however, remarkable that the peasants' relative affluence allowed the large-scale acquisition of radio, television, and other modern means of indoctrination in the village and that the telecommunication media themselves equated that affluence with the achievements of the regime.

The peasants' well-being was, of course, relative in terms of their aspirations. But it was absolute in terms of average prewar standards. The majority of Rumania's rural population was better clothed and better fed in 1962 than in 1938. And the peasantry was also literate, if not educated. The village was at last pacified by 1962, although it remained unenthusiastic about the communist order. Progress was also evident in the city. In the spring of

1962 Gheorghiu-Dej could point to the remarkable gains realized by the urban proletariat since the purging of the "anti-party group" and the Rumanization of the communist leadership. Most impressive was the growth in residential building in urban centers. Even if the housing requirements of the rapidly growing urban society (which recorded a population shift from village to city in the vicinity of 8 per cent between 1948 and 1962) could not be fully met, the construction of workers' apartments had gained momentum since 1960. The improved nutrition of the city-dwellers, officially ascribed to the socialization of agriculture, was also regarded as a plus factor by both the regime and the working class. In short, the regime's achievements, glorified by the party as a common national and socialist effort by the working class, the working peasantry, the professional and intellectual cadres, and, ultimately, the party itself, could not be denied by the proletariat. The construction of the socialist fatherland was an acceptable formula and provided incentive for the workers and a source of unquestionable support for Gheorghiu-Dej.[13]

Support was also sought from the intellectual community and the professional cadres. The technocracy, well paid and actively engaged in the rapid industrialization of the country, responded readily to the constant call for consolidation of gains and further modernization of the developing industrial society. The technocracy also favored at least the technological rapprochement with the West that the regime was anxious to promote. Emancipation from Soviet influences and control, not to mention inferior machinery and equipment, was desired as much by the professional as by the political builders of socialism in Rumania. Gheorghiu-Dej also appealed to writers and historians in his search for national legitimacy. The writers were asked, in January, to sing the glories of the party and of all Rumanians' contributions to the construction of a new, progressive fatherland. The historians were to stress historic continuity, national achievement, and the

169

role of the Rumanian party in the liberation of the country from fascism in 1944, and to minimize the significance of external factors in the shaping of modern Rumania. Whereas "bourgeois nationalism" and "chauvinism" were still prohibited in 1962, an "embourgeoisé" socialist patriotism, with distinct anti-Russian overtones, was tolerated if not encouraged. Socialist Rumania was a sovereign nation. Its sovereign rights were derived from the country's historic evolution, the "armed uprising of August 1944," and the actions of the Rumanian party's leadership, rather than from the common ideological, political, and economic bonds that it shared with the Soviet Union and the socialist camp.

In the process of national reconciliation the party decided to open its ranks to all inhabitants of the country, regardless of previous political affiliation or social position. The only requirement was present dedication to the principles of Gheorghiu-Dejism. That decision, made in May, ushered in a period of relaxation of internal police pressures, of the release of political prisoners, and of resolute pursuit of a common national effort for consolidation of Rumania's international position and domestic development. The motive force behind these actions was emancipation from Soviet domination and creation of the bases of resistance to certain Soviet pressures for reintegration of the bloc and camp through COMECON, the Warsaw Pact, and Khrushchevism.[14]

The May program of national unification was preparatory to the crucial meeting on economic integration under COMECON held in June in Moscow. The difficulties that Gheorghiu-Dej must have anticipated in Bucharest were indeed recorded in Moscow. Khrushchev and his supporters insisted on Rumania's relegation to a position of supplier of raw materials to advanced industrial countries in the bloc and opposed the Rumanians' views on each member's right to develop its own economy according to national interests and commitments. Although the dispute focused on economic problems, the issue to the Rumanians was basically political. Gheorghiu-Dej, having staked his future on the attainment of a socialist Rumania on the blueprints of 1945 and 1960, was not inclined to alter the decisions of the Third Congress and succumb to the pressures of forces inimical to his political interests. The basic hostility between Khrushchev's and Gheorghiu's views on Rumania's position in the camp and in relation to Moscow became evident to both Rumanian and foreign observers during Khrushchev's visit to Rumania shortly after the COMECON meeting. The Soviet leader publicly rejected Gheorghiu-Dej's economic and political doctrines relevant to the Rumanian road to socialism, while Gheorghiu pointedly refuted the validity of Khrushchev's. Gheorghiu's speeches in effect raised the question of "imperialistic Khrushchevism," while praising the great accomplishments of the Rumanian party and the Rumanian people.

It was not until October 1962, however, that the Rumanian leadership found it opportune to intensify its campaign against Khrushchevism, ostensibly in defense of Rumania's rights to political and economic self-determination. Khrushchev's "adventurism" and humiliation in the Cuban missile crisis persuaded Gheorghiu and his advisers that the correct Rumanian road to socialism lay in the opposite direction from Moscow's.

The basic decision to exploit Moscow's embarrassment and weakness resulting from the Cuban crisis was made at a special plenum of the Central Committee held between November 21 and 23.[15] Exploration of possible compromises for acceptance by the Kremlin and its supporters in COMECON of a formula satisfactory to Bucharest had been conducted early in November without success. At its meeting later in the month the Central Committee announced the granting of a contract for the building of the Galati steel mill to an Anglo-French consortium, the publication of a statement in support of the Albanian "heresy," and

171

the rewriting of the events of August 1944 in a manner offensive to the traditional Russian interpretation of Rumania's liberation from fascism. The sum total of the Rumanian position was that the Rumanian party was the sole legitimate ruler of a sovereign Rumanian state, the actual liberator of the country as leader of the Rumanian armed forces, the executor of the historic destiny of Rumania and of its inhabitants. Interference in Rumanian affairs, at either the state or the party level, was intolerable. Subordination of the national interest to that of the Soviet bloc was acceptable only to the extent to which the national interest was guaranteed. Gheorghiu-Dej still desisted from a direct confrontation with Moscow but, in word and deed, left no doubt that any compromise on COMECON and Rumania's position and rights in the socialist camp and Soviet bloc would have to acknowledge the validity of his tenets. Such assurances were not given by Moscow but were received from Peking.

The emergence of China as a major force in the shaping of the Rumanian independent course antedated the Cuban crisis.[16] Peking encouraged, albeit carefully, earlier Rumanian attempts to reduce dependence on Moscow. The previously cited Sino-Rumanian relations attest to China's interest in encouraging the Rumanians and the Rumanians' readiness to respond to Peking's overtures whenever appropriate to their interests. The essential element in Sino-Rumanian relations was common opposition to Khrushchev's views on the unity of the camp and Russia's role therein. Gheorghiu-Dej was more careful than Mao Tse-tung in his responses to "Russian imperialism," at least through 1962, but at no time did he fail to realize the potential leverage provided by the Sino-Soviet split. In fact, after the celebrated meeting of the internationl communist community held in Moscow in December 1960, the Rumanians regarded the so-called Moscow Declaration as an all-encompassing policy statement compatible with Gheorghiu-Dejism. The stress, in 1960, 1961, and 1962, was on the equality of members of the camp and on each member's right to determine its own socialist course. That interpretation was sufficiently ambiguous to satisfy the ideological positions of both Moscow and Peking, particularly as it avoided the spelling out of specific Rumanian stands on more controversial sections of the document. It is fair to say, however, that superficially the Rumanian interpretations before November 1962 were closer to the Russian than to the Chinese. Thereafter, the Rumanians became more responsive to Peking's attempts to exploit Gheorghiu-Dej's growing dissatisfaction with Khrushchev's refusal to acceed to Bucharest's views on COMECON and related political issues.

The Sino-Rumanian relationship was strictly political and unrelated to Rumania's historic tradition. It was not understood by the majority of the population and was not publicized by the regime. It was not regarded by Gheorghiu-Dej as providing solutions to the fulfillment of the economic goals of the Third Congress, nor was emulation of Mao's Stalinism desired at a time of national reconciliation in Rumania proper. Nevertheless, as a form of political leverage against Khrushchev, Mao's anti-Khrushchevism and extravagant demands for recognition of China's political rights within the international communist community were invaluable assets. In all probability the initiative for strengthening Sino-Rumanian relations came from Peking. In December 1962 Mao himself advised the Rumanian leaders of China's full recognition of the tenets of Gheorghiu-Dejism, of Rumania's inalienable sovereign right to shape its own destiny without external interference. In the ensuing months, the Rumanians were shifting more and more toward a neutral position in the Sino-Soviet conflict, reiterating, however, the principal Chinese theses regarding relationships among members of the socialist camp. By March 1963, the Rumanian leaders had adopted the actual Chinese interpretation of the Moscow Declaration of 1960 because of the *de facto* break with Moscow and COMECON on the vital issues of national self-determination and sovereign rights, which had occurred in February.

The official statement of March 1963 accused the Soviet Union and its supporters in COMECON of violating the "fundamental principles of the Socialist international division of labor" adopted by the organization in June 1962.[17] But this was the lesser of two charges. The other was violation of the Magna Carta of the international communist movement, the Moscow Declaration of 1960, which had proclaimed the sanctity of "observance of national independence and sovereignty, of full equality of rights, comradely mutual aid and mutual benefit" among members of the camp.

The Chinese and the politically conscious Rumanians applauded the text of the communique and its implications, albeit for different reasons. In the spring of 1963 Gheorghiu-Dej attached great significance to Peking's endorsement, as it provided an immediate guarantee against Russian political reaction. Nevertheless, he was also keenly aware of the domestic implications of his overt challenge to COMECON. As the gauntlet had been thrown at Moscow in the name of Rumanian sovereign rights, identification of the party's interests with the people's national prejudices became mandatory. Slowly but deliberately the regime sought the fusion of "bourgeois nationalism" and "socialist patriotism" into the "national interest" of all Rumanians. There was, as yet, no systematic attempt to incorporate the "bourgeois-nationalist" historic and cultural tradition into the communist one, but a few preliminary steps were taken in that direction. Intellectuals and technocrats were sent abroad to proclaim in fluent French, German or English the historic legitimacy of the communist regime and to seek recognition of that doctrine from affluent Western Europe and the United States. Westerners with past Rumanian ties were invited to Bucharest to convince themselves of the validity of the communists' claim.

174

Gheorghiu's basic purpose was to secure the economic assistance necessary for political emancipation from Moscow. But he was also willing to allow, in small doses, cultural interaction between Western European countries and the Rumanian People's Republic. It remains a matter of speculation whether these overtures to the West and the tentative reassertion of the validity and usefulness of historic relations with France, England, or Germany would have been pursued as energetically as they were within a few months after their inception had it not been for the deterioration of Russo-Rumanian relations between March 1963 and April 1964. The prevalent opinion is that Gheorghiu-Dej himself favored only a gradual restoration of ties with the West, limited primarily to economic contacts, and assigned priority to the exploitation of the Sino-Soviet conflict as the principal source of leverage against Soviet pressures. It is believed, however, that other members of the party's top leadership, including Nicolae Ceausescu, favored a more categorical assertion of Rumania's national rights and the utilization of "nationalism" as a force for securing the country's independence from the Soviet Union. These positions were not necessarily incompatible, at least as far as the common goal of emancipation from Soviet domination was concerned. Be this as it may, the dominant force in shaping Rumania's independent actions remained, at least until April 1964, the course of the Sino-Soviet conflict.

The period beginning with the statement of March 1963 and ending with the "Statement of the Rumanian Workers' Party of April 1964" was the most crucial in the divorce between Russia and Rumania. It was during these months that Khrushchev first manifested his firm determination to bring the Chinese and their supporters, the Rumanians and the Albanians, to heel and thus restore the unity of the socialist camp and of the Soviet bloc in a manner compatible with the Kremlin's interests. It was in this period, too, that he failed to attain his goals. Russian pressure on

Rumania was exerted throughout this period primarily in the form of seeking Rumanian acceptance of the wishes of the majority in COMECON and support for the convening of an international conference dealing with the Chinese "heresy." The weapons for securing Rumania's submission ranged from criticism of her reliance on the West and cooperation with Peking to the reopening of territorial questions related to Rumania's rights to Transylvania.

The confrontation between Bucharest and Moscow began with Khrushchev's attacking Rumania's obduracy on COMECON.[18] Bucharest's reply was the publication of the Chinese "25 Points," wherein Peking criticized Russia's pressurizing Rumania on COMECON. To Khrushchev's repeated criticism of Bucharest's positions Ceausescu replied on August 23 by asserting the primacy of the Rumanian party in Rumania and the country's sovereign rights. The publication of Peking's message of support of Rumania's "independent" position toward Moscow accompanied Ceausescu's statements. In the fall the Rumanians rejected Khrushchev's call for an international conference, ostensibly as champions of the unity of the socialist camp. That maneuver, evident to Moscow, provided the Rumanians with the opportunity to secure their position vis-à-vis Moscow and Peking by seeking the role of mediators in the Sino-Soviet conflict. Khrushchev, under domestic and foreign pressures himself, was temporarily disarmed by the Rumanians' tactics but remained wary of Gheorghiu-Dej's motives.

The lull in the socialist camp and Soviet bloc was short lived. The Rumanians' ideological formulation of their pragmatic position became known to the international community at large in November 1963. At that time the country's Premier, Ion Gheorghe Maurer, formally claimed for the "sovereign and independent state of Rumania" the right to mediate the Sino-Soviet dispute as the leading representative of a "third force" in the international communist movement. Maurer's premises were unacceptable to Moscow and to the Kremlin's faithful partners in COMECON, who regarded Rumania as a mere upstart disloyal to the Soviet Union. The Russian riposte is unknown, but it has been suggested that the question of territorial rights was probably raised by Moscow shortly after November. The Rumanians, apparently undaunted, persisted in reaffirming the validity of the "Maurer doctrine" by reiterating their neutrality in the Sino-Soviet conflict and their national independence throughout the fall and winter of 1963–1964.

The climax of the Rumanian policy toward Moscow and Peking occurred in February and March 1964. Khrushchev's resolution to seek a showdown with Mao forced the Rumanians into a desperate move to save their own position as a would-be independent communist state. The attempt to mediate the Sino-Soviet conflict, proposed by Gheorghiu-Dej in February and accepted for different reasons by both Moscow and Peking in March, resulted in a fruitless mission to Peking by Maurer, Ceausescu, and other high Rumanian officials. It would appear that none of the parties to the negotiations had any expectation of successful resolution of the basic conflict. The Russians agreed on the assumption that China's intransigence would compromise Peking and facilitate the re-establishment of the unity of the socialist camp under Moscow's direction. The Chinese desired to prevent the formal polarization of the international communist movement and, above all, the reassertion of Moscow's authority within the socialist camp. The Rumanians shared the Chinese views but also nurtured the forlorn hope that a temporary reconciliation of the respective Sino-Soviet positions would work to Rumania's benefit.

Whether the price of mediation was confirmation by both Moscow and Peking of Rumania's neutrality and sovereign rights or included the possible restitution by the Soviet Union of Bessarabia and Northern Bukovina is not entirely clear. It is known that upon its return from Peking the Rumanian delegation stopped in Moscow and discussed territorial problems with Khrushchev. It is also known that the Chinese had raised territorial questions of their own with Moscow, both directly and through the Rumanian mediators, and that Peking had alluded on more than one occasion to the Rumanian territories seized by Russia in the forties. It has been suggested, however, that Khrushchev reacted to Peking's specific statements and the Rumanians' allusions by urging that plebiscites be held in Transylvania as well as in Bessarabia and Bukovina to determine the righteousness of opposing claims. According to this view, Khrushchev's attitude was determined by his realization of the Rumanians' failure in Peking and his desire to bring Gheorghiu-Dej back into the fold. In any event, the relevant territorial questions were raised in Moscow and so alarmed the Rumanian leaders that they made their own determination to resist Russian pressures inimical to Rumania's "national interest" known to the international community at large. It was in the spirit of self-defense and with a view to staying Russia's hand that the celebrated "Statement" of April 1964 was issued by Gheorghiu-Dej and his associates.

The "Statement" differed from previous declarations concerning Rumania's position in the socialist camp and the international community in general in that it was direct and unequivocal in the affirmation of Rumania's rights.[19] Citing Russia as a traditional source of interference in Rumanian internal affairs, the authors of the "Statement" asserted the right of all nations, whether large or small, whether members of the socialist camp or not, solely to determine their national destinies on the basis of specific national conditions. Rumania's inalienable rights as a sovereign, independent, "neutral" socialist nation, devoted to peaceful coexistence and the unity of the socialist camp, had to be guaranteed by the international community. And having invoked the doctrine of identification of the party's with the nation's interests, Gheorghiu-Dej and his associates also sought the unequivocal support of the Rumanian people for the implementation of the principles enunciated in the "declaration of independence." In April 1964, the Rumanian communists turned to the traditional source of support of national independence against the historic enemy of Rumania and the Rumanians, the nation, and to the principal opponents of Russian hegemony in Eastern Europe, the United States and China.

In the ensuing months, the process of total national reconciliation and that of building bridges with the West gained momentum. Gheorghiu-Dej proceeded with great caution, however, partly because of his continuing suspicion of the purity of the Rumanians' "socialist patriotism" but mostly from fear of possible Russian military intervention in Rumania. It is noteworthy that the principal propaganda theme within Rumania was that of national unity and national adherence to the principles enunciated in April 1964. The material attainments of the people of Rumania also received their share of plaudits, but little was said or done with respect to internal liberalization. Only after Khrushchev's removal from power in the fall of 1964, during the period of transition to collective leadership under Brezhnev and Kosygin, did Gheorghiu encourage overt nationalist, anti-Russian manifestations. The collapse of his main enemy, who reportedly had threatened Rumania with military action in the summer of that year, persuaded Gheorghiu-Dej to take advantage of the confusion in Moscow to press his country's claims to national independence. It was in December that Rumania's claims to Bessarabia were clearly stated in an inconspicuous but widely circulated volume, *Marx on the Rumanians.*[20] The doctrine of Rumania's liberation by the Rumanian communists and all other themes regarding the primacy of the party in the construction of the Rumania of the people's historic dreams were trumpeted ever

179

more stridently after December 1964. The elections to the Grand National Assembly, scheduled for March 1965, were proclaimed symbolic of Communist Rumania's achievements, of national independence, of the brilliant future of Rumanian communism.

In the economic and diplomatic spheres at least, the achievements were remarkable. The principal indicators of national economic development attest to the great progress achieved in the decade of gradual emancipation from Soviet domination and assertion of the party's primacy in the "construction of socialism" in Rumania.[21] Although the indicators were not necessarily reflected in the inhabitants' still meager material resources, a sense of optimism prevailed in the winter of 1964–1965. The people's expectations were based primarily on the realization that the party's conflict with the Soviet Union, and corollary reliance on the support of the nation and of the West—in other words, a new nationalism and internationalism—would prevent a recurrence of the Stalinism associated with the Kremlin and Gheorghiu-Dej's own rule and conceivably provide an opening to the affluent, noncommunist world. In fact, the prevalent sentiment in Rumania at that time was one of admiration and respect for Gheorghiu-Dej's political ingenuity and shrewdness in securing Rumania's disengagement from Russia.

The politically conscious population and for that matter even the man in the street could not overlook the constant traffic of Western businessmen, primarily West German, and of foreign tourists, the highly publicized economic mission dispatched to Washington immediately after the issuance of the "Statement," or the widely heralded visit to France of Premier Maurer in July 1964. Nor could it overlook the increased independence manifested by the Rumanian delegation to the United Nations, which repeatedly voted in a manner different from other members of the Soviet bloc. Gheorghiu-Dej, his regime, and, by extension, Rumania itself were regarded by Rumanians at home and by sympathetic observers abroad as respectable members of the international community, as a "third force" in the international communist movement, as the most influential small communist nation in world affairs.

The nation's optimism was based on the assumption that the building of bridges to the West and the rallying of the national effort for the attainment of goals acceptable to the majority of the population were irrevocable commitments, that Gheorghiu's regime would seek the consolidation of the "Rumanian independent course" through implementation of the national-socialist program that the voters were to endorse in March 1965. Caution was nevertheless prevalent. The people and their leaders were conscious of Rumania's proximity to Russia, of the country's economic dependence on the Soviet bloc, of the military commitment to the Warsaw Pact. Although the possibility of military intervention was largely discounted, it was not altogether excluded. The people also questioned the regime's readiness to undertake genuine liberalization, to relax internal political pressures in a manner comparable to Tito's actions in Yugoslavia or even Kadar's in Hungary. Nevertheless, until early in 1965 the prevailing atmosphere in Rumania was one of tentative identification of the interests of the nation and the party and acceptance of the party's leadership in the resolution of internal and external affairs.

In February and March 1965, however, the bases of the party's and the nation's optimism seemed to crumble. The *de facto* outbreak of the "hot war" in Vietnam in February placed Communist Rumania in the awkward position of a country seeking economic and political support from "imperialists" inimical to a member of the socialist camp. The specter of involuntary reintegration into the Soviet bloc and socialist camp hung heavily over the regime and the people alike. The death of Gheorghiu-Dej in March cast further doubts on the viability of his policies of national independence and the possibility of their continuation under less experienced and less forceful leaders. The optimists were rewarded, however, as Gheorghiu's successor, Nicolae Ceausescu, assumed the mantle of the executor not only of Gheorghiu's policies but also of the Rumanian historical tradition as a whole. The closing of the historic circle began in fact in March 1965.

9

THE LEGACY RESTATED
The Socialist Republic of Rumania

THE "CEAUSESCU ERA" began on March 19, 1965. Nicolae Ceausescu himself was an unknown quantity to the majority of the population. He had been identified with the Gheorghiu-Dej regime to the extent that he was regarded as the number two man of the political establishment. The reasons for his rapid climb to power, which started in 1955 with his election to the Politburo of the Rumanian party, were obscure in 1965. He was earmarked as Gheorghiu's protege, as the leading *apparatchik* and faithful executor of his master's orders and policies. The more initiated expressed no opinions other than that he was a man dedicated to the pursuit of the country's independent course. Altogether it was believed when he came to power that because of his youth—he was only 47 years old—and alleged subservience to his predecessor, his regime would undertake no innovations, merely maintain the status quo implicit in the doctrinal "Statement" of April 1964. The succession in Rumania, it was thought, would be similar to that in the Soviet Union; the Ceausescu-Maurer team would be a copy of the Brezhnev-Kosygin tandem. But this was not to be the case.[1]

Ceausescu's purpose was generally similar to Gheorghiu's—to defend the sovereign interests of Rumania. But unlike Gheorghiu, he had a positive program for ascertaining and formalizing the country's independence. Gheorghiu-Dej's nationalism was born as much of political necessity as of conviction. Ceausescu's was rooted in his personal and political experience; it was not a reaction to Moscow's determination to remove him from power or to interfere in the internal affairs of a member nation of the Soviet bloc. Ceausescu came to power at a time when the Rumanian independent course was a historical and political reality. He could thus put into practice ideas and principles evolved during long years of political activity that began in the thirties and was characterized by tacit opposition to Moscow's domination of the Rumanian communist movement and adherence, whenever feasible, to the principles of democratic centralism. After his release from incarceration during World War II Ceausescu played a behind-the-scenes role in the struggle for power between the "Moscovites" and the "Rumanians," presumably on the side of Gheorghiu-Dej. It is now stated that his endorsement of Gheorghiu's policies and methods was less enthusiastic than previously assumed; in fact, that Ceausescu's prominence in the fifties and early sixties was due to the control which he exercised over the younger members of the party identified with "national" and "democratic" communism. Be this as it may, upon assumption of leadership in March 1965, Ceausescu cast himself in the role of fulfiller of the country's and the party's national and democratic historic traditions.

The essential aspects of Ceausescu's program became evident almost immediately after Gheorghiu's death. In April 1965, at a plenum of the party's Central Committee, he announced plans for the convocation of a party congress in July. The congress was to take stock of the historic and contemporary realities of the organization and, as it turned out, to translate these realities into new "democratic" programs and statutes. The redefinition of the character and functions of the party was announced by

The Socialist Republic of Rumania

Ceausescu in June, when the party's name was changed from Rumanian Workers' to Rumanian Communist. The reassumption of the original appellation, abandoned in 1948, was designed to stress the national historic continuity of the communist movement in Rumania and to assert the organization's equality with other communist parties, particularly that of the Soviet Union. The search for historic legitimacy and equality with advanced members of the socialist camp was further manifested in the dramatic announcement, also in June, of the changing of the country's name from Rumanian People's Republic to Socialist Republic of Rumania. The elevation from people's democracy to socialist republic and the substitution of "Rumanian" by "Rumania" were symbolic of national self-assertion and attainment of the penultimate goal of Rumanian communism, the national socialist state. The country's new status was to be legalized through the adoption of a new "democratic" constitution.

It is worth noting that these actions, as they affected the party and the state, represented acts of defiance of Soviet authority within the bloc and of rejection of Moscow's claim to pre-eminence in the socialist camp. As such, they were representative of Ceausescu's courage and forthrightness.

The legalizing of the Rumanian course in the face of Russian objections was not without its risks. The likelihood of Russian military intervention in Rumania was remote at a time when the unity of the camp had to be maintained in the face of "imperialist aggression" in Vietnam, but Moscow insisted on reminding Bucharest of its obligation to participate in the common fight against the "American imperialist aggressor." The leverage that Washington was able to provide in securing Rumania's position in the communist camp and the international community in general was all but lost with the intensification of the war in Vietnam. It was also difficult, in the spring of 1965, to rely on Chinese support since Peking was, at least temporarily, glossing over its

185

differences with Moscow in the common struggle against the United States and for the purpose of gaining the upper hand in Hanoi. These dilemmas and contradictions were all apparent in July 1965, when the Rumanian Party Congress opened in the presence of the leaders of the socialist camp, including Leonid Brezhnev as head of the Soviet delegation.[2]

Ceausescu avoided all forms of international partisanship. He maintained strict neutrality in the then unmentioned but evidently unresolved Sino-Soviet conflict and reiterated Rumania's commitment to international peace according to the well-known slogans of "mutual respect," "mutual advantage," and "peaceful coexistence." His political report to the congress emphasized the actual attainments and future plans of the Rumanian Communist Party in Rumania.[3] The "balance sheet of the people's great achievements" was drawn in terms of the goals of the 1960 congress and stressed the economic progress. The doubling of industrial production, the total socialization of agriculture, the growth in labor productivity, and the corollary rise in the people's standard of living were recorded and applauded. They were deemed sufficiently impressive to warrant Rumania's elevation to the rank of socialist republic. Nevertheless, the gains of the past were to be dwarfed in the next five years through continuing economic growth at an annual rate of approximately 10 per cent in industry and 20 per cent in agriculture. The noneconomic plans, the totality of the party's commitment to the "multilateral" attainment of its and the Rumanian people's historic goals, were also more ambitious than at any time in the past.

The accent was on the scientific and educational progress required for successful "completion of socialist construction." Objective scientific criteria and methods, derived from the most technologically advanced countries (of the West), were to be adopted. In the educational field, the prevalent Soviet-based institutional organization would be re-examined and replaced, whenever desirable, by tested institutions of precommunist Rumania. The recognition of the basic merits of the excellent secondary school system of interwar Rumania and the related adaptation of "bourgeois" educational values to the socialist society assumed even greater significance in the light of the revalidation of other traditional cultural values and manifestations. Speaker after speaker at the congress affirmed the progressive character of Rumanian "bourgeois" culture and the need for reviving and revalidating the national cultural tradition. The history and civilization of the nation were claimed by Ceausescu as prerequisites for the achievement of the party's and the nation's most immediate goal—an independent Socialist Rumania.

The party's pledges and program were addressed primarily to the Rumanian people. However, the substitution of national history for Marxism-Leninism, the attribution of all significant achievements to the people and the Rumanian party, rather than to the "glorious Soviet armies" and the fraternal aid received from the Soviet Union, represented *de facto* defiance of Moscow. The preamble to the Rumanian Constitution of 1952, according to which "The Rumanian People's Republic came into being as a result of the historic victory of the Soviet Union over German fascism and of the liberation of Rumania by the glorious Soviet army," was replaced by three simple sentences that the Kremlin found offensive: "Rumania is a socialist republic. The Socialist Republic of Rumania is a sovereign, independent and unitary state of the working people of the towns and villages. Its territory is inalienable and indivisible."[4] Offensive also was Ceausescu's stated intention to bring about the completion of socialist construction with Western assistance. In sum, the adoption by the Rumanian communists of the political slogan of the National Liberals of yore, "By ourselves," with all its nationalist implications, was unpalatable to the Soviet Union. It was also taken *cum grano salis* by the people of Rumania. It seemed unlikely under the international conditions prevalent in the summer of 1965 and in the light of the national experience with Gheorghiu-Dejism that Ceausescu could indeed implement his grandiose—to many, utopian—plans for Socialist Rumania.

The planned annual growth of the national income at the rate of 7 per cent, reflecting extremely ambitious economic development in industry, agriculture, and foreign trade, was contingent on political stability and the widening of economic relations with the West. These goals appeared incompatible with Rumania's own economic capabilities and resources and her overwhelming dependence on the Soviet Union and her partners in COMECON, who remained opposed to Bucharest's autarchic policies.

There were many in Rumania who also questioned the sincerity of Ceausescu's pledges to enforce "socialist legality" and to implement the principles of "socialist democracy." The limits of free literary and artistic expression had been widened during the last months of Gheorghiu-Dej's rule but had never reached those permitted by the rulers of neighboring socialist countries like Yugoslavia and Hungary. The Rumanian press remained rigorously controlled, and cultural and artistic contacts with the West were restricted to a small elite. Police repression had relaxed, but the rigidity of the state bureaucracy continued. The constitutional guarantees of individual liberty and basic freedoms were more explicit in the new constitution than in the old. But even the inclusion of a new article, whereby every citizen was given "the right to petition, as well as the right to ask the legislature to bring suit against any civil servant for offenses committed in the exercise of duty," evoked only guarded hope.[5]

It is probable that the Rumanians' traditional circumspection was enhanced by Ceausescu's own rigidity and authoritarian manner. The population lacked empathy with him, and many would have preferred Ion Gheorghe Maurer as Gheorghiu-Dej's successor despite the strength of Ceausescu's program for the consolidation of socialism in Rumania. But whatever doubts might have been entertained by the population in the summer of 1965 were soon dispelled as Ceausescu emerged as an exceptionally able, sincere, and dedicated leader of his country.

The quality of Ceausescu's leadership and the validity of the goals of his regime became apparent during the enunciation of a persuasive and principled policy toward the Soviet Union. Indeed, Rumania's relations with Russia required redefinition after Gheorghiu-Dej's death. It has generally been assumed that Moscow was hostile to Ceausescu's nationalism and sought to restrict the limits of Rumania's independence during the first months of his rule. The evidence corroborates that assumption. Brezhnev's speech at the Rumanian Party's Congress stressed Rumania's dependence on Russia and the need for unity in the face of imperialist threats to the socialist camp.[6] The Kremlin, during a hastily arranged visit by Ceausescu to Moscow in September, also imposed on the Rumanians acceptance of the inviolability of the territorial settlements of World War II. The renunciation of the veiled Rumanian claims to Bessarabia and Northern Bukovina was wrested from Ceausescu by what is believed to have been extreme pressure focusing on the reopening of the Transylvanian question and the possibility of indirect military intervention through maneuvers by forces of the Warsaw Pact on Rumanian territory.

It is evident that the visit to Russia persuaded Ceausescu and his principal associate, Ion Gheorghe Maurer, that the attainment of the goals set for the party and the state in the summer of 1965—in fact, the very future of Socialist Rumania—was contingent on immobilizing the Soviet Union.[7] In practical terms, Ceausescu sought the unification and mobilization of his own nation, the reconciliation of outstanding differences between Rumanians and "coinhabiting nationalities," and the strengthening of political and economic ties with all who could keep the Rus-

sians at bay. In a sense his conclusions were similar to those drawn
by Gheorghiu-Dej. However, Ceausescu openly invoked the doctrine of Rumanian national interest in the development of a truly
independent Rumania and proclaimed the total identity between
party, state, and nation for the realization of the historic goals of
all Rumanians and the defense of the fatherland.

In May 1966, in a speech memorable for its courage, Ceausescu
formulated the communist version of Rumania for the Rumanians.[8] He affirmed that "the Communist Party is the continuator
of the secular struggle of the Rumanian people for the attainment
of national independence, for the formation of the Rumanian
nation and the unitary national state, for the acceleration of social
progress and Rumania's forward movement on the road to civilization." He hailed the participation of all Rumanians, regardless
of social origin and political persuasion, in the historic attainment
of the aforementioned goals and condemned all forces, domestic
and foreign, who had opposed them. These included "landlord-
bourgeois" reactionaries, the Soviet party, and Russia (tsarist and
communist), all of whom were guilty of arresting Rumania's
forward movement. The seizure of Rumanian territories by the
USSR, acting in collusion with Nazi Germany, and the Russians'
justificatory arguments for that action and subsequent ones that
curtailed Rumania's national sovereignty and corollary historic
goals were denounced in terms understandable to all inhabitants
of Rumania and to interested parties around the world.

It would be erroneous to assume that the denunciation of the
enemies of the Rumanian nation was expressly designed to secure
the people's support for the execution of the party's program—
that, in effect, nationalism, with anti-Russian overtones, was
looked upon by the party as the unifying force in Rumania.
Similarly, it would be erroneous to believe that the positive response secured by Ceausescu from the Rumanian people was
primarily an expression of anti-Russian or "bourgeois-nationalist"
sentiments. There were, of course, Rumanians, particularly those

identified with right-wing political activities in the thirties, who found the new "national socialism" compatible with the old. But the majority of the politically educated and professionally active population that grew up under communism—in fact, the majority of the country's gainfully employed—was prepared to commit its energies and provide support for the consolidation of "socialist construction in Rumania" in the context of Ceausescu's actual definition of the national mission and purpose.

For several months before his speech of May 1966 Ceausescu had introduced new elements into the political and socioeconomic order. Of primary importance was the rejuvenation of the Communist Party. Aside from promoting to the party's uppermost echelons young men like Paul Niculescu-Mizil, Ilie Verdet, and Petre Lupu—all identified with democratic socialism—he substantially diversified the social and professional composition of the party's Central Committee. The number of technocrats, men of arts and letters, and university professors was increased, while a corresponding decrease in the dogmatism of the body was recorded.[9]

The party's commitment to technological and scientific progress in the pursuit of the country's modernization was also welcomed by the young and by the professional community. Ceausescu's unequivocal promise, delivered in December 1965, to commit resources for scientific and technological research and allow unhindered professional contacts and "exchanges of experience" with Western technocrats and men of science was construed as a further indication of the seriousness of purpose of his regime. It was regarded, moreover, as a sign of recognition of the need to make Western, modern experience available to the young generation of scientists, engineers, and technicians that had been deliberately isolated from such experience by Gheorghiu-Dej's caution and reliance on the "old guard," political and academic.[10]

Support was also extended to Ceausescu by the nontechnological intelligentsia, particularly the writers and artists. The granting of freedom of artistic expression to all and the *de facto* renunciation of "socialist realism" were as welcome as the reintroduction in bookstores, art galleries, and theaters of previously banned works of Rumanian and foreign authors and artists. In sum, most if not all barriers erected since World War II were removed with amazing celerity. The educated community became an asset in the completion of socialist construction rather than a suspect necessity.

Ceausescu's confidence in the population was reciprocated, not only by the educated. His constant trips to the countryside, factories, and towns, which began in the summer of 1965 and which have been an essential feature of his rule ever since, were also characterized by sensible commitments to "democratic" socialist progress. The modernization of agricultural techniques, simplification of the bureaucratic structure of the collectivized agricultural system, introduction of a program of individual incentives—all decreed in November 1965—evoked more than a modicum of rural support for his plans and rule.

The general response of the inhabitants of Rumania to his activities, plans, and deeds was favorable because of his apparent sincerity and unexpected sensitivity to the interests of the population. His Rumanianism, although clearly an asset, was not the principal reason for his success. However, the clearly nationalist manifesto of May 1966 provided his regime with an extra margin of support in the pursuit of his national policies, which, by necessity, became increasingly anti-Russian.

The consolidation of the nation to withstand Russian pressures continued unabated after May 1966. In some cases it assumed distinctly anti-Russian overtones, particularly through historical extrapolation. The revival of the nationalist school of history, initiated by the rehabilitation in 1965 of the distinguished nationalist historian Nicolae Iorga, was complete by the spring of 1966. The legendary national heroes, such as Michael the Brave, the unifier of Rumanian lands in the sixteenth century, and Stephen the Great, the defender of Moldavia's independence against foreign imperialism in the fifteenth century, became household words in the nationalist historic repertory. The most romantic interpretations of the Rumanians' historic struggles against foreign oppressors, primarily Turkish, Hungarian, and Russian, permeated historical journals, novels, and plays. Obsolete "bourgeois-nationalist" customs relevant to communist identification with the national historic traditions and, above all, patriotic songs with chauvinistic lyrics were revived and incorporated into the new political folklore. These manifestations were the theme song, the mood music, of Ceausescu's regime.

The rulers' basic purpose and political actions, however, were socialist in content even if nationalist in spirit.[11] As 1966 progressed, Ceausescu concentrated more and more on the country's economic development and the modernization of the economic and political structures to secure a sound basis for what he expected to be a protracted struggle against Soviet imperialism and Hungarian revisionism. Whether that decision was immediately connected with Ceausescu's failure to secure international support for the Rumanian doctrines on the unity of the camp and national independence is unclear, but in all probability the "objective conditions" of 1966 precluded reliance on foreign states, communist or not.

It is noteworthy that the most intensive diplomatic campaign, which began in 1965 and ended unsuccessfully in 1967, was directed toward wooing Bulgaria away from the Soviet Union. As Russia's most faithful satellite, Bulgaria presented a potential threat to Rumania. As early as 1966 Ceausescu apparently feared that Moscow would exert military pressure on Rumania by ordering maneuvers by Warsaw Pact forces on Rumanian territory. Those fears were translated into unequivocal reaffirmation by

The Socialist Republic of Rumania

Rumanian leaders of the correctness of their country's policies and formulation of the doctrine of the necessity to dissolve NATO and the Warsaw Pact as guarantees for world peace and the integrity of sovereign states. These far-reaching positions, uttered on the occasion of the so-called Bucharest Meeting of member nations of the Warsaw Pact and COMECON in July 1966, failed to sway either the Russians or the Bulgarians. The subsequent intensification of diplomatic efforts aimed at detaching Sofia from Moscow proved almost as fruitless.

The importance of the failure of Rumanian diplomacy in Bulgaria is difficult to assess. It would appear, however, that it precipitated the development of a Rumanian-Yugoslav "axis" for insuring the security of both states against a Russian partner, Bulgaria, and a potentially hostile Hungary.

Rumania's relations with Yugoslavia had become closer in the last years of Gheorghiu-Dej's rule. Gheorghiu's motivations for seeking such ties were both political and economic. The agreement of 1963 to develop jointly the hydroelectric potential of the Danube in the Iron Gates area was concluded immediately after the denunciation of the restrictive economic dictates of COMECON. Tito acted as a *porte parole* for both Bucharest and Moscow in 1964 and at that time urged moderation on both sides. After Khrushchev's fall from power, two of the principal factors for the Yugoslav-Rumanian rapprochement, the common desire to prevent the meeting of an international conference of communist parties and party-states that would permit the re-establishment of Russian hegemony in the socialist camp and the Rumanians' wish to seek economic and political alternatives to COMECON and the bloc, diminished in importance. The Yugoslavs showed signs of resenting the Rumanians' efforts to become the champions of national, independent communism in Eastern Europe, and the Rumanians sought to capitalize on their independence by competing openly with the Yugoslavs for Western

194

and *tiers monde* markets and other economic and political opportunities.

In 1966, Ceausescu sought another rapprochement with Tito in the face of Russian pressures. But the initial state visit of March 1966 was made by lesser Yugoslav representatives and was officially considered in the context of the traditional Rumanian attempts to implement the Stoica Plan for cooperation among all Balkan states.[12] The main effort of Rumanian policy at that time was still to weaken Bulgaria's allegiance to Moscow. By the fall of 1966, however, the Rumanians became increasingly anxious to strengthen their ties with Tito. The Bulgarian coolness to Rumanian overtures was definitely a factor promoting this desire. Continuing Russian pressure on Rumania for reintegration of COMECON and consolidation of the Warsaw Pact was another. The loss of the earlier Chinese crutch, subsequent to the ravages of the "cultural revolution" and China's insistence on greater Rumanian commitment to Mao's policies, was the third.

The Sino-Rumanian *refroidissement* became evident to Bucharest as well as to Moscow during Chou En-lai's visit to Rumania in June 1966. The Rumanians declined to join the Chinese in an overt denunciation of Russian revisionism and American imperialism, while the Chinese limited themselves to a routine endorsement of "independent socialist construction" by the Rumanians. The value of Chou's visit in other respects was nonexistent inasmuch as Peking, in turmoil, could provide no economic or even political leverage to Bucharest. Ceausescu therefore intensified political relations with Belgrade and economic ties with the West, both risky in terms of the continuing efforts of members of the Soviet bloc to strengthen both COMECON and the Warsaw Pact at the expense of Rumania and of her actual or potential partners, Yugoslavia and West Germany.

Moscow's plans for the summoning of a summit meeting of communist parties and states, with a view to reunifying the camp at the expense of dissident China, Rumania, Yugoslavia, and other independence-oriented parties and states, received the endorsement of the Hungarian and Bulgarian parties in the fall of 1966. That support for Moscow's plans, voiced at the respective party congresses, precipitated a meeting between Ceausescu and Tito early in December. That meeting, the first of a series, was directed specifically against Russia's plans for consolidation of its power in Eastern Europe. In the case of the Rumanians, it reflected genuine fear of reimposition of unity in the bloc by economic and political, perhaps even military, means. To minimize the impact of the economic squeeze that the members of COMECON were placing on Rumania with apparently increased intensity since 1965, Bucharest redoubled its efforts to reduce its economic dependence on the Soviet bloc.

Official statistics published in the summer of 1966 disclosed the gradual decrease of Rumania's trade with its COMECON partners and a corollary increase with the West. But the shift in trade patterns was still modest.[13] The volume of trade with the USSR declined by 8 per cent and with Hungary by 20 per cent, whereas that with West Germany and Sweden increased by 24 and 30 per cent, respectively. Nevertheless, Rumania's dependency on the Soviet bloc remained virtually unimpaired. Thus the value of trade with the USSR alone amounted to one third of the total; that with West Germany, Rumania's second most important trading partner, to less than 10 per cent. Rumania's volume of trade with the noncommunist world reached only 35 per cent of the total, while that with the Common Market amounted to only 18 per cent.

It was clearly the awareness of this politically unfavorable balance of trade that prompted Ceausescu's economic *Drang nach Westen*, which gained momentum in the fall and winter of 1966. Beginning in September, a series of new economic agreements was concluded with the West and several official statements were made in support of removing all trade barriers between Rumania and its Western partners. Belgium, England, France, Italy, and even Spain were included among the nations with which expanded trade agreements were concluded, but the principal target was West Germany. In January 1967 Rumania established formal and full diplomatic relations with the German Federal Republic in defiance of the opposition to such a move by the German Democratic Republic, by COMECON, by the Warsaw Pact members, and by the Kremlin.

It is by no means certain that the principal motivation for the Rumanian action of 1967 was economic, although the arguments for this rationale are persuasive. West Germany, at least since the summer of 1966, had intensified its own efforts to penetrate the Rumanian market, and the Rumanians responded favorably to Germany's readiness to provide industrial equipment, technological know-how, and extended credits. Significant, long-term arrangements for the building of industrial complexes by German firms were first concluded in July 1966. Later in that summer, West Germany's Economics Minister, Kurt Schmuecker, visited Rumania and signed a trade agreement advantageous to Bucharest. By the end of 1966, Rumania's trade with West Germany showed a growth of 12.5 per cent over the previous year, and the projections for future development of trade relations were even more ambitious.

It is noteworthy that a resolution of the Rumanian party's Central Committee, dated June 28, and one of the Grand National Assembly of the same date, whereby the economic targets outlined at the party congress of 1965 were raised in terms of the country's potential and interests, antedated the agreements of July. The accent on industrial growth was placed on the electronics, metal, and machine building industries, which, according to Premier Ion Gheorghe Maurer, were to account for half of Rumania's total industrial production by 1970. Whether these revisions and projections were made in anticipation of increased trade with the West, and particularly with West Germany, or whether the increase in trade was an objective necessity for the fulfillment of the regime's economic plans is difficult to ascertain. The two aspects were, however, interrelated and ultimately connected to the Rumanians' determination to "complete the construction of socialism" as rapidly as possible. Resistance to Russian pressures and the establishment of an economic basis immune to economic blackmail by Moscow and COMECON were major factors in the decisions of June 1966. Even if the desire for immunity from political reprisals was not the paramount factor in the June and subsequent search for markets and economic opportunities in the West, it assumed such significance in the winter. Russia's insistence on holding a meeting of at least the members of the Warsaw Pact, with a view to strengthening that organization and, by implication, re-establishing hegemony in Eastern Europe if not in the socialist camp as a whole, alarmed Bucharest. By January it was evident to Ceausescu that a showdown with Moscow and its loyal partners was imminent.[14]

The summoning of a pan-European conference of communist parties for April 24 at Karlovy Vary was announced in February by a preparatory commission that met in Warsaw. The Rumanians were not present in Warsaw and had no intention of going to Karlovy Vary. The Rumanian decision to refuse to accept Russian formulae for reunification of the camp was officially justified in terms of each party's "inalienable right" to determine its line and political aims. The corollary condemnation of "the practice of seeking support for one's views within other parties . . ." and of "every tendency to impose from abroad on one party a certain orientation or a certain method for the solution of problems"—actions characterized as "inadmissible interference in the party's internal affairs"—placed Bucharest squarely in opposition to Moscow. Ceausescu's brief visit to Moscow in

The Socialist Republic of Rumania

March failed to resolve the differences between Rumania and the USSR as the Rumanians declined to reunify the camp on Moscow's terms. Russian promises to the effect that Soviet-Rumanian relations would continue to be based "on respect for equality of rights, independence, national sovereignty, and non-interference in internal affairs" were less than reassuring to the Rumanians.

It is evident that the Rumanians sought reassurances from other interested parties both within and without the communist world. The formalizing of relations with West Germany in January 1967 was political to the extent to which Rumania sought the "removal of the vestiges of World War II" in Europe through recognition of all sovereign states, removal of all foreign troops from the territory of such states, and dissolution of NATO and the Warsaw Pact. The normalization of European conditions could be attained, according to Bucharest, only through general European solutions.

Rumania's insistence on the re-establishment of European relations on a nonbloc basis corresponded with her interests of disengagement and her desire to secure all the rights and privileges available to sovereign and independent states. This aspiration was unacceptable to Moscow, COMECON, and the members of the Warsaw Pact. Nevertheless, the same views were expressed during negotiations with Belgium, Holland, and other noncommunist nations, albeit within the framework of economic agreements. Ceausescu himself enunciated the principles for cooperation with the West in February 1967. He called for joint economic ventures and long-term agreements with the West and such non-committed countries as Israel, India, and Egypt, and the concurrent development of relevant political and cultural ties.

The solidifying of Rumania's bridges with noncommunist nations, however, was regarded as inadequate for meeting the political contingencies raised by Moscow's determination to re-establish hegemony in the communist world through meetings like that of Karlovy Vary. To forestall that possibility, so disastrous for Rumania, Ceausescu decided to rally all communist and workers' parties, whether in power or not, against the "reunification of the international socialist movement" according to the formulae advocated by Moscow but opposed by the Chinese and other dissidents. Before the meeting of Karlovy Vary, the Rumanians had consulted with party delegations from France, Italy, Spain, Austria, Greece, Denmark, and several other European and non-European countries in Rumania and had sent Rumanian delegations to several parties abroad. In fact, the Rumanian, Yugoslav, and Italian parties assumed, in the spring of 1967, the role of the united European opposition to Russian hegemony in the communist world. The risks inherent in this policy were apparently less than alarming to Bucharest, which continued to emphasize its independence in foreign affairs throughout 1967. Rumania alone of all members of the bloc defied Moscow's condemnation of Israel after the "Six-Day" Arab-Israeli war. Similarly, it continued to pursue a policy of neutrality in the Sino-Soviet conflict and of overt friendship with several of the Asian parties faithful to Peking. Expansion of political and economic ties with the West, at the expense of fellow socialist states of the East, exacerbated the prevalent friction and public polemics with East Germany, Czechoslovakia, Hungary, and the Soviet Union.

Nevertheless, Rumania persisted in reaffirming her devotion to her partners in COMECON and the Warsaw Pact. She justified deviations from the common norm on the basis of the inalienable rights of independent states to determine their own policies. Significantly, when Corneliu Manescu, Rumania's Foreign Minister, became the first communist President of the General Assembly of the United Nations in September, he pointedly assigned responsibility for "all international crises that gravely threaten world peace" to violations "of the inalienable right of all peoples to decide their own future." These statements notwithstanding, the Rumanian leadership was aware of the diplomatic tightrope upon which it was walking.

If Ceausescu and his associates were afraid of military intervention or some less drastic form of political pressure by the end of 1967, such fears did not inhibit them from pursuing internal policies that, like the external ones, were offensive to Moscow and its conservative allies. The essence of these policies was socialist modernization within a nationalist framework.

Throughout 1967 Ceausescu emphasized the necessity of streamlining the economic structure with a view to insuring the country's strength and prosperity. Throughout the year he stressed the need for technological progress and the improvement of the educational system. Throughout the year he insisted on the inadequacies of the centralized party and state bureaucratic organization, on the insufficiencies resultant therefrom, and on the need for decentralization and assumption of greater democratic responsibilities by local and regional groups and institutions. But it was only in December 1967 that he restated his and, by extension, the party's and the government's programs in terms of the directives of the congress of 1965 and the provisions of the Constitution. The occasion for the reformulation of his doctrine of Rumanian socialism was a conference of the Rumanian Communist Party, the first such meeting since 1945.[15]

Ceausescu's fundamental thesis in December 1967 was the incompatibility between Rumania's evolution as a national socialist state and the methods available for the continuing "completion of socialist construction." The methods were clearly inadequate, rooted in an obsolete period in the history of Rumanian socialism and unrelated to the realities of the international conditions of 1967. To modernize socialist Rumania it was imperative to adopt new organizational and ideological forms compatible with the attainment of a truly free, independent, and prosperous modern state. The specific recommendations focused on the economy since, in Ceausescu's view, the attainment of a Rumanian socialist civilization was conditional on the "raising of economic activity to a superior qualitative level." Decentralization of the economy on the basis of economic self-administration, administrative re-organization of the country into economically valid counties, readjustment of the wage-price system, evolution of long-range economic planning, democratization of the management of enter-prises and of collective farms, and a variety of other technical and administrative measures were recommended for the first time or restated in a broader context.

The accent was on increased participation by workers, peas-ants, scientists, and technocrats in the formulation of specific decisions, on the democratization of the production process. Sig-nificantly the appeal to the peoples of Rumania was based, not on the validity of Marxist doctrine, but on "fervent patriotic devotion" to the cause of the patriotic Rumanian party, the executor of the country's total historic legacy. The identification of the nation's, the party's, and the state's interests in expediting the creation of a modern Rumanian socialist civilization was to be legalized by the emancipation of key administrators from direct party control, by consolidating the leadership of the elected people's councils in a manner that would place the party's rep-resentatives on an equal footing with the people's representatives, and, ultimately, by elevating Nicolae Ceausescu to the dual post of head of the party and of the state.

The totality of identification between the nation's and the party's interest transcended similar syntheses of the past. In De-cember 1967 Ceausescu denied the validity of Gheorghiu-Dejism, inasmuch as it was rooted in Stalinism and other non-Rumanian prototypes. Gheorghiu-Dejism lacked socialist democracy, re-jected the principles of socialist equity. It relied too heavily on Soviet examples that were not compatible with Rumanian conditions and historical antecedents. Rumania's educational system, economic structure, and cultural activities emulated their Russian counterparts far too closely to insure the effective fulfillment of the national goal. In terms of the objective national and international conditions of 1967 a new Rumanian synthesis was necessary. It was for these reasons that the conference had been summoned and a revised blueprint for the "completion of socialist construction" was drawn up.

The evaluation of the shortcomings was basically accurate, but the reasons ascribed for them, as well as the proposed remedies, were not necessarily objective. Ceausescu's analysis and synthesis was political rather than "scientific." The economic reforms, although long overdue, were modest in scope compared to those in effect in 1967 in neighboring socialist countries. Decentralization was nominal, and the principal economic decisions remained the province of the all-powerful Communist Party. Even the fiscal and monetary policies adopted or ratified by the conference, characterized by increases in the cost of rents and services, as well as in income taxes and fees, and in restructuring of the wage and salary scales in a manner detrimental to the professional and technocratic cadres, could be criticized in terms of their economic rationale. The proposed reorganization of the educational system, ostensibly for improving the training of the generation that would assume the "completion of socialist construction," could not be justified in terms of the inadequacy of the present structure and inferior quality of education as such. In fact, the revamping of the educational system on the basis of that of the pre-World War II period was a deliberate attempt to maximize the excellence of a system with which the Rumanian people had identified themselves and which had been repudiated by Gheorghiu-Dej in favor of presumably inadequate and inappropriate Soviet prototypes. Similarly, the readoption of the precommunist administrative territorial system of counties (*judete*), including the very restoration of the pre-World War II names of individual counties, was motivated by the need for identification with an acceptable historical past at least as much as by the ostensible reasons of administrative and economic efficiency.

The ultimate purpose of the reformist program enunciated by Ceausescu was to secure the nation's endorsement for his national socialist policies, to obtain an unconditional mandate for his dealing with domestic and foreign problems. Traditional Rumanian values became symbolic of the Ceausescu program of socialist modernization, and he himself, symbolic of them. Ceausescu was to be identified with the major figures of Rumanian history, with men like Michael the Brave and Stephen the Great—democratic defenders of Rumanian values against foreign and domestic enemies, socially progressive rulers relying on and cooperating with the people for the attainment of eternally valid national and social goals.

The effectiveness of Ceausescu's synthesis became evident as it unfolded in 1968, as the explicit and implicit commitments of December 1967 were implemented at the risk of direct confrontation with the USSR and its partners in COMECON and the Warsaw Pact. Domestic actions were indeed characterized by socialist equity, democracy, and efficiency and by national respectability. The reform of the educational system and of the country's territorial-administrative structure, formally promulgated in February 1968, met these essential qualifications. The new penal code, adopted in April, eliminated the Draconian elements introduced during the Stalinist era, curtailed the powers of the police, and provided judicial guarantees and redress to individuals arbitrarily persecuted by the police and security organizations.

Disassociation from "undemocratic" inequitable and "non-Rumanian" practices was most dramatically illustrated, however, in the condemnation of the abuses of the Gheorghiu-Dej era. In

April, a plenum of the party's Central Committee indicated Gheorghiu-Dej for "violation of the most elementary standards of legality and justice" in the execution of Lucretiu Patrascanu in 1954 and in other instances as well.[16] Patrascanu's posthumous exoneration, followed by the rehabilitation of other victims of Gheorghiu-Dejism, including Vasile Luca, was accompanied by the dismissal of Alexandru Draghici from his official functions and the wholesale discrediting of all officials of the party and state deemed guilty of collusion with the late dictator. The corollary curtailment of the powers of the Ministry of the Interior and of the organs of the state security was intended to reaffirm Ceausescu's commitments to socialist legality and democracy. In fact, all reforms and legislative enactments of 1968 underlined the common responsibilities and efforts of all inhabitants of Rumania, whether party members or not, in the construction of Socialist Rumania on the foundations of an idealized "progressive" historic Rumania.

The "historic foundations" were strengthened in 1968. The invoking of historic antecedents in the justification of current policies, internal and external, was most manifest during the celebration of historic anniversaries, such as the 109th of the unification of Moldavia and Wallachia and the 120th of the revolutions of 1848. It is doubtful, however, that these celebrations and the equating of the Communist Party and its leaders with the "progressive Rumanian" leaders of the past were as instrumental in securing the Rumanians' allegiance to Ceausescu's regime as the very essence of Ceausescu's actual domestic and foreign policies. The element of confidence in the purposes of the party and the government, more than any other factor, secured the nation's support for actions that involved actual hardships and potential catastrophe.

The hardships, as well as the risks, were immediately connected with the rapid deterioration of Rumania's relations with the Soviet

The Socialist Republic of Rumania

Union and the Soviet bloc. The reasons for the growing isolation of Rumania from the bloc were directly related to Russia's insistence on conformity and unity under Soviet direction and Rumania's counterinsistence on safeguarding and promoting its own national interests. The first evidence of an overt rift between Moscow and Bucharest was the failure of both sides to renew the Soviet-Rumanian treaty of friendship, cooperation, and mutual assistance upon its expiration, twenty years after its conclusion, in February 1968. Ceausescu regarded the original treaty as legalizing Rumania's role as a satellite of the USSR and allegedly demanded reformulation of the provisions of the original document in a manner compatible with the realities of 1968. The Kremlin, determined to reassert its authority over the socialist camp and thus limit Rumania's freedom of action, was apparently equally opposed to legally recognizing the validity of Rumania's independent course. The failure to renew the treaty was symptomatic of the inevitability of continuing conflict. The summoning by Russia of a preparatory conference of communist parties in Budapest for the purpose of determining the agenda for another Moscow conference was clearly designed to consolidate Soviet control over the camp and to bring dissidents back into the fold. The Russian action placed Rumania in a position from which it could hardly extricate itself and led to the first public confrontation between Bucharest and the rest of the bloc.

That confrontation, which occurred in Budapest in February 1968, was provoked by Moscow. The Kremlin encouraged a direct attack on Rumania's independent policies toward Israel by the subservient Syrian Communist Party, and at least tolerated criticism by other servile parties of Rumanian economic cooperation with West Germany. The virulence of Soviet-inspired denunciations of Communist China and, by implication, of "neutral" Rumania was deemed by the Rumanian delegation to violate the agreement reached by all participants at the Budapest conference regarding immunity from attack by any "fraternal party" and prompted the exodus of the Rumanians from the conference. A few days later, at a meeting of the Warsaw Pact nations in Bulgaria, the Rumanians once more rejected Soviet-imposed uniformity by refusing to endorse the other members' recommendation for acceptance of the Russian formula for nonproliferation of nuclear weapons.

Attempts to gloss over the conflict by verbal reiterations of loyalty to the socialist camp and international organizations specifically restricted to the Soviet bloc could not obscure the reality of the critical turn in Rumanian-Soviet relations. The Rumanians were not invited to the meeting of other members of the bloc held late in March in Dresden, where matters affecting COMECON, the Warsaw Pact, and Czechoslovakia's liberalization program were discussed. Rumania's exclusion from the bloc became painfully evident during the following months, when the Czechoslovak problem assumed paramount importance to the Kremlin and its conservative allies. The Rumanians failed to attend any of the consultations concerning Czechoslovakia and did not participate in the Warsaw Pact operations that eventually resulted in the invasion of Czechoslovakia in August 1968.

It is a matter of speculation as to whether the decision to exclude Rumania from the affairs of the bloc after the Warsaw Pact meeting held in Sofia in March was intended as a firm warning to Bucharest by Moscow or whether it was sought, at least in part, by the Rumanians themselves. According to Rumanian sources, Ceausescu was surprised at Moscow's failure to invite the Rumanians to the Dresden meeting, since Bucharest had pledged continuing support to the Warsaw Pact pending dissolution of all military blocs in Europe. After Dresden, however, it is probable that the Rumanians declined to associate themselves with the Warsaw Pact maneuvers, which were designed to intimidate dissidents from Soviet and allied orthodoxy. In fact, the evidence tends to point to an awareness of the dangers to both Rumania and Czechoslovakia and, perhaps, even to Yugoslavia, created by Moscow's resolution to exert military pressures through the instrumentality of the Warsaw Pact. The plenum of the Central Committee of April 1968 decided to strengthen the Rumanian armed forces and to equip them with domestically produced weapons. Precautionary diplomatic measures were undertaken immediately thereafter to safeguard Rumania's independence. These assumed the form of consolidation of economic and political relations with the West and of military ties with Yugoslavia.

It is uncertain whether Ceausescu feared Soviet military action against Czechoslovakia and Rumania at the time of the visit of General de Gaulle in May. But it is certain that he entertained few hopes for meaningful resolution of the differences between Moscow and Bucharest at that time. The Rumanians declined de Gaulle's overtures to disassociate themselves from regional alliances and join the Europe of his dreams. Ceausescu's commitment to European policies was restricted to those compatible with the interests of the socialist camp and obligations vis-à-vis the Warsaw Pact and COMECON. This compatibility did not exclude the strengthening of economic and political relations with other nations if such actions would advance Rumania's well-being and the ultimate cause of universal peace. Ceausescu's caution was dictated by the reality of Rumania's relationship with Moscow and by awareness of the utopian nature of de Gaulle's plans. Nevertheless de Gaulle's presence was exploited by the Rumanian regime to reaffirm the eternal brotherly ties binding Latin nations and validity of the historic Western, chiefly French, roots and orientation of Rumanian civilization. The principal pro-Western drive of Bucharest in the spring of 1968 was, however, focused on securing technological assistance from West Germany and the United States and long-term credits through the World Bank, all for the development of the country's industrial and military power.[17]

The Socialist Republic of Rumania

The fact that the pro-Western moves, particularly the consolidation of relations with Germany, came under direct attack by Poland and other partners of Moscow did not alter Bucharest's policies. More offensive to the Kremlin, however, were Rumania's attempts to consolidate its ties with Yugoslavia and to seek the revival of the Little Entente.[18] With respect to Yugoslavia, Rumania's actions were unequivocal. Ceausescu shared Tito's apprehensions over the maneuvers of the Warsaw Pact forces and the possibility of military action against Czechoslovakia. In all likelihood the thought of military intervention in Rumania must have crossed the minds of the Rumanian and Yugoslav leaders during their meeting late in May and early in June. At that time they restated the identity of their views on national sovereign rights, peaceful solution of European problems, and the need for liquidation of both NATO and the Warsaw Pact. It was also then that the decision was made not only to strengthen the Yugoslav-Rumanian axis but also to seek the inclusion of Czechoslovakia into a common defensive perimeter against potential aggressors. The Rumanians appear to have been particularly eager to reduce the possibility of intervention by Russia in Czechoslovakia and allegedly were persuaded that the restoration of the Little Entente would minimize the likelihood of violation of the territorial sovereignty of its members by major powers "exerting dictatorial pressures on their smaller allies."

If indeed Ceausescu entertained the illusion of Soviet restraint in June 1968, he was evidently more realistic in August. His visit to Czechoslovakia, a few days after Tito's and only a few days before the Soviet invasion of that country, was a desperate attempt to forestall military action. His plea to his allies in the Warsaw Pact was based on the sovereign rights of independent states to determine their own destinies. No mention was made of regional alignments or even bilateral agreements that did not conform to the interests of the bloc and the camp. He was counting, like the Czechoslovak leaders, on Moscow's restraint in the face of solidarity by members of the communist camp. His efforts were to no avail, however, and on August 21 Rumania was faced with its gravest crisis of the twentieth century.

For two weeks after the invasion of Czechoslovakia the Rumanians lived in terror, fearful of Russian military action against their country. But for the first time in the twentieth century they responded with spontaneous enthusiasm to the call for national mobilization. That call was issued by Nicolae Ceausescu on August 21 and reiterated daily in the name of the defense of the fatherland against would-be aggressors.[19] Ceausescu, invoking Rumania's traditional defense of its sovereignty and independence against foreign powers and likening himself to the national leaders of the past, defied the Soviet Union and its allies by promising military resistance should the Warsaw Pact forces cross Rumania's borders. To what extent the unity of the inhabitants of Rumania and the certainty of resistance to the armies of the "fraternal socialist countries" by the Rumanian forces deterred the Kremlin from invading Rumania is unknown. But these considerations must have played a part in Moscow's decision to limit its attacks to threats and diatribes. Nor is it easy to ascertain whether the support given to Ceausescu by the people of Rumania in the hour of crisis reflected actual identification with his cause or fear of another "liberation" by the "glorious Soviet armies." What is certain, however, is that all Rumanians became aware in August 1968 that their own future and that of their country was anything but secure. The immediate danger passed in September, but the Brezhnev doctrine of limited sovereignty for members of the socialist camp and the Soviet armed forces remained. The inhabitants of Rumania also learned in August 1968 that the staunchest defender of their country's independence was Nicolae Ceausescu. These "objective conditions" have brought the party, the government, and the nation together to face the uncertain future.

EPILOGUE
Continuity and Change

O N MARCH 2, 1969, 13,577,143 inhabitants of Rumania cast their ballots in the election of a new Grand National Assembly. The vote was sought by the Rumanian Communist Party as a mandate for its policies, domestic and foreign; as an expression of confidence in the attainments of the party during the last quarter of a century and its ability to attain the ultimate goal of all inhabitants of Rumania—an independent, affluent, and democratic socialist republic. Of the total, 13,543,499 voters cast their ballots for the candidates of the Front of Socialist Unity. Did their votes represent an actual endorsement of Nicolae Ceausescu's policies? Did they indicate appreciation of the achievements of the Communist Party since the country's liberation" in 1944? Or did these voters, in the last analysis, express their determination to defend their country in a moment of peril and, *à faute de mieux*, entrust their fate and their hopes to the sole and ultimate source of power in Rumania, the Rumanian Communist Party and its nationalist leaders?

There are no certain answers to these questions, but in all probability the magnitude of the endorsement of the party's candidates is a more accurate reflection of the actual support enjoyed by the rulers of Rumania among the population at large than

211

that claimed and recorded in previous elections. It is also probable that the voters of March 1969 took stock of the achievements and problems of their rulers and on the basis of these factors delivered a vote of confidence in Nicolae Ceausescu's rule. Indentification of personal and communist interests, recognition of progress, and acceptance of the communist order were, in one form or another, reflected in the vote.

In objective terms, the greatest achievement of the Rumanian communists has been the modernization of the country. The statistics presented to the electorate in 1969 must have been persuasive to all born in the twentieth century. In terms of pre-World War II standards, Rumania was industrialized. The gross industrial output was 12 times greater in 1968 than in 1938; the industrial labor force had doubled. Other relevant statistics reflected similarly spectacular advances. Even in terms of the beginnings of the planned economy in Rumania, specifically in those of 1950, the statistics were impressive. And the rate of progress was still gaining momentum in 1969. In agriculture too, both production and mechanization had risen markedly since the eve of World War II. The gross output of Rumanian agriculture was 40 per cent larger in 1968 than in 1938; the net output, some 25 per cent greater. The number of tractors rose from 4,000 to 100,000 in the 30-year span.

Rumania's foreign trade, reflecting economic progress, recorded major gains and diversification. The educational system had become that of an industrial state. Illiteracy was virtually eliminated by 1968. The number of educational institutions of all kinds was nearly twice as large as in 1938. Educational opportunities were indeed available to all who sought them.

Technological progress had reached the village. The radio, movies, even electric appliances—all unknown to the peasantry before World War II—plus television were available in the countryside. The automobile was still a secondary means of transportation in 1969, as it was in 1938, but the oxcart and the horse-drawn wagon were on the way out. The realities of the industrial society were visible to all in 1969, and the prospects for even more rapid industrialization and corollary socioeconomic benefits were appreciated by most inhabitants of the country.

It is uncertain, however, to what extent modernization related to industrialization was an asset to the communists in their search for popular support in 1969: to what extent it secured the vote of confidence of the population. Statistical considerations notwithstanding, the increase in the country's gross national product has not filtered down to the rank and file of the technocracy, industrial working class, or peasantry. To the majority of the population the country's industrial transformation is not a blessing or a source for enthusiastic support of the regime responsible for industrialization. The peasant, still representing some 60 per cent of the total population, may be reconciled to the collectivization of agriculture and the relative prosperity resultant from the rational utilization of the land. He may even enjoy the fruits of electrification and mechanization. He is clearly appreciative of the opportunities opened to his children by the industrial and technological evolution of the country. But ultimately the majority of the rural population, which had been engaged in agricultural pursuits before the communist era, which had owned its land as private property, cannot be fully persuaded of the validity of socialist progress. In all likelihood the peasant would forego most of the benefits of industrialization for a return to "normalcy." And normalcy is equated with private ownership of his land and meaningful observance of the traditions of rural society not associated with socialist modernization. Thus the reasons why the peasants cast their votes for Ceausescu's regime must be sought elsewhere than in devotion to industrial progress.

What is true of the peasant is also true of all but the technocracy and the industrial working class. The professional groups other than those immediately connected with industrialization, the intellectuals, the governmental bureaucracy, the pensioners, know that wages are low, prices are high, and housing is insufficient, as a result of industrial urbanization; the necessities of life, are more difficult to obtain in 1969 than in 1938. It is not that these persons oppose modernization but that modernization has not benefited them as much as it did other members of the society. Their vote in 1969 was based on different considerations.

On the other hand industrial progress and the regime's commitment to consolidation and the completion of "socialist construction" were probably crucial factors in the confidence expressed in the regime by workers and technocrats. The new generation of workers, engineers, technicians, and others associated with industrialization is proud of Rumania's achievements. It does not have the ideological commitment to communism that many of the older workers still entertain or the identification with the precommunist industrial order known to the previous generation of workers and technocrats. The old have been absorbed by the new, and all, in one way or another, have benefited, materially and professionally, from modernization. The commitment of these workers to further industrialization is more profound than their loyalty to any leader, Ceausescu included. Their support, voiced in 1969, was given to the industrial modernization unleashed by the Rumanian communists and accelerated by Ceausescu's regime.

It is undeniable, however, that the vast majority of the voters was aware in 1969 that Rumania's commitment to industrial progress was irrevocable and that the present and future international position of their country was linked to that progress. During the electoral campaign much was said by Ceausescu and other leaders about the country's unprecedented standing in the international community. The new prestige was ascribed as much to industrial as to political modernization. These claims were undeniably correct. Rumania in 1969 carried on the diplomatic relations of an industrial state with virtually all nations in the world. It was a respected member of the international community. The historic epigrams and bon mots ridiculing the character of the people and of their rulers had disappeared from the glossary of political jokes. Corruption, prostitution, ignorance, deviousness—all implicit in the derogatory evaluation that "Rumanian is not a nationality but a profession"—were no longer relevant to the assessment of the country's achievements. If anything, Rumania's foreign policy, based as it was on the national interest of a sovereign industrial state, was, in the estimation of a majority of observers of international affairs, among the most sophisticated in the world.

There can be no doubt that Rumania's international posture was a source of pride to the country's inhabitants. Nor can there be any doubt about the population's associating this international prestige with the policies of Nicolae Ceausescu and Ion Gheorghe Maurer. It is, however, questionable whether that pride, translated into votes of confidence in March 1969, was based on sober realization of the actual achievements of Rumanian communism or, instead, on patriotic or nationalist sentiments that could have been converted into support for any regime threatened by an external power. The answer to this question rests ultimately on the degree of identification by the people of communist Rumania with historic Rumania.

Ceausescu's thesis that the people's historic aspirations have been fulfilled by his regime has apparently gained acceptance to the extent to which the people no longer regard Rumanian communist rule as alien. The coincidence between the regime's and the people's nationalism, although not complete, is evident in the separation of Rumanian from non-Rumanian interests. Thus the Rumanian population and its rulers alike, although not necessarily for identical motives, are determined to safeguard their interests against attack by foreign enemies. However, the nationalism of the leadership does not actually coincide with that of the masses.

The majority of the population, although accepting as inevitable and, in fact, tolerable the nationally oriented communism of Ceausescu, has not so far sublimated its "bourgeois" nationalism into "communist" nationalism. To the majority of the population the Russians are doubly dangerous as uncivilized foreigners and as uncivilized communists. Hence the destruction of Ceausescu's regime would be resisted for fear of reimposition of a political order alien to the country's historic tradition by an alien and inimical power.

To the leadership, however, the Russians are only the would-be executioners of the executors of an international political and socioeconomic revolution, alien to Rumania's historic tradition but made compatible with that tradition by adaptation to the country's "objective conditions." And among the "objective conditions" nationalism, of an anti-Russian and anti-Hungarian variety, was and remains paramount.

There can be little doubt that to the average Rumanian pride in the regime's achievements in international affairs rests primarily on the anti-Russian character of Rumania's independent course. The average Rumanian felicitates Ceausescu and takes pride in being a member of the same nationality as the man who, like David and like earlier Davids in his country's history, has stopped through ingenuity and courage the Goliath from the East. Fewer are those who identify their nationalism with that of their rulers in terms of traditional hostility toward the "Hungarian revisionists" as such. Indeed, the anti-Hungarianism of both ruler and ruled has become a function of associating Hungary with the Soviet Union, of regarding Kadar as a tool and an instrument of Russian leaders opposed to Rumania's independence. Fewer still are those who endorse Ceausescu's foreign policy and resultant international prestige because of Rumania's actions with respect

to Communist China and other member states of the socialist
camp. Instead, those concerned with such matters extend their
support to Ceausescu because of the reidentification of Rumania's
contemporary and traditional policies within a European context.
It is indeed the Europeanism of Communist Rumania—the regime's readiness to join the noncommunist European community
in matters of national interest, in short to rejoin the Europe identified with Rumania's historic tradition, Latin and Western—that
has given credence to Ceausescu's views on historic continuity.
The people's confidence in Ceausescu's regime is based ultimately
on the belief that the coincidence between the interests of the
rulers and of the subjects in matters affecting national sovereignty
and independence will in time result in genuine reconciliation
between communist dogma and practices and the "bourgeois"
values of the population within the frame work of the historic
Rumanian state.

It is precisely in terms of such expectations that Ceausescu's
popularity has to be measured and his role in the history of twentieth century Rumania assessed. If indeed the expectations of the
people of Rumania are justified, the views on the historic continuity of the Rumanian communist regime enunciated by the
present leadership may also be accepted as valid. But is a synthesis
of national communism and bourgeois nationalism possible? And
if it is, is it likely to be achieved in Rumania in the twentieth
century?

These questions may be answered by separating the specific
communist elements from the historic ones and appraising the extent to which the former have altered the course of Rumania's
evolution in our century. On the assumption that the industrialization and corollary modernization of the country would have
gained momentum after World War II under all circumstances,
would today's Rumania have been substantially different under
a noncommunist regime? In all probability the industrialization

of society would have proceeded more slowly and the social reorganization been less drastic as a consequence. But the disintegration of the village and the mechanization of agricultural production would have occurred with resultant unrest among the peasantry. Although it is certain that the modernization of the village would not have entailed collectivization, it is doubtful that the peasants' prosperity would have been greater under a noncommunist government than under the communist regime.

In all likelihood, except for the crucial question of ownership of industry, the problems connected with industrialization would have been similar no matter what regime had been established at the end of World War II. The urbanization of the country, the increase in the size of the working class, the training of an industrial technocracy, and the acquisition and rational utilization of resources would not have been materially different. The experience of countries like Greece or even Italy and France, which underwent the crisis of rapid industrialization after the war, has shown that there are greater similarities than differences in the achievement of industrialization and in the impact on those engaged in the process. Similarly, the status of the professional classes would not have been vastly different in a noncommunist Rumania from what it is today except in terms of the social origins of a few of its members and, in certain areas, of the freedom of intellectual expression.

It must be recognized, however, that today's Rumania is vastly different from its "bourgeois-landlord" prototype and, even more significantly, from its Soviet prototype of the late forties and fifties. The contrast between prewar and contemporary Rumania is evident only to those who knew the Rumania of the twenties and thirties and have been affected by the postwar changes. In the late sixties, thirty years after the outbreak of World War II, memories are blurred and the resemblances between communist and noncommunist Rumania sufficiently obvious to obliterate the evident differences. In fact, two generations are unable to remember and evaluate the relative merits of the two systems today. And these two generations, starting with the one born in the late twenties, occupy the principal positions in the new social and political order. Their attitudes are those of modern men who have either maintained, regained, or acquired the Rumanian characteristics of those striving for modernization and change in the thirties and early forties. Indeed, the best that precommunist Rumania had to offer has reappeared in the sixties of our century. In the process of modernization the values and mores of the *ancien régime* have fallen by the wayside in all countries, communist or not. They are regretted by the beneficiaries or exponents of those values and mores, and the forces of change are resisted. Such resistance has virtually disappeared in Rumania, partly because of the passage of time but mostly because of the conscious reassumption of the forms of the past that are compatible with the present.

On the other hand such classical Rumanian forms identified with the "bourgeois-landlord" order as the absentee landlord, the party boss, the rural clergy, and the king have either disappeared or lost their premodern character and significance. The destruction of the "bourgeois-landlord" class may have been limited to communist Europe. But the Rumanian bourgeoisie was small at the end of World War II and the landlord class even smaller. It is true that both played an inordinately powerful role in the conduct of the country's affairs, but it is also true that the "bourgeois-landlord" order was not representative of the national interest and did not enjoy the full support of the population. The demand for modernization and change was almost universal in postwar Rumania. Few inhabitants of the country sought to return to the thirties or the early forties. The Rumania of the interwar years was obsolete.

It is fair to say, however, that the pattern for modernization,

the search for a New Rumania, was to be found in Western prototypes and Rumanian experience. In 1944 most of those seeking
change and all of those seeking continuity rejected modernization and social revolution *à la russe*. It was, in fact, the brutal
destruction of national traditions, the violent eradication of national aspirations, the imposition of an alien order by representatives of a foreign and hostile power that created the crisis of
postwar Rumania rather than the modernization inherent in communist doctrine and practice. Thus, the de-Rumanization and
dehumanization of the anticipated and generally desired socioeconomic and political revolution provided the basis for both
oppression by the agents of Russian communist imperialism and
resistance by the people of Rumania.

It is in this context, then, that the question of Ceausescu's claims
to historic continuity and the fulfillment of national traditions and
aspirations has to be judged. It is also in this context that the degree of acceptance of these claims by the population must be
evaluated.

Whatever the argument may be in favor of identifying the
Rumanian communist with the Rumanian historic tradition, the
validity of that contention is questionable. Certainly until the
sixties the principles and practices of Rumanian communism were
rooted in those of Soviet Marxism-Leninism. The Rumanian communist and the Soviet communist practices and traditions were
essentially similar and bore only the most superficial resemblance
to the historic tradition of precommunist Rumania. These factors
account for the *de facto* rejection by the population of the thesis
of continuity as orginally formulated and enunciated by Gheorghiu-Dej's Stalinist regime. It is true that the doctrine of socialist patriotism as it evolved into that of national communism in the
early sixties provided a basis for acceptance of the "nationalist"
element inherent in Gheorghiu-Dejism. But the corollary identification of Communist Rumania with historic Rumania was not

generally accepted by the population. Too many elements in the structure of the state, the nature of the leadership, and the ideological, cultural, and international orientation of the regime were alien to the historic tradition if not incompatible with it. Gheorghiu-Dej was, in the last analysis, an "old-guard" Stalinist, a party boss, whose nationalist policies were admired for their ingenuity rather than for their sincerity. Gheorghiu-Dej was neither a modernizer nor a social reformer. He was an emancipator of Rumania from Russian domination but not from Stalinism. The people's identification with Gheorghiu's Rumania was one-dimensional— nationalist, derived from fear of the Soviet Union.

Identification between the people of Rumania and Ceausescu's regime, on the other hand, is multilateral and therefore permits identification of Ceausescu's Rumania with the national historical tradition. Through repudiation of Stalinism in all forms, including Gheorghiu-Dejism, and unequivocal assertion of the validity of the Rumanian historic experience and the party's contribution thereto, Ceausescu has evolved the doctrine of fusion of party, state, and nation as the total synthesis of the historic aspirations of all inhabitants of Rumania. If indeed modernization was inevitable and generally desired after World War II, the "socialist solution" to Rumania's problems was not necessarily incompatible with that primary purpose. The chief reason it was thought incompatible by the population was that it used alien forms and alien methods borrowed from or imposed by the Soviet Union. Thus, according to Ceausescu's doctrine, the elimination of the borrowed and imposed when incompatible with the aspirations of the people, and the substitution therefor of forms and methods compatible with the aspirations and experience of the inhabitants of Rumania, are prerequisites for legitimizing the Rumanian communist order.

There is much merit to this doctrine, and the acceptance of its validity by the inhabitants of Rumania is a reflection of its plausibility. The legitimizing of the "progressive," modernizing elements contained in the country's historic experience at all levels of civilization—technical, educational, political, and economic—and the assigning to them of a specific place in the link of the chain leading to the Socialist Republic of Rumania made contemporary "socialism" Rumanian in form if not in origin. It is evident that this fitting of communism into a Rumanian mold is historically imperfect. Even if the "bourgeois-landlord" order was ineffectual and discriminatory, it was more directly rooted in the country's historic experience than socialism and certainly more than communism. It is conceivable, in fact likely, that any "bourgeois-landlord" regime would not have been able to bring about the modernization of Rumania after World War II and that this process would have been conducted by the Social Democratic Party. It is also conceivable that a socialist order rather than a communist one would have been established in Rumania by the sixties of our century. But, before the establishment of Ceausescu's rule, it was inconceivable to the population of Rumania that the Communist Party would have truly collaborated with the socialists and other "progressive" forces in the country to bring about a "socialist" (rather than "communist") Rumania. Ceausescu's measures and policies, whether determined by political expediency, the realities of the international situation, or genuine conviction that "socialism" was the inevitable synthesis of the Rumanian historic experience and national aspirations, at least cast doubts on the theory of essential incompatibility between Rumania's historic evolution and the contemporary communist order.

It is indeed possible to argue that Ceausescu's "socialism" is the quintessence of true Rumanian socialism; that the Socialist Republic of Rumania is not atypical of the country's experience; that his rule is indeed comparable with that of enlightened Rumanian rulers of the past. Rumania has never been exposed to the conditions that made possible the establishment of a "bourgeois" democratic society. The democratic experience in Rumania was limited, artificial, and unrepresentative of the historic tradition. The fruition of the democratic potential of the country was restricted by the socioeconomic and political order both before World War I and in the interwar years. But it was also limited by the geopolitical factors prevalent in the interwar period and clearly after World War II. Under these circumstances authoritarianism, paternalism, nepotism, and other historically based mores alien to the Western democratic tradition were integral components of the country's historic experience. The communists have done away with most of the stagnant and "nonmodern" practices except for authoritarianism, which they have strengthened through the importation and implementation of the worst forms of Stalinism. In the process, however, they have modernized the economy and have established the bases for further evolution of the modern industrial state.

The humanizing and Rumanianizing of authoritarian rule validates the view that politically the regime is not un-Rumanian. The reassumption of historic Rumanian forms of internal organization, the reorientation of the country's international relations in a manner representative of historic interests, old and new, and the promise of continuing adherence to Rumania's socialist and national interests may not have obscured the fact that much of "Socialist Rumania" is still Russian communist in origin and is likely to remain that way for some time to come. Nevertheless, there is much expectation among the peoples of Rumania that Ceausescu's Rumania will become increasingly more socialist in form and, consequently, a genuine synthesis of their aspirations. Surely these aspirations did not encompass the establishment of a socialist state in 1944. But by 1966, the ever larger number of politically educated Rumanians had taken stock of the "objective conditions" of Rumania and of the world. Under the circumstances they have come to regard Ceausescu as an exceptionally able and dedicated leader and to have confidence in his determination to secure Rumania's gains and make the socialist order increasingly more compatible with the aspirations of all inhabitants.

To the extent to which the present Rumanian regime is able to satisfy the requirements of the population and preserve the country's independence, to the extent, then, to which Ceausescu's plans are realized, will the validity of the thesis of historic continuity be proved or disproved. Before the end of the twentieth century the Socialist Republic of Rumania may very well be the Rumania of its people's historic dreams. That possibility, weighed in terms of contemporary conditions and trends, accounts for the overwhelming support given to the candidates of the Front of Socialist Unity by the Rumanian electorate on March 2, 1969.

NOTES

Chapter 1
The Historic Legacy: Greater Rumania

1. Nicolae Ceausescu, *Raport cu privire la proiectul de Constitutie a Republicii Socialiste Romania* ["Report Concerning the Draft Constitution of the Socialist Republic of Rumania"] (Bucharest: Editura Politica, 1965), pp. 31-32.

2. Henry L. Roberts, *Rumania; Political Problems of an Agrarian State* (New Haven: Yale University Press, 1951); Hugh Seton-Watson, *Eastern Europe Between the Wars, 1918–1941* (Cambridge: Cambridge University Press, 1945); Constantin C. Giurescu, *Istoria Romanilor* ["History of the Rumanians"] (Bucharest: Fundatia Regala pentru Literatura si Arta, 1940–1944), 4 vols.; Lucretiu D. Patrascanu, *Sous trois dictatures* (Paris: Vitiano, 1946); Charles Upson Clark, *United Roumania* (New York: Dodd, Mead, 1932); Robert W. Seton-Watson, *A History of the Roumanians* (Cambridge: Cambridge University Press, 1934); Alexandru D. Xenopol, *Istoria Romanilor din Dacia Traiana* ["History of the Rumanians of Trajan's Dacia"] (Iasi: Saraga, 1896), 12 vols.; Nicolae Iorga, *Histoire des Roumains et de la romanite orientale* (Bucharest: Imprimeria Statului 1937–1944), 9 vols.

3. The problem of the Rumanians' disappearance, with its broad historical and political implications, is discussed with intelligence and restraint in George I. Bratianu, *Une enigme et un miracle historique: le peuple roumain* (Bucharest: Dacia, 1942), 2nd ed.

225

4. This thesis, expounded with vigor by nationalist historians before World War II, has been adopted by communist historians also, albeit in a somewhat different context, in recent years. The most complete statement is contained in Constantin Daicoviciu et al., *Din Istoria Transilvaniei* ["From the History of Transylvania"] (Bucharest: Editura Academiei, 1961), 2nd ed., 2 vols.

5. See, for instance, Seton-Watson, *History of the Roumanians*, pp. 16-49.

6. The most intelligent discussion of the problems of the Rumanian provinces is contained in Academia Republicii Populare Romine, *Istoria Rominiei* ["The History of Rumania"] (Bucharest: Editura Academiei, 1961), Vol. II.

7. Seton-Watson, *History of the Roumanians*, pp. 61-74, provides a typical interpretation of Michael's rule and activities.

8. The Graecization of Rumanian life and politics has not been studied systematically. In the absence of a comprehensive account of the Phanariote period in Rumanian history the reader is referred to the most objective, if not the most exhaustive, treatment currently available: Academia, *Istoria Rominiei*, Vol. III.

9. A comprehensive analysis is contained in Daicoviciu et al., *Istoria Transilvaniei*, I, 254-298. A summary, in French, will be found in the abridged version of the Rumanian text prepared by Constantin Daicoviciu and Miron Constantinescu, *Breve histoire de la Transylvanie* (Bucharest: Editions de l'Academie de la Republique Socialiste de la Roumanie, 1965), pp. 153-172.

10. A good basic statement on the problems of the Rumanian population and on the history of Transylvania in general may be found in Daicoviciu and Constantinescu, *Breve histoire*, pp. 86-172.

11. See Keith Hitchins, "Samuel Clain and the Rumanian Enlightenment in Transylvania," *Slavic Review*, XXIII, No. 4 (1964), 660-675.

12. A comprehensive discussion of these problems is contained in Stephen Fischer-Galati, "The Origins of Modern Rumanian Nationalism," *Jahrbücher für Geschichte Osteuropas*, XII, No. 1 (1964), 48-54.

13. John C. Campbell, *French Influence and the Rise of Rumanian Nationalism* (Ph.D. dissertation, Harvard University, 1940), remains the fundamental work on Rumanian nationalism in this period.

14. Andrei Otetea, *Tudor Vladimirescu si miscarea eterista in Tarile Romanesti, 1821–1822* ["Tudor Vladimirescu and the Hetairist Movement in the Rumanian Provinces, 1821–1822"] (Bucharest: Institutul de Studii si Cercetari Balcanice, 1945), provides a brilliant analysis of the social and national forces at work in the Rumanian provinces in the first quarter of the nineteenth century.

15. The classic, and still largely valid, statement on Russo-Rumanian relations in this period is by Jean C. Filitti, *Les Principautes roumaines sous l'occupation russe (1829–1834); Le reglement organique* (Bucharest: Imprimerie de l'Independance roumaine, 1904).

16. Very little work has been done by Rumanian and foreign scholars on the socioeconomic problems of the Rumanian provinces and Transylvania during the first half of the nineteenth century. Whatever information is available has been ably synthesized in Academia, *Istoria Rominiei*, III, 933-1151.

17. A comprehensive treatment of the Revolution of 1848 and its immediate antecedents will be found in Academia, *Istoria Rominiei*, IV, 1-179. For an excellent critical discussion on the role of the intellectuals in 1848 the reader is referred to John C. Campbell, "The Influence of Western Political Thought in the Rumanian Principalities, 1821–1848: The Generation of 1848," *Journal of Central European Affairs*, IV (1944), 262-273.

18. A review of these problems is found in Stephen Fischer-Galati, "The Rumanians and the Habsburg Monarchy," *Austrian History Yearbook*, III, Pt. 2 (1967), 430-449; Andrei Otetea, "The Rumanians and the Disintegration of the Habsburg Monarchy," *ibid.*, pp. 450-476, and in the comments to these papers by John C. Campbell and Raymond Grew, *ibid.*, pp. 477-490.

19. Excellent studies on these problems include those by Thad W. Riker, *The Making of Roumania; A Study of an International Problem, 1856–1866* (London: Oxford University Press, 1931), and by Paul Henri, *L'abdication du prince Cuza et l'avenement de la dynastie de Hohenzollern au trone de la Roumanie* (Paris: Alcan, 1930). On the agrarian question and related social and economic problems the best work, although somewhat dated, is that by David Mitrany, *The Land and the Peasant in Rumania; The War and Agrarian Reform (1917–1921)* (London: Oxford

University Press, 1930). Good bibliographical references are contained in Roberts, *Rumania*, pp. 387-389.

20. An excellent brief discussion of these problems will be found in Seton-Watson, *History of the Roumanians*, pp. 346-382.

21. On the peasant revolt and its antecedents consult N. Adaniloaie and Dan Berindei, *Reforma Agrara din 1864* ["The Agrarian Reform of 1864"] (Bucharest: Editura Academiei, 1967), and *Marea Rascoala a Taranilor din 1907* ["The Great Peasant Revolt of 1907"] (Bucharest: Editura Academiei, 1967). Its consequences are discussed by Fischer-Galati, *The Rumanians*, pp. 445-447.

22. *Ibid.*, pp. 444-449; Otetea, *The Rumanians*, pp. 464-475.

23. The best study of these problems is by Erich Prokopowitsch, *Die Rumänische Nationalbewegung in der Bukovina und der Dako-Romanismus* (Graz: Böhlaus, 1965). Also, V. Liveanu, *1918; din istoria luptelor revolutionare din Rominia* ["1918; From the History of Revolutionary Struggles in Rumania"] (Bucharest: Editura Politica, 1960) contains valuable materials.

24. The classic summary statement by Seton-Watson, *History of the Roumanians*, pp. 432-520, is essentially sound.

25. Bratianu's policies, attitudes, and motivations have been carefully studied by Sherman D. Spector, *Rumania at the Paris Peace Conference; A Study of the Diplomacy of Ion I. C. Bratianu* (New York: Bookman Associates, 1962). It should be read in conjunction with Seton-Watson, *History of the Roumanians*, pp. 534-547, and Roberts, *Rumania*, pp. 3-39.

Chapter 2
The Legacy Tested: The "Democratic" Twenties

1. The problems concerning the treatment of minorities, particularly in Transylvania, have never been either fully or impartially analyzed. Heated controversies continue to this day with resulting inflammation of political issues. A routine but factually accurate statement concerning the problems of minorities is contained in Joseph S. Roucek, *Contemporary Rumania and Her Problems* (Stanford: Stanford University Press, 1932), pp. 183-214.

Notes: The "Democratic" Twenties

2. The fundamental statement on these problems is by Roberts, *Rumania*, pp. 25-93.

3. *Ibid.*, pp. 32-35.

4. On the "Communist threat" consult Ghita Ionescu, *Communism in Rumania, 1944–1962* (London: Oxford University Press, 1964), pp. 1-21. A succinct statement on these and related problems may be found in Stephen Fischer-Galati, *The New Rumania: From People's Democracy to Socialist Republic* (Cambridge, Mass.: The M.I.T. Press, 1967), pp. 1-16.

5. Roberts, *Rumania*, pp. 32-39 and 89-97.

6. In addition to Roberts' distinguished survey and analysis of Rumanian politics in the interwar years the reader is referred to two other volumes: *Politics and Political Parties in Roumania* (London: International Reference Library Publishing Company, 1936) and Institutul Social Roman, *Doctrinele partidelor politice* ["The Doctrines of Political Parties"] (Bucharest, 1924).

7. Ionescu, *Communism in Rumania*, pp. 17-22, and Roberts, *Rumania*, pp. 246-252.

8. An excellent discussion of these problems is contained in Eugen Weber, "Romania," in Hans Rogger and Eugen Weber, eds., *The European Right: A Historical Profile* (Berkeley: University of California Press, 1966), pp. 501-544.

9. A good summary of Rumanian foreign relations is contained in Roucek, *Contemporary Roumania*, pp. 135-182.

10. On the so-called "Liberal Period" consult Roberts, *Rumania*, pp. 94-129.

11. Differing interpretations of the "Peasantist Period" are contained in Roberts, *Rumania*, pp. 130-169; Ionescu, *Communism in Rumania*, pp. 32-34 and 38-40; and Fischer-Galati, *The New Rumania*, pp. 9-16. The author has accepted Roberts' careful and judicious analysis and conclusions as valid, subject to such corrigenda as recent disclosures and re-examination of the evidence tend to justify.

12. In addition to the data contained in Roberts the reader is referred to the excellent general discussion of the "international experience" of the East European countries in this period given in Seton-Watson, *Eastern Europe*, pp. 362-378.

Notes: Authoritarianism, Dictatorship, War

Chapter 3
The Legacy Tested: Authoritarianism, Dictatorship, and War

1. The most authoritative statement is by Roberts, *Rumania*, pp. 170-222.

2. A highly informative discussion of the impact of the depression is contained in Roberts, *ibid.*, pp. 176-186.

3. Important materials on the Grivita uprising may be found in Partidul Comunist din Romania, *Documente din istoria Partidului Comunist din Romania* ["Documents from the History of the Rumanian Communist Party"] (Bucharest: Editura de Stat Pentru Literature Politica, 1953), 2nd ed.

4. The most succinct discussion and penetrating analysis of Rumanian fascism and the Iron Guard is by Eugen Weber, "Romania," in Hans Rogger and Eugen Weber, eds., *The European Right*, pp. 501-574.

5. An essentially positive appraisal may be found in Fischer-Galati, *The New Rumania*, pp. 13-15; one basically negative in Ionescu, *Communism in Rumania*, pp. 50-61. Neutral and informative is the work of Andreas Hillgruber, *Hitler, Konig Carol und Marschall Antonescu* (Wiesbaden: Steiner, 1954).

6. See Roberts, *Rumania*, pp. 192 ff.

7. *Ibid.*, pp. 223-225.

8. Weber, "Romania," pp. 546-548.

9. Codreanu's doctrine is contained in Corneliu Zelea Codreanu, *Pentru legionari* ["For Legionaries"] (Bucharest: Editura Miscarii Legionare, 1940). A German version may be found in Corneliu Zelea Codreanu, *Eiserne Garde* (Berlin: Brunnen, 1942).

10. Fischer-Galati, *The New Rumania*, pp. 12-15.

11. There is an excellent discussion of these problems in Weber, "Romania," pp. 548 ff.

12. On the Carolist dictatorship consult Roberts, *Rumania*, pp. 206-222.

13. On the fascist period consult Roberts, *ibid.*, pp. 223-241.

14. General Antonescu's political views are succinctly stated in Ion Antonescu, *Generalul Antonescu catre Tara, 6 Septemvrie 1940–22 Iunie 1941* ["General Antonescu to the Country, 6 September 1940–22 June 1941"] (Bucharest: Imprimeria Nationala, 1941).

15. A sober appraisal of Antonescu's rule is contained in Roberts, *Rumania*, pp. 233-241.

16. Consult Fischer-Galati, *The New Rumania*, pp. 15-16.

17. Stephen Fischer-Galati, "France and Rumania: A Changing Image," *East European Quarterly*, I, No. 2 (June 1967), 107-114.

18. Ionescu, *Communism in Rumania*, pp. 61-68, contains interesting thoughts and data on these problems.

19. Roberts, *Rumania*, pp. 242 ff.; Ionescu, *Communism in Rumania*, pp. 71-86.

Chapter 4
The Legacy Transformed: Continuity, Change, and Legitimacy

1. The significance attached by the communists to the "liberation" of Rumania is indicated by the publication of numerous monographs and collections of articles on that topic. Most noteworthy are *23 August 1944: Culegere de articole* ["23 August 1944: Collection of Articles"] (Bucharest: Editura Politica, 1964); *Contributia Romaniei la victoria asupra fascismului* ["Rumania's Contribution to Victory over Fascism"] (Bucharest: Editura Politica, 1965); Ion Popescu-Puturi et al., *La Roumanie pendant la deuxieme guerre mondiale* (Bucharest: Editions de l'Academie de la Republique Populaire Roumaine, 1964); A. Petric and Gh. Tutui, *L'instauration et la consolidation du regime democratique populaire en Roumanie* (Bucharest: Editions de l'Academie de la Republique Populaire Roumaine, 1964). A somewhat different interpretation is contained in Ionescu, *Communism in Rumania*, pp. 83 ff., and in the classic indictment of Soviet and Rumanian communism by Reuben H. Markham, *Rumania under the Soviet Yoke* (Boston: Meador, 1949). See also Roberts, *Rumania*, pp. 242 ff., and Fischer-Galati, *The New Rumania*, pp. 17 ff.

2. A good summary of these problems is contained in Ionescu, *Communism in Rumania*, pp. 83-99.

3. The most comprehensive official survey, that by Institutul de Istorie a Partidului de pe linga C.C. al P.M.R., *Lectii in ajutorul celor care studiaza istoria P.M.R.* ["Lessons to Guide Students of the Rumanian Workers' Party History"] (Bucharest: Editura Politica, 1960), leaves too

231

many questions unanswered. The several corollary collections of documents, most notably *Documente din Istoria Partidului Comunist din Romania*, are too fragmentary to allow the piecing together of a meaningful story. Ionescu's synopsis comprising the introductory chapter to *Communism in Rumania*, pp. 1-68, is most valuable but too brief. This is also true of Roberts' survey of the history of Marxist parties in Rumania in his *Rumania*, pp. 243 ff.

4. Much insight into these problems may be gained from a study of the data contained in Ionescu, *Communism in Rumania*, pp. 40-46 and 350-357; in Institutul de Istorie, *Lectii*, pp. 289-299; and particularly in *Studii*, XVI, No. 1 (1963), devoted exclusively to the events of 1933.

5. A more detailed discussion of these and related matters is contained in Fischer-Galati, *The New Rumania*, pp. 4 ff.

6. An excellent summary statement will be found in Ionescu, *Communism in Rumania*, pp. 87 ff.

7. See Fischer-Galati, *The New Rumania*, pp. 26 ff.

8. Ionescu, *Communism in Rumania*, pp. 96 ff., provides a good factual summary of the events of this period.

9. A sober and intelligent appraisal of the significance of the establishment of the Groza regime is found in Roberts, *Rumania*, pp. 258 ff.

10. See Fischer-Galati, *The New Rumania*, pp. 28 ff.

11. On these points consult the major speech of Gheorghe Gheorghiu-Dej of November 30, 1961, contained in *Scinteia*, December 7, 1961.

Chapter 5
The Legacy Transformed: The Loss of National Identity

1. A good summary account of the principal developments during this period is contained in Ionescu, *Communism in Rumania*, pp. 107 ff.

2. A most interesting evaluation of the roles played by Patrascanu and Gheorghiu-Dej in those years is contained in the far-reaching speech of Nicolae Ceausescu of April 27, 1968, published in *Scinteia*, April 28, 1968. See also Fischer-Galati, *The New Rumania*, pp. 25 ff.

3. An excellent discussion of the agrarian reform of 1945 is contained in Roberts, *Rumania*, pp. 274-299.

4. Statistical details may be found in Ionescu, *Communism in Rumania*, pp. 111-112, and in Roberts, *Rumania*, pp. 293-298. The most authoritative analysis of Rumanian agrarian problems is by John Michael Montias, *Economic Development in Communist Rumania* (Cambridge, Mass.: The M.I.T. Press, 1967), pp. 87 ff., but the discussion is very technical.

5. A carefully drawn account of Gheorghiu-Dej's activities in this period is contained in Fischer-Galati, *The New Rumania*, pp. 24 ff.

6. Ionescu, *Communism in Rumania*, pp. 114 ff.

7. Montias, *Economic Development*, pp. 19 ff., and Ionescu, *Communism in Rumania*, pp. 112 ff., provide valuable details.

8. The diplomatic aspects of the period are well discussed by Ionescu, *Communism in Rumania*, pp. 115 ff.

9. On these problems consult Fischer-Galati, *The New Rumania*, pp. 17 ff., and the bibliographical references on pp. 18 and 19. See also *East Europe*, XII, No. 3 (March 1963), 51.

10. The materials relevant to the October conference will be found in *Scinteia*, October 18-22, 1945.

11. See Gheorghiu-Dej's report in *Scinteia*, October 20, 1945.

12. An interesting interpretation of the results of the election is contained in Robert Lee Wolff, *The Balkans in Our Time* (New York: Norton, 1967), pp. 287-289. See also Ionescu, *Communism in Rumania*, pp. 123-125.

13. Interesting discussions of these problems may be found in Roberts, *Rumania*, pp. 300 ff., and Wolff, *The Balkans*, pp. 289 ff.

14. An excellent interpretation of the provisions of the peace treaty, with summaries of the principal provisions, may be found in Ionescu, *Communism in Rumania*, pp. 128 ff.

15. The events leading to the establishment of the republic are discussed with care by Ionescu, *ibid.*, pp. 131-143.

Chapter 6
The National Legacy Abandoned: Stalinism, Socialism, *Satellitenstaat* (1948–1952)

1. A most comprehensive explanation of the events and practices of that period was provided by Nicolae Ceausescu himself in April 1968.

Notes: Stalinism, Socialism, *Satellitenstaat*

The far-reaching speech, made on April 27 in connection with the rehabilitation of "certain Party activists," condemns the then prevalent Stalinist practices in unequivocal terms. The text of the speech may be found in *Scinteia*, April 28, 1968.

2. A detailed review of the role of religion in Rumanian life and of the communist policies toward religion is contained in Stephen Fischer-Galati, "Religion," Stephen Fischer-Galati, ed., *East-Central Europe under the Communists: Romania* (New York: Praeger, 1957), pp. 132-147. See also Rumanian National Committee, *Persecution of Religion in Rumania* (Washington, 1949).

3. A comprehensive study of these problems is contained in "Literature and the Arts," Fischer-Galati, *Romania*, pp. 165-181. A brief but excellent review of the problems of the intellectual community may be found in Ionescu, *Communism in Rumania*, pp. 175-180.

4. A detailed review of the Rumanian educational system may be found in "Education," Fischer-Galati, *Romania*, pp. 148-164. See also Rumanian National Committee, *The Perversion of Education in Rumania* (Washington, 1950).

5. In attacking the educational system the communists hoped to root out the obscurantist and elitist traditions associated with education in Rumania. Indeed, historically the function of primary schools—at least in the village—was to preach and reinforce the dogmas of "nationality" and "orthodoxy." Secondary education, normally inaccessible to children of peasant or worker origin, was reserved for the urban bourgeoisie, intelligentsia, professional groups, and political elite. Here, orthodoxy and nationality were less relevant than emulation of the West and grounding in Western values through rigorous academic pursuits. The secondary school was a prerequisite for higher education, usually pursued abroad and in France. Only those who could not qualify for or afford university training outside Rumania attended Rumanian universities, the traditional hotbeds of "bourgeois nationalism" and, in the thirties, of militant "fascism."

6. A summary of the divergent positions is contained in Ionescu, *Communism in Rumania*, pp. 94 ff., and Fischer-Galati, *The New Rumania*, pp. 1 ff.

7. The most authoritative discussion of these problems is by Montias, *Economic Development*, pp. ix, 1 ff.

8. The most explicit official statement on these matters is by Ceau-

sescu in the speech referred to in note 1 above. See also Ionescu, *Communism in Rumania*, pp. 151-158.

9. Fischer-Galati, *The New Rumania*, pp. 35 ff., provides a careful review of these problems.

10. A detailed analysis of the struggle for power in that period is contained in Fischer-Galati, *ibid.*, pp. 39-43.

11. See Gh. Gheorghiu-Dej, "Für die Reinheit der Partei," *Für dauerhaften Frieden, für Volksdemokratie!*, June 23, 1950.

12. A recorder of the absurdities of "socialist realism" in that period lists among the most successful works produced the "Second Peace Sonata," "Ballad to Gheorghiu-Dej and the Brotherhood of the Rumanian People and the National Minorities," "Alarm on the Rumanian Railroads"—all musical compositions—and "Maria Zidaru, President of a Collective Farm," "Our Beloved Party Leader Gheorghiu-Dej," and "Rumanian Delegation of Peasants in Moscow"—all in the plastic arts. Other examples may be found in "Literature and the Arts," Fischer-Galati, *Romania*, pp. 180-181.

13. Revealing statistics are provided by Montias, *Economic Development*, of which the following table, from p. 5, indicates the per capita production of selected industrial commodities in 1929, 1938, and 1950:

	1929 Prewar Territory	1938 Prewar Territory	1938 Postwar Territory	1950 Postwar Territory
Electric power (kilowatt-hours)	30.9	57.8	72.4	130
Iron ore	5.1	7.1	8.9	24
Pig iron	4.1	6.8	8.5	20
Steel (crude)	9.3	14.1	18.2	34
Coal (brown and bituminous)	173	151.7	181.1	238
Cement	18.1	23.6	32.7	63
Petroleum	275	336	422.7	310
Sulfuric acid	1.5	2.3	2.8	3.2
Sugar	6.1	7.0	6.1	5.3
Cotton cloth (millions of square meters)	n.a.	n.a.	6.7	9.1
Woolen cloth (millions of square meters)	n.a.	n.a.	0.8	1.3

14. Ionescu, *Communism in Rumania*, points out on p. 201 that the ratio of machine tractor stations to collective farms was 102 to 56 in 1950 and 138 to 1,027 in 1951.

15. Interesting factual data on these matters are provided by Ionescu, *ibid.*, pp. 208 ff.

16. On these points consult Fischer-Galati, *The New Rumania*, pp. 39 ff.

17. The speech is in *Scinteia*, June 4, 1952.

18. Nevertheless, Gheorghiu-Dej's "men," Moghioros, Apostol, Stoica, and Parvulescu, constituted, with Gheorghiu-Dej himself, a working majority in the Politburo.

19. This thesis was presented most eloquently by Gheorghiu-Dej himself in 1961. See *Scinteia*, December 7, 1961.

Chapter 7
The National Legacy Reclaimed: Socialist Patriotism
(1953–1960)

1. Ceausescu's speech is contained in *Scinteia* of April 28, 1969. An interpretation of the speech and its implications may be found in Radu Constantinescu, "Why Patrascanu Was Rehabilitated," *East Europe*, 17, No. 8 (August 1968), 6-9.

2. On these matters consult Fischer-Galati, *The New Rumania*, pp. 44 ff.

3. The "New Course" is analyzed by Ionescu, *Communism in Rumania*, pp. 219 ff., and by Montias, *Economic Development*, pp. 38 ff.

4. See especially pp. 38-53 of Montias, *Economic Development*.

5. *Scinteia*, August 23, 1953.

6. An analysis of these problems may be found in Fischer-Galati, *The New Rumania*, pp. 47 ff.

7. Consult Ionescu, *Communism in Rumania*, pp. 226 ff.

8. See note 1, above. Also Fischer-Galati, *The New Rumania*, pp. 48 ff.

Notes: Socialist Patriotism

9. There is little reason to doubt the accuracy of Ceausescu's account of the problems of that period as presented in his speech of April 27, 1968. *Scinteia*, April 28, 1968, contains the speech in its entirety.

10. On these problems consult Fischer-Galati, *The New Rumania*, pp. 50 ff.

11. All relevant materials may be found in *Scinteia*, August 23–August 26, 1955.

12. Gheorghiu-Dej's summary statement at the Congress may be found in Gheorghe Gheorghiu-Dej, *Raportul de activitate al comitetului central al Partidului Muncitoresc Romin la congresul al II-lea al partidului* ["Report of the Central Committee of the Rumanian Workers' Party at the Second Party Congress"] (Bucharest: Editura de Stat Pentru Literatura Politica, 1956), pp. 5-160. A comprehensive summary of the proceedings of the congress is contained in Ionescu, *Communism in Rumania*, pp. 240 ff.

13. See note 1, above.

14. An intelligent appraisal of the impact of the Twentieth Congress on Rumanian communism is contained in Ionescu, *Communism in Rumania*, pp. 255 ff.

15. *Scinteia*, March 29, 1956.

16. Consult Fischer-Galati, *The New Rumania*, pp. 57 ff.

17. Consult Ionescu, *Communism in Rumania*, pp. 267-287, and Fischer-Galati, *The New Rumania*, pp. 62 ff.

18. The divergences between Moscow and Bucharest are clearly illustrated in the joint declaration on the negotiations held in Moscow between November 26 and December 3, 1956, published in an English version in *Soviet News*, December 4, 1956.

19. On these and related matters consult the excellent study by Robin Alison Remington, *The Changing Soviet Perception of the Warsaw Pact* (Cambridge, Mass.: Center for International Studies, Massachusetts Institute of Technology, 1967), pp. 36 ff.

20. See Montias, *Economic Development*, pp. 187 ff.

21. *Ibid.*, 167 ff.

22. A comprehensive discussion may be found in Fischer-Galati, *The New Rumania*, pp. 66 ff.

23. The most intelligent discussion of these problems is contained in Remington, *Changing Soviet Perception*, pp. 43 ff.

24. See Fischer-Galati, *The New Rumania*, pp. 69 ff.

25. A perceptive discussion of these matters will be found in Montias, *Economic Development*, pp. 53 ff.

26. On these points consult Ionescu, *Communism in Rumania*, pp. 288 ff.

Chapter 8
The National Legacy Reclaimed: National Communism
(1960–1965)

1. *Declaratie cu privire la pozitia Partidului Muncitoresc Romin in problemele miscarii comuniste si muncitoresti internationale adoptata de Plenara largita a C.C. al P.M.R. din aprilie 1964* ["Statement on the Stand of the Rumanian Workers' Party Concerning the Problems of the International Communist and Working-Class Movement Adopted by the Enlarged Plenum of the Central Committee of the RWP Held in April 1964"] (Bucharest: Editura Politica, 1964).

2. A comprehensive summary of the proceedings of the Congress is contained in Ionescu, *Communism in Rumania*, pp. 316-331.

3. See in particular Montias, *Economic Development*, pp. 203 ff.

4. *Ibid.*, pp. 187 ff.

5. Gheorghiu-Dej's lengthy report at the Congress is available in Gheorghe Gheorghiu-Dej, *Raport la cel de al III-lea congres al Partidului Muncitoresc Romin* ["Report at the Third Congress of the Rumanian Workers' Party"] (Bucharest: Editura Politica, 1960), pp. 5-126.

6. On these points see Fischer-Galati, "Rumania and the Sino-Soviet Conflict," Kurt London, ed., *Eastern Europe in Transition* (Baltimore: Johns Hopkins, 1966), pp. 268 ff.

7. Ionescu, *Communism in Rumania*, pp. 318-321, contains an excellent discussion of these problems.

8. All relevant economic problems are analyzed with much insight by Montias, *Economic Development*, pp. 53 ff. and 135 ff. A briefer statement may be found in Ionescu, *Communism in Rumania*, pp. 321 ff.

Notes: The Socialist Republic of Rumania

9. *Ibid.*, pp. 322-335. Gheorghiu-Dej's statement has been published in several versions. The official version is contained in *Scinteia*, December 7, 1961.

10. A review of these problems will be found in Fischer-Galati, *The New Rumania*, pp. 84 ff.

11. *Scinteia*, December 7, 1961.

12. Agricultural problems, in political and economic context, are discussed by Montias, *Economic Development*, pp. 87 ff.

13. The nature of the party's achievements and their political significance are revealed in the various speeches made by Gheorghiu-Dej between December 1961 and June 1962. See Gheorghe Gheorghiu-Dej, *Artikel und Reden, June 1961–Dezember 1962* (Bucharest: Politischer Verlag, 1963), pp. 206-447.

14. Fischer-Galati, *The New Rumania*, pp. 86 ff.

15. The official communique relative to the plenum will be found in *Scinteia*, November 24, 1962.

16. These problems are discussed in detail in Fischer-Galati, *The New Rumania*, pp. 90 ff.

17. *Scinteia*, March 9, 1963.

18. On these points see Fischer-Galati, *The New Rumania*, pp. 94 ff.

19. See note 1 above. An excellent English version of the "Statement" is contained in William E. Griffith, *Sino-Soviet Relations, 1964–1965* (Cambridge, Mass.: The M.I.T. Press, 1967), pp. 269-296.

20. A. Otetea and S. Schwann, eds., *K. Marx—Insemnari despre romani* (Bucharest: Editura Academiei, 1964).

21. An extensive analysis of the indices and their significance will be found in Montias, *Economic Development*, pp. 231-247 and 248 ff.

Chapter 9
The Legacy Restated: The Socialist Republic of Rumania

1. See Stephen Fischer-Galati, "Nicolae Ceausescu: Rumania's Leader," *Communist Affairs*, 2 (1967), pp 23-26.

2. The proceedings of the Congress are contained in *Congresul al*

Notes: The Socialist Republic of Rumania

IX-lea al Partidului Communist Roman ["The Ninth Congress of the Rumanian Communist Party"] (Bucharest: Editura Politica, 1966).

3. *Ibid.*, pp. 21-104.

4. The two texts may be found in Jan F. Triska, ed., *Constitutions of the Communist Party–States* (Stanford: The Hoover Institution, 1968), pp. 362 and 378, respectively.

5. Article 35. *Ibid.*, p. 383.

6. *Congresul*, pp. 294 ff.

7. Fischer-Galati, *The New Rumania*, pp. 114 ff.

8. "Partidul Comunist Roman–Continuator al Luptei Revolutionare si Democratice a Poporului Roman, al Traditiilor Miscarii Muncitoresti si Socialiste din Romania" ["The Rumanian Communist Party–Continuator of the Revolutionary and Democratic Struggle of the Rumanian People, of the Traditions of the Workers' and Socialist Movement in Rumania"], *Scinteia*, May 8, 1966.

9. *Congresul*, pp. 735 ff.

10. "Expunere cu Privire la Imbunatatirea Organizarii si Indrumarii Activitatii de Cercetare Stiintifica" ["Statement Regarding the Improvement of the Organization and Guidance of Scientific Activity"] will be found in Nicolae Ceausescu, *Romania pe Drumul Desavirsirii Constructiei Socialiste* ["Rumania on the Road of Completion of Socialist Construction"] (Bucharest: Editura Politica, 1968), I, 219-245.

11. Ceausescu's numerous speeches made in this period reflect these fundamental positions. See Ceausescu, *Romania*, I, 251 ff., and II, 5 ff.

12. The significance attached by Rumania to these problems is reflected in the publication of a semiofficial volume on "Rumania and the Balkan Entente" in 1968. See Cristian Popisteanu, *Romania si Antanta Balcanica* ["Rumania and the Balkan Entente"] (Bucharest: Editura Politica, 1968), particularly the introduction by George Macovescu on pp. 5-18.

13. Montias, *Economic Development*, pp. 182 ff.

14. On these problems consult Remington, *The Warsaw Pact*, pp. 36 ff.

15. See Ceausescu's comprehensive statement to the Conference "Raportul cu Privire la Masurile de Perfectionare a Conducerii si Planificarii Economiei Nationale si la Imbunatatirea Organizarii Administrativ-Teritoriale a Romaniei" ["Report Concerning Measures for Perfecting

the Direction and Planning of the National Economy and the Improvement of the Administrative-Territorial Organization of Rumania"], presented on December 6, 1967, and published in Ceausescu, *Romania*, pp. 504-611.

16. See *Scinteia*, April 28, 1968, and May 6, 1968. A succinct interpretation of these events is offered by Radu Constantinescu, "Why Patrascanu Was Rehabilitated," *East Europe*, 17, No. 8 (August 1968), pp. 6-9.

17. The principal source of information for developments in this period is *Scinteia*, which provides complete texts of the statements of Rumanian and foreign officials.

18. The publication of a brief volume on the Little Entente by Eliza Campus at this time was symbolic of Rumania's interest in possibly reviving that international understanding. See *East Europe*, 17, No. 9 (September 1968), 50.

19. *Scinteia* carried all pertinent statements made late in September and provides details mirroring the tension and hopes of the population and the leadership.

BIBLIOGRAPHICAL NOTES

THIS BOOK is based primarily on sources in the Rumanian language. Specific references to selected sources in Rumanian have been provided in the notes. The compilation of an exhaustive bibliography of all Rumanian materials consulted, however, appears unnecessary. The student of Rumanian affairs able to use sources in Rumanian is referred to the excellent bibliographical essay contained in Henry L. Roberts, *Rumania: Political Problems of an Agrarian State* (New Haven: Yale University Press, 1951), pp. 381-399, and the annotated bibliographic guide by Stephen Fischer-Galati, *Rumania: A Bibliographic Guide* (Washington: The Library of Congress, 1963). He may also consult the bibliographic references listed in the latest studies on contemporary Rumania by John Michael Montias, *Economic Development in Communist Rumania* (Cambridge, Mass.: The M.I.T. Press, 1967), pp. 307-310, and Stephen Fischer-Galati, *The New Rumania: From People's Democracy to Socialist Republic* (Cambridge, Mass.: The M.I.T. Press, 1967), pp. 119-120. All these bibliographies contain complete references to works on Rumania in all languages.

Studies relevant to twentieth century Rumania in English and other western languages are, however, few in number and generally poor in quality. The outstanding contribution to the literature on the history, politics, and economic problems of Rumania in our century is Roberts' work cited above. Less sophisticated but nevertheless informative is the monograph by Joseph S. Roucek, *Contemporary Roumania and Her Problems: A Study in Modern Nationalism* (Stanford: Stanford University Press, 1932). Roberts' study has been supplemented with respect to developments since 1948 by several symposia and a few monographs. Of the symposia, Alexandre Cretzianu, ed., *Captive Rumania: A Decade of Soviet Rule* (New York: Frederick A. Praeger, 1956), and Stephen Fischer-Galati, ed., *Romania* (New York: Frederick A. Praeger, 1957), are the most comprehensive. Representative of the monographic literature are Ghita Ionescu, *Communism in Rumania 1944–1962* (London: Oxford University Press, 1964) and the companion works by Montias and Fischer-Galati published by The M.I.T. Press in 1967 and referred to above.

In addition to these fundamental studies the reader will find relevant materials in article form in the specialized periodical literature, particularly in the *Revue Roumaine d'Histoire, Südost-Forschungen, Revue des Etudes Sud-Est Europeennes, Slavic Review, East European Quarterly, Journal of Central European Affairs, Canadian Slavic Studies,* and *Balkan Studies.*

Finally, mention should be made of two classic works on Rumania in English: R. W. Seton-Watson, *A History of the Roumanians: From Roman Times to the Completion of Unity* (Cambridge, England: Cambridge University Press, 1934), and David Mitrany, *The Land and the Peasant in Rumania: The War and Agrarian Reform, 1917–1921* (London: Oxford University Press, 1930). These studies, although published many years ago, retain much of their original validity.

INDEX

Index

Index

247

Index

N